Understanding Pope Francis

Key moments in the formation
of Jorge Bergoglio as a Jesuit

Javier Cámara

Sebastián Pfaffen

Printed by CreateSpace,
An Amazon.com Company

Understanding Pope Francis.
Key moments in the formation of Jorge Bergoglio as a Jesuit

Javier Cámara e Sebastián Pfaffen

First English edition, September 2015.

270 p. – 22,86 x 15,24 cm.

Printed by CreateSpace, an Amazon.com Company

Available on Amazon.com

Available in Kindle – eBook format

ISBN-13: 978-1517161583
ISBN-10: 1517161584

Original Spanish title:

Aquel Francisco

Copyright © 2014 by Editorial Raíz de Dos S.A., Córdoba, Argentina

Translated by Peter M. Short

English edition and notes by Luis F. Escalante

Full of gratitude, I dedicate this book to the seven most important people in my life:
my parents, Titilo and Negra.
They always dreamt it. Here it is.
To my spiritual father, Peter Short, today, far away, but always close.
The four women through whom God makes me a happy man each day: my wife Mónica
and my daughters Juli, Agus and Miqui.

Javier Cámara

To my wife Elizabeth and my children Ivo, Irina, Tobías, Ignacio and Clara,
knowing that this book is one more grace from our loving Father.
To my parents and brothers and sisters, with the hope that this humble work will help in
the constant and passionate seeking of Truth, Goodness and Beauty.

Sebastián Pfaffen

INDEX

Chapter 6

Chapter 7

PRESENTATION

I have the pleasure of presenting this work of two known cordobese journalists, Javier Cámara and Sebastián Pfaffen, who have set about to speak to us of the years Pope Francis resided or passed through the city of Córdoba, as a Jesuit novice, as provincial of his Order and an a resident priest in the house the Society of Jesus has in the center of this city.

The way they have gone about this endeavor is characterized by their seriousness, their professional competence, their eyes of faith, their sympathy with and love towards the Holy Father. The result of this effort is the presentation of an image of today's Pope where the work of God and his providence that worked in him to prepare him for the service that was conferred on him March 13, 2013.

At that time, God our Lord, joyfully surprised all faithful Catholics, but he especially surprised the then archbishop of Buenos Aires, Cardinal Jorge Mario Bergoglio, calling him to be the new bishop of Rome. It was when he was preparing to resign from his position at the head of the Archdiocese he was called "from the end of the world" to a very singular service: to be the successor of the apostle St. Peter and Pastor of the universal Church.

God's work in the Cardinal and the providential preparation we mentioned were seen right away in his gestures, in his teaching and in his proposals, which offered and offer the whole Church consolation, illumination, renewed enthusiasm and much joy.

This providential preparation was developed "on the run"; in his action as a pastor of one of the largest diocese in Latin America. His gestures, his teachings, his proposals are not improvised or an act. On the contrary, they are nothing more than a show of the coherence and of the dedication with which the Pope carried out his former pastoral job and that he now offers to the whole Church.

Personally, I can give reliable witness to his kindness toward people, his interest in the situation of others, his delicate, exquisite and effective charity toward all.

It is a joy to have this work which helps us understand and appreciate better the successor of St. Peter, Pope Francis. This knowledge and this love should oblige us also to accompany him with our prayer answering his constant request; "Pray for me".

+ *Carlos José Ñáñez*
Archbishop of Córdoba - Argentina

PROLOGUE

Córdoba was a double desert experience for Pope Francis. First in his novitiate: the desert that fascinates, where we Jesuits are freely taken to be seduced by the Lord who calls us to His encounter, to be "Companions of Jesus", to follow his path, to feel with his sentiments, to see with his eyes, to strip ourselves of the mantles we bring from the world and take up the washbowl, pitcher and towel, and "bowing down", wash the feet of the brothers and sisters.

Accompanying and bowing down are two gestures that certainly mark the pontificate of Francis, a man of "who has encountered the Lord" in the intimacy of prayer, and a man "who has encountered the people" in the "closeness" that clearly marks his pastoral style. He is also a man used to lowering himself before human miseries.

Fr. Pedro Arrupe, who was the Superior General of the Jesuits, used to say that our place usually is where there is most sorrow. Francis clearly understood this not only intellectually but also showing it through his heart. And although a long time has now past, it is probable that it was in that Novitiate in the neighborhood of Pueyrredon in Córdoba where he drank in these lessons.

Life and the mysterious pedagogy of God are strange at times and Córdoba again received Jorge Bergoglio in very different circumstances. This time it was a desert of exile, or as he described it, a "time of darkness, of shadows", "a moment of interior purification". Writers speak of a *second journey*, the mystics call it a *second conversion*.

Beyond the circumstances that provoked it and that Javier

Cámara and Sebastián Pfaffen delve into in these pages, it is clear that Francis went through the desert of being put on the "side of the road" during these years, the solitude of not being a protagonist and the silence of the heart. But the desert is not a place designed to stay in. One passes through to reach the other side. That way the exile turns into an exodus.

In the parable of the vine, Jesus tells us that all pruning, whether it comes from God or is permitted by Him, serves to give us more life. And if it is true –as Benjamin Gonzalez Buelta says—that God cannot tie an arm that cuts, nor stop the blade of the axe, He can turn a cut destined to kill into one destined to give life. The pruned plant looks dead, but the sap of God, His grace, works "in hiding". And suddenly, fruit of this "presence" the Spring erupts, fragile but unstoppable; and then the time of surprises where an incredible vitality comes forth which is impossible to stop or hide. That is the sensation we felt on that afternoon in March of 2013 when we saw Jorge, now Francisco, come out onto the balcony of the world ready to serve.

Javier and Sebastian speak of this in this book. They do it with the rigor of those who do not improvise and the wisdom of those who can glimpse, with wonder, the Mystery of God incarnate in this unique page of history.

Ángel Rossi SJ

PROLOGUE to the english edition

Jorge Bergoglio, Pope Francis, has generated a lot of attention since his election on March 13, 2013. Much has been said and written about him already. There are those who see him as a great hope for reform in the Church, others see his simplicity and spirit and love of poverty as refreshing. Still others are pleased that the first non-European Pope was elected and see a new "universality" in the chair of Peter. He has also generated a lot of controversy. Who is Jorge Bergoglio? What will he mean for the future of the Church? Although this book will not answer those questions completely, certainly Javier Cámara and Sebastián Pfaffen have focused on events and circumstances of Bergoglio's life that will give you a glimpse into the heart and mind of the 366th Pope. And they have done it with the help of Francis' own clarifications.

When Jorge Bergoglio was ordained as auxiliary bishop of Buenos Aires, as the authors point out, he chose a motto, as all bishops do, that he kept when he was elected pope: "*Miserando atque eligendo*" "Looking upon him with mercy and choosing him" which is taken from a homily on the call of St. Matthew by St. Bede the Venerable. It is interesting that the Holy Father should be so taken by a homily on the apostle who was called from his life as a tax collector, particularly since he is today usually described as a mix between the reformer John XXIII and the *poverello* of Assisi. And although a case can be made for comparing Jorge Bergoglio to all three of these saints, it is doubtful he was drawn to this motto because of the apostle of whom it is written, but rather because of the Lord who showed such mercy.

Francis is, first and foremost, a Jesuit who takes very seriously the discernment of spirits the founder of his Order so eloquently and practically described especially in his Spiritual Exercises. And one cannot take discernment of spirits seriously without recognizing the mercy of God in all.

Writing a prologue for the book of his professor and colleague Miguel Fiorito, precisely on the discernment of spirits, Bergoglio wrote: "St. Agustin, speaking to the Lord, tells Him: 'You seek those who escape from you and you escape from those who seek You'. This is a classic Christian paradox: to conquer God is to let oneself be conquered by Him, to discover by what road he is coming to us and allow Him to reach us.

This means a battle against our desire to find God more in our human condition than in His divine signals. The traces left by our accomplishments or failures and not the marks of the God's action; the traces of our sorrows and not the signs of his abundant blessings; the traces of our sins and not the signals of His forgiveness."[1]

This book reveals some of the signs of God's action in his life, and how this son allowed himself to be reached by Him.

The mercy of God is at the center of Bergoglio's life, but not only the mercy he has received from God but the mercy Jesus asks us to bestow on others. It is not a strained effort at charity in Bergoglio but, as the book describes in many stories, it is the fruit of one who has made the criteria of the Gospel his own. From his famous "Who am I to judge?" comment to "God never tires of forgiving us", Francis shows his capability of making visible the love of Jesus who was "a friend of publicans and sinners".

Now he is the one who invites us to seek that mercy, indeed to never tire in seeking it. In his words: "we are fragile and have to return to confession again, all of us. But He never tires. He always takes us by the hand again. This is God's love, and we must imitate Him! Society must imitate Him, and take this path."[2]

Peter Short

---

[1] Miguel Fiorito SJ, *Discernimiento y lucha espiritual* (Buenos Aires, Agape Libros, 2010) page 7.
[2] Pastoral visit to Castrovillari penitentiary, June 21, 2014.

INTRODUCTION

—Hello?

—Hello? Yes? Who's speaking?

— Jorge Bergoglio.

—Who?

—Jorge Begoglio.

—Really?... the Holy Father?

—Yes! Do you want me to say it in a Cordobese accent?

Monday February 3, 2014, before noon, Jorge Bergoglio, Pope Francis, called my home on the phone. Eight months earlier, in July of 2013, I had begun to investigate about the days the now Pontiff of the Church had spent in Córdoba, as a novice, between 1958 and 1960, and then as a priest between 1990 and 1992.

Before long the story I was developing overwhelmed me and I sought out my friend and colleague Sebastian Pfaffen, who as a special envoy of Channel 12 of Córdoba was an eye witness in Rome of the historical conclave that elected the first argentine and Latin American pope, the same man who had been living in Córdoba for some years. In this way Sebastian became co-author of this book and we began to write this story *in the first person plural.*

In December of 2013 we found out that the archbishop of

Córdoba, Carlos Ñáñez, was going to the Vatican to see Francis. An e-mail was enough for this pastor, with admirable kindness and generosity, to tell the Holy Father that two cordobese journalists were writing a book on him and his link to this province, its history and its people.

Days later, Bishop Ñáñez responded the message to tell us that the Holy Father was willing to collaborate and Francis himself gave him a piece of paper with an e-mail address where we could send a written commentary of what we wanted to do.

On Monday, February 3, 2014, as we said, with the simplicity of a father who is calling his children to say hello, pope Francis called home and changed the blood pressure of those who heard him as well as the proportions of this journalistic work.

We never had a formal interview with the Pope. But he cleared up several doubts and gave us a few commentaries and very important memories on some of the things we were investigating and sharing with him. It was an unforgettable, incredible, unimaginable experience. Or can one say he is "prepared" to speak with the Pope, or hear the successor of St. Peter, the servant of the servants of God, for many the most important man in the world, ask him: "say, when do you want me to call?"

Francis always surprises. And in this book he will, for example, when he tells us, among other things, when and where he met Perón and Evita, and at the same time clarify once and for all, what is his true –and too often very manipulated– relationship with peronism.

Who is this Pope Francis? Who is Jorge Mario Bergoglio? Who was this *Eminentissimum ac reverendissimum Dominum Gerorgium Marium Sanctae Romanae Ecclesiae Cardinalem* Bergoglio? Who is this man from Buenos Aires who became, almost without anyone expecting it, the most important argentine in history?

When on March 13, 2013 the French cardinal proto-deacon Jean-Louis Tauran, fighting his Parkinson's disease, announced that

Bergoglio had been elected pope, many people fell to the ground, on their knees, weeping with emotion; some of them, on the same old cordobese tiles that the new Pope of the Catholic Church had walked years earlier.

The history that links Bergoglio to Córdoba, the days that Francis passed in this city and province as a Jesuit novice and later as a priest of this Ignatian order, are vital to understand his pontifical gestures as well as his understanding of God, of the Church, of life, of history, of politics and of himself. Here, during his novitiate, the young Bergoglio shaped his life in the ignatian spirituality, the one that offers people of faith a radical devotion to the Gospel of Jesus and a Cosmo vision of the world –of ones own life and that of others— that is impossible to box into worldly categories of right or left, orthodoxy or heterodoxy, of conservative or progressive. Bergoglio, Pope Francis, lives and encourages others to live according to the spiritual discernment that he makes each day in prayer, speaking with God, with Jesus, with the Virgin Mary and seeking the intercession of St. Joseph, his favorite patron.

Everything that he has managed and manages, everything that is related to power, to authority, to the interpersonal relationships, has been screened by his disciplined discernment of spirits. A discernment that understands that everything that comes from God, the good, the true, the beautiful, always has to respond to the itinerary of the incarnate Jesus. What does this mean? That for the man who today guides the Church, things are from God when they follow the way of Jesus: the way of humility, of service to others, of lowering oneself, of humiliation and of the cross.

In his second stay in Córdoba, exiled, silenced and silent, cast aside because he became a stone in the shoes of others, Bergoglio took on this evangelical itinerary of silence and humiliation. It was a time of "interior purification" the Pope says today. Through the work and grace of Providence, in which he believes and hopes, the rejected stone became over the years the corner stone, into the stone upon which Jesus himself builds his Church.

This corner stone that today touches the world, is the same person who in 1958, when he made his novitiate in the building the Jesuits had in the Pueyrredon neighborhood of the city of Córdoba, ate lunch on his knees, kissed his superior's feet, showered in cold water in the cold of winter and would go a month without speaking – except with his superior—, during his spiritual exercises that all the young Jesuits had to make.

He is that novice who wept when he found out that the sick man who lay dying in the Córdoba hospital, who he was caring for, had a wife who was unfaithful to him with a doctor, in a situation that he still remembers and calls "the social wound of infidelity".

This Pope who is reforming the Roman Curia is the same young man who prayed his rosary below the trellis that still stands in the patio of the apartment buildings where the novitiate once stood, at 1500 Buchardo Street. The same man who on Saturdays and Sundays in the morning went to "the ravines" of the Pueyrredon neighborhood looking for poor children to give them catechism, to play games with them, and share a cup of *mate* and a piece of bread.

It is the same one who, as a young novice, was surprised by the popular piety of the people of Impira, in the remote part of the province of Córdoba, Argentina; faithful who, for the patronal feast day, sang hymns to the Virgin patroness of their town with overflowing emotion. The Pope still remembers the melody and some of the words of this pious hymn.

It is the same man who, in Río Segundo, Córdoba, found a priestly model at that time of a "man to man" pastor, who he still remembers and admires.

He is the man who as vice-chancellor of the Córdoba Catholic University, headed an ordering of the economy and placed as a priority the payment of the retirement accounts that were owed, so that no professor or employee would pass into retirement without receiving payment.

That Bergoglio, this Francis, is the same who lived two years in a cold, noisy room, without a private bath, in the Residence of the Society in Córdoba, whose window can be seen today from the pedestrian street of Caceros, in the center of Córdoba city. He is the same man who at that time rolled up the sleeves of his black Jesuit habit to clean the elderly, sick or dying religious brothers. The Pope, nothing less than the Pope, is that same serous man, with a low profile, quiet, who between 1990 and 1992, could be found by anyone in Córdoba walking the streets and central pedestrian walkways going to the Basilica of Our Lady of Ransom, where he would often go to pray before the image of St. Joseph with the Christ child that is over the tabernacle.

The Supreme Pontiff of the Catholic Church, spiritual leader of millions of faithful, is that priest who remained cooking all night so that a young poor couple from Córdoba could offer to their relatives a plate of food worthy of a humble wedding party.

Francis is all this, and much more. He is one of the most important men in the world who one day after the first telephone conversation with one of the authors of this book, which was the same day all the papers in the world learned that he had scheduled and confirmed his meeting with the president of the United States and with the Queen of England, he called a second time to say he had forgotten to mention an "important" person in his cordobese history: Cirilo Rodríguez, the religious brother who was the doorman, who 56 years ago had opened the door of the Novitiate of the Pueyrredon neighborhood.

For these reasons, the thesis of this book is that Pope Francis would not exist, such as we know today, without those two intense years of Jesuit formation in the cordobese novitiate, and without the two later years of "interior purification" that Fr. Jorge Bergoglio passed in the Major Residence of the Society of Jesus.

It is not a matter of belittling the vital importance that his family life had on his childhood or adolescence, or his experiences as pastor, or professor or superior outside of Córdoba. Much less do we want to underestimate his undeniable quality as one born and raised in

Buenos Aires. But we do want to show that these years in the interior of Argentina were "defining" moments in the life of the man who today is the supreme Pastor of the Church. We try to tell all of this on these pages. And he, the Pope, knows about it, and agrees.

When we asked him what these two prolonged stays in Córdoba, his years of formation, his visits and actions here as Provincial, meant for his religious life, he responded with conviction: "My years in Córdoba determined, in some way, a spiritual strength. Since I went first as a novice, and after this I spent two years there as a priest, between '90 and '92, that were like a night, with some interior darkness, the years also helped me in my later apostolic work and strengthen me as a pastor".

That Córdoba is the place where Pope Francis was strengthened as a pastor is very important, for this reason we wrote this book. For this reason the book makes sense.

In summary, this work shows Pope Francis in his years of formation as a novice and also his work as a Jesuit priest; it shows the bright moments and the shadows that he lived through; the people that he knew and who in some way "marked" him; in the trials, challenges, desolations and consolations. It shows him in the landscapes, streets and buildings that he encountered and still remembers. It shows a Pope "who came from the end of the earth", walking the same streets that all cordobese walk each day, as a gleeful warning that God's Providence goes on in every corner of the world, and it moves in each human heart, wherever we are. Even in Córdoba.

CHAPTER 1

WITH FAITH IN THE GENES

Coming from the Turin of Don Bosco

"The beautiful ship *Principessa Mafalda* sunk off the coast of Bahía, Brazil, yesterday at 19:15 hours. Four hundred of the sixteen hundred on board were saved" read the terse cable of the Associated Press (AP). The boat was the Titanic of its time, the only one capable of uniting Italy with Argentina in only fourteen days, and so was the preferred ship of the immigrants who arrived on those shores to "get rich in America". In that ship Rosa Margarita Vasallo, her husband Giovanni Bergoglio and their only son, Mario Francisco wanted to travel. If that had happened, this story would never have been told and this book never written.

Rosa is the beloved Nonna Rosa of the today Pope Francis; Giovanni, the grandfather; and Mario Francisco, who at that time was 21 years old, son of both of them, who with the passing of time would become the father of the 266th pope of the Catholic Church.

"They arrived in the *Giulio Cesare* (the other Italian boat that replaced the one that sank), but they should have sailed on the ship that went down. You have no idea how many times I have thanked Divine Providence for this", Jorge Mario Bergoglio confided to the Salesian priest and Cordobese historian Cayetano Bruno, in a letter written in Córdoba in 1990. On January 25 of 1929, in the suffocating heat of a summer morning in Buenos Aires, an elegant woman stepped off the boat in a coat with a fox fur collar. It was an article of clothing totally inappropriate for the temperature of the morning, but the woman would have preferred to faint from the heat than risk losing what was hidden in the lining of the coat: the entire savings of the family. The money that Rosa carried was fruit of several years' work in the Italian Piedmont province as well as the hope of their new life in Argentina. The Bergoglios had sold everything they had in Turin including the fashionable store which was their work. It was precisely the delays in these sales that caused their missing the ship which providentially saved their lives.

Rosa Margarita had met the grandfather of the future pope in Turin, or *Torino* for Italians. Before this, each on his own had arrived from the countryside to the city, seeking the progress that the industrial revolution had promised. But they did not only seek progress, they also sought God. Rosa was actively involved in the recently-formed Catholic Action, to the point of giving conferences on Christian commitment. "One of these conferences —Bergoglio remembered in a letter to Fr. Bruno— was published under the title 'St. Joseph in the life of the single woman, the widow and the married woman'. It appears that my grandmother said things that were not well received by the political class of her time –remembers the grandson in another paragraph—. They once closed the hall where she was to give a conference, so she gave it on the street, standing on a table".

Giovanni began working in a café, but, soon after marrying Rosa, they began their own food business. In 1908 Mario José Francisco was born to them, the father of the Pope, who was privileged to do something few other children of the countryside could: study in order to be an accountant. Mario spent the majority of his time in Italy on the corner of Via Garibaldi and Corso Valdocco, in Turin. "The proximity of the Salesian church was the reason he would seek out the priests there", wrote the Pope in a letter, a copy of which he kept and today allows us to know some of the details of his family's history.

The place where Jorge Bergoglio's father grew up is significant: Turin is the city where the Salesian Congregation was born, founded by Giovanni Melchiore Bosco (1815-1888) a priest, writer and educator known as Don Bosco who became world famous for his enormous human and spiritual work with children and young people[3]. Mario José Bergoglio was one of those who benefited from this work. From his teenage years in Italy until his death in Argentina, he always had at his side some priest of Don Bosco's congregation that accompanied him and his descendants, among them, the future Pope.

In 1922, three of the four brothers of Giovanni Bergoglio decided to immigrate to Argentina, a country where everyone saw as promising peace and prosperity. They left behind a Europe ravaged by the Frist World War, with serious economic challenges and with the risk of seeing themselves involved in another war. They settled in Paraná, capital city of the province of Entre Ríos, Argentina and began a construction company. The results were impressive and it was demonstrated by the building they constructed to house the whole family. "It is still called the Bergoglio Palace, a four story house where my grandparents, my father and his brothers all lived, each on a separate floor", Francis himself told the authors of this book.

The Bergoglio Palace is located on the corner of Andrés Pazos and San Martin, and over the façade on the Pazos Street side one can still see initials that link the building with the last name of the Pope "AVB", the "B" is for "Bergoglio".

"It is one of the most beautiful buildings of the city; it has four floors with excellent furnishings and apartments for the families, as well as luxurious offices", reads an article in the first edition of the magazine *Revista Social de Paraná*, that appeared in May of 1928, and quoted by the newspaper *El Diario* of Paraná in an article published when Francis was elected. "I don't think that the political situation was the motivating factor in the migration to Argentina" Bergoglio explained in that letter to Fr. Bruno. "A brother of my grandfather was already living in Paraná and his business was going well. They came to be a part of the family business in which four of the five Bergoglio men worked. For this reason, distinct from his other travel companions, the newly arrived were not forced to

---

[3] Don Bosco was canonized by Pope Pius XI on April 1, 1934, and declared by John Pail II "Father, Teacher and Friend of all young people". The Salesian work is present in thirty countries. In Argentina it was charged with the evangelization of the Patagonia and was responsible in the formation of two Blesseds: Artémides Zatti and Ceferino Namuncurá.

stay in the famous Immigrant Hotel, where hundreds of passengers were obliged to stay on their arrival, fleeing from Europe. The grandparents and father of today's Pope travelled on quickly to Paraná where they took part in the family business. However the prosperity abruptly ended in 1932. They could not overcome the great human loss and the effects of the Crash of Wall Street that occurred in 1929. The financial crisis paralyzed the construction industry, lowered property value, stopped sales and increased unemployment. Argentina was suffering what would be called the "infamous decade" and the Bergoglios had to face the economic recession together with an even greater loss. "The president of the company, my grandfather's brother (Miguel Lorenzo Bergoglio) became sick with leukemia and linfosarcoma, and died. Both situations, the recession and his death, destroyed the company" remembers Fr. Jorge, in that letter of 1990. They lost everything and had to sell even the cemetery mausoleum that the family held.

One of the great uncles began over; the younger went to Brazil, and Giovanni moved to Buenos Aires where he received help from a great friend, Fr. Enrique Pozzoli. The Salesian priest would later on be a key figure in the history of the Bergoglio family and, even more so, in the life of the future Pope Francis.

The priest introduced them to a person who loaned them 2000 pesos. With this money, Giovanni was able to buy a store in Flores, a section of Buenos Aires that the young Mario José knew very well since he had gone there as the accountant of the family business, travelling from Paraná to do errands.

In the store, "dad, who had been *Raggionere* in the Bank of Italy and an accountant in the construction company, made deliveries of groceries with his basket" tells Jorge's father in that letter written in Córdoba. Giovanni worked at this job until he could get a job in another company. "They began again with the same tranquility with which they had come".

The new store of the grandfather was not the fancy store they had in Italy, but it was a type of work they knew well. Between his deliveries on a bike and his work as an accountant, Mario José made time to cheer on the soccer team of the San Lorenzo club. It had been founded in 1907, also by a Salesian priest, Fr. Lorenzo Massa, who baptized it with the name of St. Lawrence the martyr. The club was in the area of Buenos Aires called Almagro and it was in this same neighborhood where Mario met his wife, in 1934, during a Mass in the Salesian oratory. The Pope himself recounts this family history: "When (my father) came to Buenos Aires he stayed with the Salesians on Solis Street, and it was there that he knew Fr. Pozzoli who immediately became his confessor. He joined the group of young men that surrounded the priest, where he came to know the brothers of mom and through them mom, with whom he married on December 12, 1935".

The parents of the future pope, Mario Bergoglio and María Regina Sívori, were married in the Basilica of St. Charles and María Auxiliadora. A year later, on Christmas day of 1936, in the same church they baptized their first son, Jorge Mario, who had been born on December 17. The priest in charge of administering this sacrament of Christian initiation was Fr. Pozzoli.

Later four other children of the couple would arrive: Oscar Adrian, Marta Regina, Alberto Horacio, and María Elena. In several interviews, the then Cardinal Bergoglio recalled how when he was 13 months old, his mother had her second son. "Mom was unable to keep up with taking care of the two of us and my grandmother, who lived around the corner, took me to her house in the morning and brought me back in the afternoon". From her he was able to learn the Piedmont dialect, similar to Italian, a gift that he never thought would be so useful in the last stages of his life.

During these years he also had the opportunity to learn some words in Genovese from a maternal uncle, although Bergoglio himself made clear that he was an "old rascal" that taught them songs that were less than clean, for which the only words he knows of that dialect are phrases that are "not repeatable".

His infancy passed living in the house at 531 Membrillar Street, in Flores. It was a tranquil area, with a lot of trees and it was just a few blocks away from the basilica of St. Joseph, something that was of great importance for the Bergoglio family.

"They nurtured us on God from the time we were very young children", says María Elena Bergoglio, younger sister of Francis, and the only one of the four siblings of the Pope that still lives. She recalls that their father always prayed the rosary when he got home from work. As children they accompanied him in the first mystery (of the five that are meditated upon in the rosary), but with the passing years began to be a part of the whole ritual. Sundays, on the other hand, there were no exceptions: no member of the family could miss Mass or the meals, which also were part of the tradition.

Among the closest family members, the favorite for Jorge Bergoglio was his *Nonna* Rosa, whom he always mentions, even as Pope. "It was she who taught me to pray, who impressed upon me the faith, she told me stories of the saints", explained Bergoglio, when as Cardinal, he gave an interview in the radio of the parish of Our Lady of the Miracles of Caacupé, in slum *21*. In the letter to Fr. Bruno, Bergoglio says without hesitation that his grandmother was "the woman who had influenced his life the most".

Nonna Rosa was a column of support for the family and religious life of the Bergoglios. This relationship for such a young boy who is now Pope was so special that it undoubtedly contributed to his continually seeking respect and protection for the elderly, for those who are "in one of the extreme ends of their existence".

The Pope himself told the authors a story of one of the pious incidents that he experienced with his grandmother: "When I was a boy, on Good Friday my grandmother would take us to the candlelight procession and at the end, when the image of the dead Christ would pass, our grandmother would kneel and tell us: 'Look, He is dead, but tomorrow he will rise!' This is way the faith entered us".

With time, Bergoglio would find a name for this living faith that he experienced as a child. "Popular piety" will become a key resource for his life and his faith. So much so, that already designated Archbishop and created a Cardinal by John Paul II, he elevated it to the category of a "precious treasure of the Catholic Church in Latin America", when he was chosen to coordinate the redaction of the final document of the Fifth Conference of the Latin-American Episcopate which took place in Aparecida, Brazil, in 2007.

Those religious festivals that he participated in thanks to his grandmother had a great impact in his heart: "I remember the processions to which I was brought from home, especially the procession of Saint Rose in which we always took part; the Good Fridays, when grandmother would take us to the candlelight procession; the procession of María Auxiliadora. Since I was a child I have participated in popular piety".

Bergoglio confided once that as a child he enjoyed collecting cards, reading, playing soccer and accompanying his father who played basketball at the San Lorenzo club. At the same time, he loved to listen to the opera with his mother on Saturdays at 2 o'clock in the afternoon, as well as to cook. He himself tells us of a painful event in the family that gave him a notable ability to cook. In February of 1948, for several months, his mother lost mobility after giving birth to her last daughter, the fifth "branch" of the family tree. This situation obliged them to collaborate with all the household chores. When they arrived home from school, their mother met them with all the ingredients for dinner laid out on the table. They had only to roll up their sleeves and follow the directions given by their mother, seated in a corner of the kitchen. "In this way we learned how to cook. We all know how to make at least *milanesas*", Bergoglio himself told us while he was Cardinal. With time, he was able to learn how to make delicious *paellas*, a meal which he would serve his brothers of the Company of Jesus almost every 31st of October when they would celebrate the feast day of the Coadjutor Brothers because of their patron saint, the Jesuit brother Alonso Rodriguez who entered the glory of God on that date. His mother's health problems forced another decision that would be important for the future pope. His father signed him up as a boarding student (together with his brother Oscar) in the Wilfred Baron of the Holy Angels School in Ramos Mejía, and his sister was put in another boarding school, María Auxiliadora School.

Attending a Salesian school would mark Jorge forever. In fact, it was there while he was in sixth grade, he felt the first call to the priesthood. In this regard, Fr. Jorge would write in 1990, when he was in the city of Córdoba: "I spoke with the famous 'fisherman' of vocations, Fr. Martinez, but then I began high school and it ended".

"In love" and a hard worker

"The only letter that he wrote me cost me a good walloping from my father. 'He had drawn a white house with a red roof and above it was written: 'This little house is the one I will buy when we get married. If I do not marry you, I will be a priest', this is what he wrote me and was faithful to his word". The story is from Amalia, a woman in Flores who was interviewed by dozens of Argentine journalists the day after her "beloved" from infancy was elected pope. They were only 12 and it was a platonic love that did not prosper beyond that first declaration of love. He was still a boy, but that same year, his father signed him into high school and told him: "It would be good for you that you begin to work also; I will get something for you to do during your vacation". His father's idea troubled him since he remembers that they did not have any pressing economic needs that would justify such a decision. "There was nothing that we didn't need, we didn't have a car nor did we go on vacation, but we did not have any serious needs." But still he obeyed his father and a little while later began to do cleaning chores in the accounting office where his father worked; three years later he worked in a sock factory, and during the last months of high school, in a chemical analysis laboratory.

Several times, remembering that decision on the part of his father to instill in him love of study and also of work, Bergoglio thanked him: "Work was one of the things that benefitted me most in life and, particularly in the laboratory; I learned the good and bad of all human endeavors".

At that time he would work from 7 to 1 p.m., and then he had lunch and went to school until 8 p.m. The chemical laboratory analyzed animal fats, water and food. Bergoglio collaborated doing the chemical control of the food samples that were sent from the factories. There he met Esther Ballestrino de Careaga, whom the Pope remembers as "an extraordinary boss". She was an expert chemist, a militant communist who during the Argentine dictatorship suffered the kidnapping of a daughter and a son in law. She was one of the founders of the "Mothers of the Plaza de Mayo", she was also kidnapped and assassinated (thrown into the sea from a military plane) together with the French religious sisters Alice Domon and Léonie Duquet. Her body was found on a beach on the coast of Buenos Aires and buried in a common grave; years later she was found and identified by an Argentine Team of Anthropologic Forensics which also worked in the common graves that the military dictatorship "sowed" in Córdoba.

The Pope studied in the Industrial Technical School number 12, which at that time was located in a family home and had very few students. There he learned Chemistry and Physics, although his companions point out that he excelled in literature, psychology and most of all in religion.

His friends remember him playing soccer and basketball after class, but they insist that he was better in intellectual pursuits. They tell us he always had a book in his hand, sometimes he even went to the neighborhood plaza and read for hours. Others are grateful for his help in their studies, even some who were not classmates. All agree that he was a good student, polite and always orderly, although when he went to the plaza he had no difficulty taking his school coat off and playing with the others.

Peronist?

When Juan Domingo Peron became president of Argentina for the first time on June 4, 1946, Jorge was 9 years old. Although certainly the president himself exacerbated the political tension in the country, his first term and the circumstances that surrounded it also enabled an improvement in the life of workers and the middle class. The spread of collective bargaining, unionizing, the advance of social projects, housing projects and the building of schools and hospitals were all part of an economic plan to expand the internal market"[4], which in turn helped the peronist party reach its height of popularity in 1949 and 1950.

Some critics have suggested that during his adolescent years, Jorge Bergoglio was punished for wearing on his High School uniform a pin of the peronist party. This story helped fuel the theory that Francis was a "Peronist Pope", a phrase that the Argentine government, run by the peronist party in 2013, proposed after changing its tune when the initial criticism of the Pope of the more left-leaning wing of the party's fell flat.

The Pope revealed to us that the story of the pin "was not true". When the story of the "Peronist Pope" was installed in the Argentine press, a historical operative of the Peronist party (Partido Justicialista) Julio Barbaro was interviewed incessantly because of his friendship with Bergoglio since they were children. He said: "we are both part of the same story that at times is twisted... Bergoglio was a part of the real world around him and shared the thought of those around him, that often was peronist, but he was clearly an enthusiast of religion, never of politics."

To clarify things, the Pope himself explained in this way his relationship with politics: "I always was interested in politics." In a conversation, he spoke about the origin and evolution of this interest, and he began with the history of one of his grandfathers: "I come from a family of the Radical Party, my grandfather was a Radical of the 90s", said the Pope, referring to the beginning of the political party that won national elections in Argentina nine times.

To illustrate the influence of that "Radical" grandfather in his life, the Holy Father remembered a story that he told in the book "*Sobre el Cielo y la Tierra*" ("On Heaven and Earth"), that is a collection of dialogues he had with his friend the rabbi Abraham Skorka: "My

---

[4] Mónica Deleis, Ricardo de Titto, Diego Arguindeguy, *El Libro de los Presidentes Argentinos*, page 206.

maternal grandfather was a carpenter and once a week a man with a beard came to sell him aniline. He would stay a long time chatting with my grandfather in the patio while my grandmother served them *mate* with wine. One day my grandmother asked me if I knew who this 'Don Elpidio', the aniline salesman was. As it turns out he was Elpidio González, who had been vice president of the nation[5]. It impressed me a great deal that an ex vice president of the nation now earned his living selling aniline. It is a sign of honesty."

Aside from this family influence, Bergoglio would also explore for himself the world of political ideas: "Later on, as a teenager, I delved a little into the leftwing –the pope told us mischievously—, reading books of the Communist Party that my boss in the laboratory gave me. Esther Ballestrino de Careaga was a great lady who had been of the Paraguayan Febrerista Revolutionary Party. After that I accompanied a group of young people with different political experiences. At that time, the political party centers set up in different parts of the cities were places of political culture. Now they are probably being used to teach cooking or sewing, workshops etc... but in those years the political culture was greatly promoted. I liked to go to these places. There was a period where I would wait anxiously for the newspaper *La Vanguardia*, which was not allowed to be sold with the other newspapers and was brought to us by the socialist militants. Obviously I also frequented the groups of peronists. But I never affiliated with any political party".

A couple of stories that have never been told took place at this point in his life, for example how he came to meet personally Juan Domingo Peron on one occasion and on another met María Eva Duarte de Peron, better known as "Evita": "The only time I met Peron was when I had to go as the flag-bearer of my school to a reunion of schools at Colon Theater. I was in High School at the time. They put us on a stage together with the other flag-bearers and there I saw him close up. I also saw Eva close once. It was when I entered the Peronist Party center on Córdoba Street, in Buenos Aires together with my brother to get some pamphlets on the party for a school project. She was there and she

---

[5] Elpidio Gonzalez was vice-president of Argentina during the years 1922-1928 during the presidency of Marcelo T. de Alvear.

greeted us but nothing more."

The Holy Father does not deny the close relationship the original Peronist doctrine had with the social doctrine of the Church. "In the original peronist position there is a link to the Social doctrine of the Church –Francis told us–. One should not forget that Peron brought his writings to the bishop of Resistencia (Chaco, Argentina) Nicolás De Carlo so that he could make sure that they were in line with the social doctrine of the Church".

The Pope remembered that this bishop was accused of being "peronist" and he gave his version: "Bishop De Carlo may have been a sympathizer with the party, but he was an excellent pastor. The first did not have anything to do with the other". To illustrate this, he recalled a famous episode that happened in April of 1948, which involved then president Peron and the bishop of Resistencia: "Peron was on the balcony of the Seminary in the city of Resistencia –recalled the Holy Father— and at the end of his speech wanted to clarify something. He mentioned that some accused Bishop De Carlo of being a peronist and he said 'this is a big lie, Peron is De Carlista'. De Carlo was the one who helped Peron with the Social Doctrine of the Church".

The vocation

"It was 'Day of the student' and for us the first day of spring. Before going to the party I went to the parish church where I usually went. I found a priest I did not know and felt the need to go to Confession. For me it was an experience of encountering someone. I found someone who had been waiting for me for a long time". This is the way Jorge Bergoglio as pope, describes his vocation.

It was September 21, 1954 and Bergoglio was almost 17. He had left his home heading for the train station in the Flores area of Buenos Aires. The plan was to meet with his friends and celebrate the Day of the Student, but suddenly everything changed when he knelt in the confessional in front of Fr. Carlos Duarte Ibarra.

"After that confession I felt as though something had changed. I was not the same. I had heard what was like a voice, a call: I was convinced that I had to become a priest" said Francis during the Vigil of Pentecost on May 18, 2013.

He never arrived at that meeting with his friends because, almost without realizing it, he had replaced it with a much more transcendental meeting. That day he did celebrate the beginning of spring... but that of his priestly vocation. Several years after that experience, in a letter written to Fr. Cayetano Bruno, Bergoglio described this as the day he "was thrown from the horse", like Paul of Tarsis in the Acts of the Apostles. "I made my confession by chance and there the Lord was waiting for me 'miserando atque eligendo' (looking at him with mercy and choosing him)"[6].

That young man returned to his house in Flores to meditate on that which, 60 years later he would repeat as the Universal Pastor of the Catholic Church: "We say that we have to seek God, go to Him to ask His forgiveness, but when we go, He is already waiting for us, He is there before us. In Spanish we have a word that describes this well: the Lord always "primerea" (gets there first)".

From the moment of this "encounter" until his entering the seminary some time will pass and even more until he decided to become a Jesuit.

"For a while it all ended there", explained Bergoglio, since from then on he dedicated himself to finishing high school and then continued to work in the laboratory. His decision to become a priest was kept in secret. He would only speak about it with Fr. Duarte Ibarra, who died a year after that confession, and so took the secret to the tomb, or to heaven... since he had forgiven the sins of a future Pope.

---

[6] A phrase taken from a homily of St. Bede the Venerable, who lived from 672 to 735. The homily was on the scene taken from the Gospel where Jesus calls St. Matthew: "*Vidit ergo Iesus publicanum et quia miserando atque eligendo vidit, ait illi Sequere me*" that recalls the following passage: "Jesus saw a man called Matthew, seated at the table of the tax collectors, and said to him 'Follow me'. He saw him more with an interior look of his love than with his physical eyes. Jesus saw the publican, and He saw him with mercy and choose him (*miserando atque eligendo*) and he said to him 'Follow me', which means 'Imitate me'".

"When Jorge finished High School, his mother had asked him what he wanted to do and he told her he wanted to study medicine. So mom fixed up a room where he would be able to study in peace", recalled his sister María Elena. The problem came when his mother entered the room for the first time. "She went in to clean and found theology and Latin books. So she asked him: 'Son, what are these books? Weren't you going to study medicine?' And Jorge answered: 'Yes, but medicine of the soul'".

Bergoglio remembered that the first one to know about his decision to be a priest was his father. He knew that his dad would understand better than his mom and that was the way it went. Regina did not have a good reaction to the news. She told him she did not see him as a priest, that he should wait a while longer, and should finish college first. According to Bergoglio, she saw the decision as a loss, while his father received the news with joy from the first moment.

In that letter to Fr. Bruno in 1990, Bergoglio revealed the sly tactic that he used at the time: "Since I saw where the conflict was heading, I went to see Fr. Pozzoli and told him everything. He examined my vocation. He told me to pray, to leave everything in the hands of God and gave me the blessing of Our Lady of Perpetual Help". Just as the young Jorge imagined, his parents brought their son's vocational difficulty to their life long confessor and friend. His dad brought the idea up: "Why don't we go ask Fr. Pozzoli?" –Bergoglio remembered his father asking— "and I, with my best straight face said yes. I still remember the scene. It was December 12, 1955".

Jorge's parents were celebrating 20 years of marriage and the celebration consisted in a small Mass, where the only ones present were the priest, the couple and their 5 children. After the Mass, Mario invited Fr. Pozzoli to have breakfast in *La Perla de Flores* bar. The following is from Bergoglio himself: "Fr. Pozzoli, who knew what was going to be discussed, accepted right away…and half way through breakfast the topic was brought up. The priest explained that to continue at the university is a good thing, but that one should take things as God sends them… and he began to tell stories of different people's vocation without taking sides in the matter, and ended telling the story of his own vocation". The Pope continued: "At this point my parents had softened their position. Of course, Fr. Pozzoli did not ever say that they should let me enter the seminary nor did he demand of them any decision; he understood that his role was simply to soften their position. He did that and the rest came on its own."

The one who was most happy was his grandmother Rosa. "Well, if God is calling you, may you be blessed", she responded adding that no one would reproach him if he decided to return home and the doors would be always open for him. And so, in 1956, at 19, Jorge Bergoglio entered the Metropolitan Seminary of Devoto in Buenos Aires. His mother did not go with him and although they were not angry with one another, she would not accept his decision for many years. She thought he had made a rash decision.

Yet, Jorge had taken many long months to meditate on that call first "felt" in the sixth grade and then more intensely on that first day of Spring in 1954. In fact during that period he delved into political interests, motivated by his boss in the laboratory where he worked who introduced him to the thought of leftwing intellectuals, but the Pope himself remembers today that "it never went beyond the intellectual plain" and he never was a communist.

For Bergoglio that period of contemplation was a moment of solitude before the call of God. He spoke about it while archbishop and repeated it while Cardinal and again as Pope. During that confession he felt like the publican Matthew when Jesus looked upon him with mercy and chose him. This meditation burned into his soul so deeply that it has accompanied him during his whole life and transformed itself into the seal and motto of his pastoral and priestly mission.

In the Metropolitan Seminary of Devoto

The echoes of the so-called "*Libertadora*" revolution that led to the downfall of the second government of Peron were still felt as well as the political tension exacerbated by the execution by firing squad of 27 military personnel and civilians that had tried to revolt against the *de facto* government led by Pedro Eugenio Aramburo.

It was in this climate of tension, which began in Buenos Aires and extended to the whole country, that Jorge Bergogio entered the Metropolitan Seminary of Our Lady of the Inmaculate Conception.

Today, in the Seminary of Devoto there are students of the Faculties of Philosophy and Theology of the Catholic University of Argentina, whose rector is from Alcira Gigena of the Province of Córdoba, Victor Manuel Fernandez, recently appointed Archbishop by Pope Francis.

Considering what happened soon in his life, it is clear that although the young seminarian had discerned clearly a priestly vocation the particular characteristics of the vocation were not yet clear. He began studying with a group of seminarians some of whom had more of an attachment to studies than to the spiritual or pastoral life, and others with more capability for the spiritual or pastoral life than for studies. Bergoglio had an inclination for the three aspects, but in the light of his later decision might have experienced something missing in his spiritual formation and in the radical nature of his surrender to Christ. He was in the seminary, but he continued to search.

Visits to his family home in Flores and the participation in some family reunions that were allowed by the Seminary, caused some disturbance in his interior life; so much so that at one point he was even "bowled over" for a while by the beauty and intelligence of a young lady of his age. Bergoglio himself wrote about it in the book he wrote with the rabbi Abraham Skorka: "It never crossed my mind to get married. But when I was a seminarian I was dazzled by I girl I met during my uncle's wedding. Her beauty and intellect surprised me…. So I was "bowled over" for some time and it kept me distracted. I could not even pray and when I tried to, the girl kept popping into my head".

From the experience, Bergoglio remembered how it finally passed and the conclusion he drew from it: "I had to rethink my option again. I choose again, or better said, allowed myself to be chosen by the religious life. It would not be normal not to pass through these kinds of trials."

Before, during and after this distraction, Bergoglio noticed that he liked the distinctiveness of some of his Jesuit professors. He quickly realized that this mix of wisdom, devotion, spirituality and commitment had to do with a level of discernment that he had not yet reached. He considered that the key could be in the Spiritual Exercises that were so revered by his professors and formation directors of that time. And yet it was Providence that rushed the decision that would be very important in his life.

The call of St. Ignatius

Almost a year and a half after entering the Villa Devoto Seminary, Bergoglio caught a serious bought of pneumonia that almost killed him. It was during this time that he experienced what he would much later call "travelling in patience". When already a Cardinal he said: "We have to realize that we cannot give birth in life without pain (...) in all things that are really important and allow us to grow, we must pass through moments of suffering. Suffering is something that breeds fruitfulness".

In his room in the Sirio-Lebanese Hospital of Buenos Aires, young Jorge suffered a lot of pain, fevers and fear during an illness that led doctors to recommend a high-risk operation. They took out the top half of his right lung.

His seminarian companions accompanied him night and day. They donated various pints of blood during "person to person" transfusions typical of the time. One of those who visited him and donated blood was Msgr. José Bonet Alcón, now a recognized expert in Canon Law, who declared that Bergoglio demonstrated during those days to be a young man of great virtue and with a large capacity to take on suffering. Fr. Enrique Pozzoli was also present during that difficult time in his life.

It was during one of the painful "healing" sessions which consisted in pouring a saline solution with a probe on the wounds left by the removal of the piece of the lung, that a nun who was a friend, named coincidentally "Dolores", told him something that comforted him a great deal. It also gave him the transcendent dimension that he needed: "With your suffering you are imitating Jesus". This difficult situation, the comforting words of this religious sister and the significant presence of his spiritual director, helped him make the decision that would mark his future as well as that of many others.

More than a pastor in some parish in Buenos Aires, Bergoglio wanted to be a missionary, he even dreamt of spreading the Gospel in Japan. This desire became stronger each time he would hear the stories of his Jesuit professors. It was frequent as well that the best students of the Metropolitan Seminary often followed the steps of St. Ignatius of Loyola. They were drawn by the discipline, obedience and the image of this "front line of the Church".

In the midst of this trial, between the hospital and the Seminary, the young Jorge made a decision that the Pope recounted to us in detail: "I decided to leave the Metropolitan Seminary and enter the Jesuits after they operated on my lung. I was clear in my decision, and it was then that Fr. Pozzoli invited me to go to Tandil on vacation with the Salesian students, so that I would not spend so much time at home and I could better prepare to enter the Company. I think I traveled to Tandil on January 25, 1958".

With the Salesian Aspirants the young Jorge shared activities in the outdoors, choir practice, some Latin classes, walks, soccer matches, campfires and theatrical performances at night. He did this without neglecting his strict schedule of meals, house cleaning and daily Mass, among other things.

In this atmosphere of celebration which at the same time was ordered and religious, Bergoglio recovered a large part of his pulmonary capacity and was strengthened in his Jesuit vocation. This experience was a "warm up" that the wise priest Fr. Pozzoli invited his beloved spiritual son do so as to be better prepared, physically and spiritually for the hard and demanding routine that he would face with the Jesuits. It was, as the Pope admits, another small gift of Providence Who uses inscrutable ways to help those who hope in Him.

The young Bergoglio was ready to take a step that would be transcendental for his life. The boy from Flores had obtained spiritual fruits from the physical pain and experience of suffering, as well as clarity as to his future. He had learned from suffering. He had entered into patience. Bergoglio understood this sometime later, reading the book "A Theology of Failure" by the Jesuit priest John Navone. In this book, Jorge found a reason for the many trials that he had to face during his life. Navone explains in the book how Jesus "enters into patience". Bergoglio explains it himself in "*El Jesuita*": "In the experience of our limits, in dialogue with limits, patience is formed. Sometimes life leads us not to "do" but to "suffer", supporting and carrying our limitations and those of others. To pass through patience is to be responsible for what matures in time. To pass through patience is to allow time to mark and mold our lives."

The experience that was gained in the light of these meditations led him to accept that life is a continuous learning experience, it means to take time, and allow others to unfold their life; it means –also— to give up the pretense of attempting to solve everything, and consider as relative the mystique of efficiency. It means, as later Fr. Jorge will say, to favor time over space; a phrase in his teaching that many people will remember.

On Sunday, March 9, 1958, in the room of his parents' home in the neighborhood of Flores, Jorge finished packing the few things in his bag that he had to bring with him, according to the indications he received from the Jesuits. Two changes of clothing would be enough for the trip he had been planning for the last few months. He asked his father if he had the tickets with him and his mother if she was ready to go. Jorge said goodbye to his brothers and sisters as well as to the walls of the room that had been his for 12 years. "One should not be attached to material things", he told himself. His mother took him by the arm and together they rode in a taxi to the Retiro train and bus station. In the Jesuit novitiate of Barrio Pueyrredón, in Córdoba, no one imagined how far the young novice who was about to enter would go.

CHAPTER 2

IN THE NOVITIATE OF CÓRDOBA

The year was 1908. In one of the offices of the Major Residence of the Company of Jesus, in the center of the city of Córdoba, where the Jesuit novitiate was at the time, a Scottish businessman and a Spanish priest talk business. The scot, Arturo Hughes, an expert in land measurement for the Registry of the Province of Córdoba, is trying to convince the Spanish priest (who has lived in Córdoba for some years) to move the house of formation of the Society of Jesus to an unpopulated area to the northeast portion of the city that he wants to organize and baptize "English Quarters". The priest, Fr. José María Bustamante, well known for having founded the Congregation of religious sisters of Adoration of the Blessed Sacrament, as well as for his tireless preaching of the Spiritual Exercises throughout the province, is now an elderly man, but he has not lost his intelligence or his prudence. As a superior of the Society of Jesus, he knows that the population is growing rapidly and that, sooner or later, it will be difficult to find in the center of the city the peace and space necessary to form the Jesuit novices, scholastics and "regents".

Three years have passed since that meeting. Fr. Bustamante is no longer there, he passed away in 1909. The insistence of Mr. Hughes and meditated decision of the Jesuits begins to show the first fruits of that business conversation in the area referred to as the English Quarters, still deserted and full of ravines and landfills[7]. Building has begun of what will be the enormous Holy Family Novitiate (see picture n. 1), whose walls, a half century later, when the area is renamed Pueyrredon, will house a young novice who will become Pope.

---

[7] Efraín U. Bischoff, *Historia de los Barrios de Córdoba.* Pages 279-291.

Picture 1 - The new Jesuit novitiate in 1915, in the middle of the *English Quarters*, today Pueyrredón. *Picture by kind permission of Remo Bordese.*

Arriving in Córdoba and the beginning of his life as a Jesuit

"I entered the novitiate in the neighborhood of Pueyrredon on March 11 1958, —the Pope recalled to us—. But I arrived to the city of Córdoba a day earlier, with my parents".

Mario Jose Bergoglio and Regina Sívori accompanied their firstborn son to the door of the novitiate where he would spend the next two years. Although he had been in the province four years earlier, the young man did not know the capital city. During a trip with the youth group of St. Joseph parish in Flores, they had gone to the city of Villa Carlos Paz, without stopping in the capital city. Now, they arrived and made their way to an unknown area in the capital.

"We arrived and stayed in a hotel close to plaza San Martin in the center of the city. We spent March 10th visiting some people we knew in the city, among them Fr. Urtiaga, as I recall. The next day, they took me to the Pueyrredon area and left me at the novitiate".

That Tuesday, March 11, Jorge knocked on the double-door of the formation house. They were opened by a smiling religious brother who was the doorman, Cirilo Rodriguez, who would win the heart and mind of the future Pope with his humility and kindness.

As he did with everyone who came to the door, Br. Cirilo invited Jorge and his parents to wait in the visitors' room to the side of the entrance of this immense building that took up a city block. Then he went calmly to look for Fr. Gaviña, the Novice Master. Fr. Cándido Gaviña was born on May 17, 1910 in Carmen de Areco, Buenos Aires, and was ordained a priest on August 24, 1938. He was quickly sent to Columbia where he lived a few years; after returning to Argentina he spent some time in the Immaculate High School, in the province of Santa Fe, and then was named Novice Master in Córdoba. Later he occupied other responsibilities in the Jesuit province, including Provincial (1958-1963). Finally Gaviña was called to Rome, to the General House, where he was secretary to Fr. Pedro Arrupe[8]. He died there, in the Eternal city, on January 16, 1982, when Bergoglio was rector in the Maximo College, in San Miguel, Province of Buenos Aires.

The reception for the young aspirant was brief, as were the words with which he said goodbye to his parents. During their short conversation it was made clear to the parents that during the next two years, he could have visits but always in Córdoba and never for very long. Except for rare circumstances, the new novice would not be able to travel to Buenos Aires to visit his parents or brothers and sisters. Regina Sívori's heart pounded and her emotion erupted in tears. She knew it would not be possible to come back to Córdoba to visit for only an hour. She made an effort to hide her emotion and she supported herself on her husband. Both understood that they were giving away their son and that is always painful. At that time and for the next few days they would have to recall the words of Fr. Pozzoli about the deep happiness of those who with humility and generosity allow themselves to be won over by the call to "follow Him more closely". Their firstborn had accepted that call.

---

[8] Fr. Pedro Arrupe was born in Bilbao, Spain, on November 14, 1907. He was a Jesuit missionary priest in Japan with life experiences, witness and teaching that will lead him to be elected Superior General of the Company of Jesus in 1965, a responsibility he had until 1983. In Japan, during World War II, he was persecuted and imprisoned for being falsely accused as an American spy. He lived through the explosion of the atomic bomb at Hiroshima, where with his knowledge of medicine, he converted the Novitiate into a field hospital to attend hundreds of victims of this deflagration. He resigned as Superior General in 1983 because of health problems. He died in Rome, Italy on February 5, 1991.

The Holy Father still remembers the first moments of his entering into the novitiate, that first encounter with Gaviña in the entrance hall and details of the relationship that he would have with the one who for a few months would be his Novice Master. "I remember that Fr. Gaviña received me, who was at that time the Novice Master, although in a few months he would be named provincial –recalled the Pope—. Gaviña was a very reserved, a very serious man, very good and very delicate. But we did not understand one another well; in fact, at one point, sometime later he would suggest that I leave the Novitiate. I remember telling him once that I could not stand his way of acting, he was very Columbian in his mannerisms and I was very direct, so we did not get along well".

When the Novitiate door shut after Mario Jose Bergoglio and his wife Regina left, Fr. Gaviña told Jorge to follow him. As was done with each new member, the Novice Master assigned him an "angel", that is, a second year novice who would show him around the building and would respond to questions and doubts regarding the new life he was beginning. Since assigning an "angel" was more a custom than a rule, there is no record of who was the one assigned to Bergoglio. And with so many "angels" flying around his life, Francis does not remember.

The tour of the building had to be quick. The strict time schedule of the Novitiate did not leave much free time. Order was also an important tool in the formative process of the Jesuits of that time as it is now, who, if they are to follow one of the principle counsels of their founder should try to do all *Ad maiorem Dei gloriam,* that is "for the greater glory of God", as St. Ignatius taught.

The "angel" led Jorge through the four corners of that enormous religious complex that occupied the block with its façade on Buchardo Street. Today, this land is occupied by three department buildings, a supermarket and paradoxically, a Mormon Church. The only thing left standing today of the Jesuit building that was surrounded by dirt roads is the entrance arch (see picture n. 2) that is now an entrance to one of the apartment complexes and one of the three monkey puzzle trees that adorned one of the patios of the religious house. The rest of the buildings were demolished years later after a decision was taken by Bergoglio himself as Provincial.

Picture 2 - Entrance arch of the demolished novitiate (1974)

Going back to that Tuesday, March 11, 1958, Jorge had seen the entrance hall, and also the visitor's room where he said good bye to his parents. The *angel* repeated to him that if anyone were to come visit him at the Novitiate, no matter who he was, he had to see the person there. No visitor could go further into the house without the expressed permission of the superior.

These rooms were in the principal wing of the building that had two floors with high ceilings. Across the street today stand Holy Family Jesuit Institute and Sebastian Raggi School, which have the same building structure.

The priest's rooms were on the ground floor, among them those responsible for the formation of the students; while the novices and juniors had their room on the second floor on the wing of the building whose windows overlooked Lamadrid Street. The rooms were enormous and very cold in the winter as those who lived there remember. "Here is where you will sleep", the *angel* told Bergoglio with the formality that was used between the brothers, and he indicated his bed, between two others that had a few things that had already been left on them by the other recent arrivals. There were two or three young men in each room.

They then left the dormitory to see the rest of the second floor. Each room had a sign on it indicating its use: they passed through the infirmary, where there was a brother who knew some first aid and how to attend the sick; the chapel right in front of the stairs; the library, where they were to study; classrooms with room for twenty students; and on one of the ends of the hallway, a smaller, warmer chapel that had two statues in marble, one of the Blessed Virgin Mary and the other of St. Ignatius of Loyola.

Guided by the second year novice, the young Bergoglio became familiar with the whole house. They went down the same stairs they came up and saw the laundry room and the priest's quarters. They went out and crossed the patio to the southern wing where there was the kitchen, run by the brother cook, and the huge refectory with a large table set in the shape of a U that could seat up to ninety people.

Picture 3 – Novitiate's basketball court. *Picture from a video by kind permission of José Ravalli.*

In another patio there was a basketball court, with cement tile flooring and wooden backboards (see picture n. 3). On the far western part of the block, there was a dirt soccer field surrounded by trees. Fifty six years later, the Pope remembered the place: "The best part of the building on Buchardo Street –and my favorite— were the basketball court and the soccer field. We played a lot of sports, several days a week".

Pope Francis always loved soccer. His father would take him to the stadium to watch games, which is where he developed his "passion" as a fan of the San Lorenzo Club. As a child "Jorgito" Bergoglio would play soccer with his friends and classmates in the Herminia Brumana plaza in the Flores area, near his home. But it seems he was always better at prayer and theology. "He had two left feet", says Hugo Morelli, a childhood friend who was humorously cited in the book: *Francisco, Vida y Revolución (Francis, Life and Revolution)*, by Elisabetta Piqué.

The last part of the tour his *angel* gave the future Pope was the enormous community church which could be entered directly through the novitiate or from Buchardo Street.

Construction on the huge church began in 1926 and 1927 (see picture n. 4); and although it was never finished according to its plans, in 1927 it began to be used for the liturgy with a provisional tin roof and an incomplete dome that would never be completed.[9]

Picture 4 – The roof of the church demolished in 1974 when Bergoglio was Provincial. *Picture from a video by kind permission of José Ravalli.*

The young novice was surprised to see that the church was not finished and although only thirty years old, it was greatly deteriorated (see picture n. 5). His guide told him that in 1927 the community had run out of money for the construction and decided to inaugurate it such as it was, with a temporary roof that usually leaked when it rained. Since it was not finished, the main altar was very simple, small and without an altarpiece. A dark curtain formed the backdrop of the crucifix. On each side of it

---

[9] The Holy Family church was blessed in 1931, and on December 24, 1938 it was made a parish by the decree of the then archbishop of Córdoba Fermín Emilio Lafitte. The first pastor was the Jesuit Telésforo Andía, who remained in the office until 1944. Cfr. *Los jesuitas en Córdoba* –Córdoba, 1937– written by Fr. Sebastián Raggi.

two large paintings hung, depicting scenes of the Gospel. In front of each of the paintings were plaster statues of angels that held electric candles in their hands.

Picture 5 – Front of the Holy Family Church, still incomplete.
Picture from a video by kind permission of José Ravalli.

Jorge's eyes were drawn to a beautiful collection of statues that represented the Holy Family on a side altar. Already Bergoglio had a special devotion to the Blessed Virgin and St. Joseph and what was better than to have them there, together with the Child Jesus, where he would participate in Sunday Mass together with the Jesuit and parish community of the neighborhood. These three statues are found today on the wall behind the altar of the parish church that was built years later on the corner of Buchardo and Deheza Streets, in front of where the old church stood. Bergoglio could never have imagined that only fifteen years later, he would have to make the decision to sell these buildings and its land in a difficult stage of his priestly life that would also mark his relationship with Córdoba. Not even the Novitiate building would be saved from the destruction even though at the time it was still being used for classrooms by the Catholic University. This is part of the history that at the moment the two novices getting to know the building could not have foreseen.

Bergoglio asked his guide why some people referred to the neighborhood as the *English* Quarters and others as *Pueyrredon*. His *angel* replied that the name of the area had changed a while before to *Pueyrredon* but that some people, especially the older residents, could not get used to the change.

In fact, the change was made official in August of 1950 with the passing of Ordinance 3993. This law reflected the nationalist political tension that was promoted by the peronist central government. In this case it was an excuse to change the foreign name for the name of a man who was Governor of the province in 1810 and later Supreme Director of the United Provinces of Rio de la Plata: Juan Martin Pueyrredon.

History and politics always go hand in hand, sometimes they reflect one another, and sometimes they are manipulated. The young Bergoglio knew this, and although at this time he was more concerned about what was going on in his soul, he was not ignorant of what was going on in the country.

Just fifteen days earlier, on February 23, 1958, there had been national elections where the Intransigent Radical Party formed by Arturo Frondizi and Alejandro Gomez had won by a wide margin (44,8% of the votes). The Peronist Party did not participate due to the restrictions still placed upon it by the *de facto* president Pedro Eugenio Aramburo.

It could have been the first elections in which Bergoglio participated but he was in Tandil vacationing with the Salesians at the time.

The situation in the country was difficult; a recession was beginning, with the reduction of the reserves and a deficit in the trade balance[10].

Those that were companions of now Pope Francis during those years agree that the novices did not discuss party politics in the house of formation. The daily routine was very intense, concentrated upon their Novitiate training, and there was very little time to talk anyway.

Still, the priests in charge of formation and the superiors were aware of what was going on in Córdoba and in the country. There were priests living in the Novitiate very committed to social causes (among them for example Fr. Sebatian Raggi, founder of the Worker Association),

---

[10] Cfr. Mónica Deleis, Ricardo de Titto, Diego Arguindeguy, *El libro de los Presidentes argentinos*, page 234.

and others that were working in or collaborated with the Catholic University of Córdoba that was just beginning. Almost all of them read the newspaper *Los Principios* that was brought to their door each morning. Through this newspaper and through the contact that the priests had with their faithful as well as the institutions where they worked, the priests found out about the political and institutional events going on and some of it reached the novices.

At that time, when the now Pope went to the area hospitals (Córdoba and Transito Caceres hospitals) to visit and attend the sick, he must have known of the doctors' strikes in all the clinics and hospitals of the province, seeking higher pay and relief from the firing and incarceration of union bosses. These union conflicts, that had as their catalyst the popular unrest due to the removal of the 1949 Constitution, mobilized workers also from the Judicial Ministry, bankers and even the police.

On February 16, 1960, when Bergoglio was preparing to make his first vows of poverty, chastity and obedience, the city of Córdoba became the center of violence in the country. The minister of the economy of the nation Alvaro Alsogaray and the secretary of war, General Rodolfo Larcher came to visit the city. For their "welcome", in a crime that was never resolved, the gas tanks of the Shell-Max Company were blown up, with fifteen persons killed and around twenty more wounded. People spoke of a terrorist attack, or an attack that was organized by members of the peronist party and even of the possibility of a self-inflicted attempt by the provincial government to provoke unrest. The suspects were freed a year and a half later, for lack of evidence. The case was never clarified.

Still the Air Force mobilized pressure on President Frondizi to intervene the province and remove the governor before his term ended. On June 15, 1960, when Bergoglio was already in Chile as a scholastic, Governor Zanichelli handed over the power of the province to the government appointed receiver Juan Francisco Larranchea.

While all this was happening outside the Novitiate, inside the young Bergoglio investigated the details of Jesuit spirituality, this way of living that teaches one to put himself under God, the great Sculptor's, chisel. Within the walls of the novitiate the Divine Artist was beginning to perfect His work.

Friends, companions and teachers in one place

That religious community of Pueyrredon was important for the Society of Jesus in Argentina for the number of members it contained as well as for the quality of its members. According to the Jesuit records, in March of 1958, there were eighty five men living there: thirty one priests (between superiors, those responsible for the formation, the pastor, ministers and tertians – the priests in the final stages of Jesuit formation); forty one students (novices and scholastics, among them Bergoglio); and thirteen assistant brothers (religious that cannot celebrate the sacraments but are in charge of different responsibilities in the Order such as the cooking, attending the door, the sacristy, etc.)

Another eight novices entered with Bergoglio that March 11, and three more would enter later on that year. Aside from the Pope, the group was formed by Agustin López, Alejandro Antunovich, Horacio Lescano, Luis Casalotto, Eugenio Orlinski, Santiago Frank (who was a diocesan priest who entered the novitiate to become a Jesuit), and another two young men named Sintes and Pautasso. Nine months later Juan Gabriel Wille arrived, but as many of the others, he left before ordination as a priest.

Of this group the ones that completed their formation and were ordained priests for the Society of Jesus were: Bergoglio, Casalotto, Lopez and Antunovich; but Casalotto ended up incardinating in the clergy of the diocese of Buenos Aires; Lopez died during the 80's in the Jesuit house of San José del Boqueron, in the province of Santiago del Estero; and Fr. Antunovich passed away years later in the province of Corrientes.[11]

[11] Alejandro Antunovich SJ was born in the town of La Paz, Province of Entre Ríos, Argentina on August 10, 1935, and he died in Corrientes, in the Jesuit community of Itá Ibaté, on July 14, 1993. Fr. Augustin López was born in Santa Fe, Santa Fe, Argentina in 1940 and died at the Colegio Máximo, in

The Pope remembers that Casalotto was the closest friend he had during his novitiate years. "He was very close to "Gringo" Casalotto who later left the Society of Jesus and is in the diocesan clergy. Yes; we were close companions with Casalotto and also with some others who later left the Society such as Horacio Lescano. Together we formed a close knit group".

Today, Fr. Luis Jeronimo Casalotto lives in Boulogne, in the province of Buenos Aires. He still remembers his friendship with Bergoglio and the hardships of the novitiate. "I have many memories but they are too much to tell you over the phone", the priest told the authors. Later, his brother Dante Casalotto and his wife Olga (residents of San Vicente, in the city of Córdoba) explained that health problems have prohibited him from being the active priest he had been up to a few years ago. He can almost no longer walk and at times prefers to remain in absolute silence. Yet when asked about the friend of his youth who in now Pope, he said: "I am happy that Bergoglio is the Pope and it is a great honor for me that people say I was his friend, his colleague. I, too remember him as a close friend. And from what I can see, he is doing things well as Pope. I hope he can continue on for many years because the Church needs someone like him".

The other member of the group of novices that the Pope remembers well is Horacio Lescano, who entered the novitiate the same day as Bergoglio (see picture n. 6).

San Miguel, Buenos Aires on August 7, 1980. Both had been ordained priests on December 19, 1970 by Bishop Enrique Angelelli, with whom they had studied and deepened their knowledge of the importance of popular piety that Bergoglio emphasizes continually.

Picture 6 - Horacio Lescano, one of the classmates of the Pope, around end of March, 1958. He left the Company before priestly ordination. *Picture by his kind permission.*

Horacio has his own important history, since after being in formation for 13 years, when he was about to be ordained a priest, he was told by one of his superiors that he would be happier if he left (become a layman). "And Father was right", he assured the authors, from his home in Villa Cabrera, in the city of Córdoba, where he was interviewed for this book. After leaving the Society and returning to lay life ("something that was very difficult for me" he indicated), he met the woman who today is his wife, who gave birth to five children and now has some grandchildren and who have made him a happy man. Yet, every time he can, so as not to lose contact, Lescano calls his friend and ex-companion in formation Fr. Carlos Cravenna, and asks him if there is space in the Residence for a couple of days of spiritual retreat. In this way Lescano (see picture n. 7) increases his happiness tremendously because if there is anything this friend of the Pope has not lost, in spite of his experience, is his Christian faith and hope.

Picture 7 - Horacio Lescano at home showing his diary. *Picture by his kind permission.*

"I met Jorge Bergoglio the day we entered the Novitiate and I was impressed by the very diplomatic style of that serious and intelligent young man who today impresses the world with his smile and gestures that are typical of Jesuit spirituality". Horacio remembered that the first year novices had contact and worked at times with those of the second year. With effort, he remembered some of their names: Nicolas Zacowicz, Jorge Gonzalez Manent, Alejandro Henin, Vidal Llanos (who already passed away), Andrés Swinnen, Juan Carlos Constable y Aldo Scotto. Some left the Society shortly after joining, some were ordained but later left the ministry; the others continue to serve in the Order such as Frs. Swinnen (in Holy Family parish, in the city of Córdoba), Constable (at this moment in St. Joseph of Boqueron) and Scotto (in Holy Martyrs parish in Posadas, province of Misiones Argentina).

When we interviewed him, at a certain point Horacio Lescano excused himself for a moment to look for a "treasure" he had put away. Minutes later he returned with an old notebook in his hands and told us a story to add to this book. "Since I was young I had the habit of writing something each day, so my "diary" has many volumes", he explained. In the notebook numbered 7, on May 17, 1958, the then Jesuit novice wrote his impressions of each of his companions in formation. "I remember that it was a Saturday, so I had a little more time to write", he explained before showing us what he wrote. He wrote a commentary on each of the novices, in alphabetical order, on those pages that are now yellow with age. There are notes on "Anasagasti" ("from Uruguay", Lescano remembers without showing us what he wrote); "Adamo"; "Amado"; "Artigas"; "Antunovich"; "Bergoglio"; "Casalotto"; "Espil"; "Frank"; "Gonzalez Manent"; "Longo"; "Macagno"; "McAdam" ("he was English, who later was assigned in the province of Missions and then left the Order" he pointed out); "Martilotti"; "Orlinski"; "Puricelli"; "Rey"; "Sanchez"; "Sintes"; "Swinnen"; "Zacowicz".

The authors of this book, curious, read what was written about Bergoglio. There is a prophetic tone in what was written in 1958: "I like him –Lescano wrote of the man who is now Pope–. What will he be? He is really intellectual. A philosopher or a theologian? I like talking to him". (see picture n. 7).

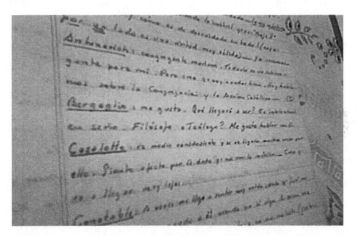

Picture 8 – Diary of Horacio Lescano of 1958 with the following description: "Bergoglio: me gusta. Qué llegará a ser? Es intelectual en serio. Filósofo o Teólogo? Me gusta hablar con él".

It is extraordinary: the question that this novice asked about his companion found its remarkable answer fifty five years later.

In March of 1960, the now Fr. Carlos Cravenna joined the community, and so was able to share a few days with Bergoglio before he left for Chile. The very friendly disposition of Fr. Cravenna who at this moment exercises his ministry and lives in the Major Residence of Córdoba, as well as the stories of Lescano, of Fr. Swinnen and of Pope Francis himself, gives us a good idea of the daily life of that community that housed and formed the Pope.

All four emphasize an important detail: on July 9, 1958, Fr. Gaviña, until then the Novice Master, was elected Provincial and Fr. Francisco Zaragozí[12], who had been provincial for the six years before, now took the position of Novice Master in the novitiate in Córdoba. Cravenna described Zaragozí as "a very austere person, physically similar to St. Ignatius of Loyola in that he was short and a little bald. He was also very parsimonious; he only said "yes" or "no". It was a triumph if he made any other gesture".

In spite of his parsimony, Bergoglio got along very well with this Novice Master, certainly better than the former one. The Pope himself expressed it in his conversations with us: "Fr Zaragozi and I understood each other well, and in fact, years later I chose him as my assistant priest during my ordination to the priesthood".

The Jesuit Catalogue records that beginning in July of 1958, Fr. Zaragozi not only took charge of the novices but also became the rector of the Holy Family community, director of the Apostolic School of the Coadjutor Brothers, and director of the Friends of the Society Association.

Aside from Zaragozi, there were other important priests to help in different aspects of the formation of the students, as well as in other Jesuit works and in the Holy Family parish.

The Pope and those who were his companions remember Fr. Antonio Aznar, well known in the ignatian religious order for his work in the west of the province of Córdoba where he preached the Exercises of St. Ignatius to hundreds of people as did the Blessed "Cura" Brochero. In fact

---

[12] Francisco Zaragozí was born in the locality of Altea, Spain, on January 30, 1904. Son of immigrants, he entered the Company of Jesus and was ordained a priest in Argentina on December 23, 1933. As Fr. Provincial, it was he who sent Fr. Jorge Camargo in order to take care of "the University things" which ended up creating the Catholic University of Córdoba. He was, aside from this, the Novice Master and even a pastor in the city of Montevideo, Uruguay. He died there on January 20, 1986.

Fr. Aznar was one of the first to promote the cause for the canonization of Brochero, writing two books and several articles about the apostle of the sierras of Córdoba.[13]

Another was Fr. Oscar Dreidemie, founder and first director of the National Jesuit Museum of Jesus Maria (province of Córdoba), and the clinic of Sinsacate. Because of his knowledge and experience he became the national delegate of Museums. It is in part due to the silent work of this man that in the year 2000, several Jesuit residences and ranches in Córdoba were declared World Patrimony of Humanity by UNESCO.[14]

Fr. Cravenna also remembers the advice that Fr. Matías Crespi offered; he had been a great missionary in the Patagonia and underlined the importance that the priests be close to the faithful while evangelizing, something that he had sought to do among the poor in the southern part of Argentina.

Of the many important examples, Pope Francis noted two: "Among the priests at the Novitiate in Córdoba I remember Fr. Sebatian Raggi, founder of the Worker Association and Fr. Carmelo Gangi who was a great preacher and did very good pastoral work".

Fr. Gangi, who has since died, was in charge of the parish that the Jesuits had in the area of Guiñazú, in the very north of the city of Córdoba, until the 80's. Together with Fr. Raggi, the real *character* of the house, they worked a lot for the School of the Workers Association of Holy Family that is named now, appropriately, Fr. Sebastian Raggi School.

Fr. Raggi has his own story, known and appreciated by Pope Francis, since he was able to learn from him, a man committed to the spiritual and social well-being of the people. Born in 1879, ordained a priest for the Society in 1912, he made his final vows with the Order in 1915. Fr. Raggi was seventy when Bergoglio arrived to the novitiate and he walked with a cane. He was a confessor and spent a lot of his time

[13] Fr. Antonio Aznar wrote the books: *El Cura Brochero, vida heróica y santa* (1964) that has 100 pages; and *El Cura Brochero en su apostolado sacerdotal, su vida espiritual y legendaria en heroísmos,* Paulinas (1951), that has 205 pages, with a prologue by G. Martinez Zurivía and an appendix with photographs.
[14] As was decided by the Annual Assembly of UNESCO held on November 29, 2000 in the city of Cairns, Australia.

writing the history of the novitiate building as well as his own memories. Long before, in 1921, he had founded the Workers Association of the Holy Family. This association was aimed at alleviating the poverty and ignorance of many of those employed at the train workshops and their families for the lack of education and social assistance.

The Pope and his novitiate companions remember these great priests, from whom they received counsel, spiritual advice and example of religious life that was also part of their formation. It was an intense and profound process that was supported by the strict routine and some customs that would mark forever the man who leads the Catholic Church from the Chair of Peter.

The strict schedule of "Brother" Jorge

Imagine dear reader, an enormous dining room with high ceilings and walls and large windows, and with a table in the form of a U. All those dining are religious men. There are nearly eighty of them, all dressed in a black cassock, and at the head of the table sit those of greater age, some of them quite elderly. Look closely dear reader: the rest of the places are occupied by men of different ages: from fifty year old adults to young men of just eighteen. No one is speaking, except the novice who is standing close to the head of the table reading in a loud and clear voice the life of a saint. But focus even more the imagination. The reader will notice that one of the novices has not yet sat down but with plate in hand is moving along the table "begging" for food from those who already have their plates full and are eating. Follow the young man who was chosen, precisely on this day to do penance by eating only what the others have given him as an act of charity. One might be surprised even more when one realizes that the "beggar" has filled his plate and he has returned to his place. But there is no seat for him: the young man kneels on the floor, puts his plate on the table and eats his meal kneeling, like a beggar. Can you imagine, dear reader, who he might be?

Jorge Bergoglio's life as a Jesuit novice, just as with all the other "brothers", was ordered by a strict regimen, full of rules, motivations, exercises and penitential customs each with their meaning. These requirements aimed at maturing and strengthening the ignatian religious spirit of the novices. They also were meant to increase humility as well as the consciousness of their belonging and abandonment to the Will of God, to the will of the Creator that is expressed in prayer, in the voice of the priests in charge of formation and in the learning of the Constitution of the Society of Jesus as well as the teachings of St. Ignatius.

Pope Francis told us a little about those first months of formation: "In general, it was a period where we were closed in, a very strong interior effort, with a rigorous schedule and in silence. It was a very ordered life, a very austere one, in which there was good climate and in which I felt very much at home".

Almost all those that lived in the novitiate at that time that we could consult seem to agree with the assessment of Bergoglio. Lescano y Cravenna noted that everything was ordered toward the interior life of the novices who had to "apprehend", that is to say, understand and live deeply certain principles of St. Ignatius. They can be summarized in the following sayings of the founder of the Society: *"It is necessary to make ourselves indifferent to all created things, in all that is within our freedom to do and is not prohibited; in such a way as to not desire on our part more health than sickness, riches more than poverty, honor than dishonor, a long life more than a short one, and so on with everything else; desiring and choosing only that which leads us to the end for which we have been created".*

"Each has been created to praise and serve God, our Lord".

"What satisfies the soul is not knowing a lot, but rather feeling and savoring things interiorly".

According to Fr. Swinnen, who was already in the novitiate house for a year when Bergoglio arrived, the novitiate that they made "was closer to the novitiate made in the time of St. Stanislao Kostka in the year

1560 in as much as the demands and hardships were concerned, than that which is lived in the novitiate of the Society today.

Swinnen remembers that a lot of the activities, rules and demands were established according to what was written in a small book called the "*Costumbrero*" or "Book of Customs" that each Jesuit house had and which was "obeyed to the letter". Years ago, this book, which had as many versions as there were provinces of the Order, was used to unify and regulate the exterior life of the sons of the Society of Jesus throughout the world with the aim of emphasizing the identity of the Order. Smiling, Fr. Andrés assured us that following the *Costumbrero* was so important at one point that, during the canonical visits of the superiors to the different communities, in the written reports there was often a reference to the non-compliance of what the *Costumbrero* required. Swinnen remembers having read in one report the provincial complaining because the community did not put butter out at breakfast "as the *Costumbrero* stipulates".

The *Costumbrero* with the title: *General and ordinary practices in the Loyola novitiate for the years 1856-1857* describes in detail the life of this Spanish novitiate, its schedule and routine: *Rise, offer works, prayer, order room, hear and help at Mass, prayer of the divine office or the parvulo, talk, exercise of modesty and conferences. Manual duties. Writing exercises. Memory exercises. Examination of conscience. Lunch. Recreation. Rest. Give lessons. Catechism, music and ceremony of the Holy Mass. Walk in silence. Visit to the chapel. Spiritual Reading. Afternoon meditation. Activities for after evening recreation. Retiring and taking discipline. Particular practices: monthly retreat. Practices for the instructors.*

In the same book there are also forty two rules about clothing, food and shoes.

Except for a few minor differences, this was the routine that was used in the novitiate of Córdoba when the Pope lived there.

At 6 in the morning the porter passed by the rooms ringing a bell.

Immediately the novices began to pray the *Te Deum*[15] in Latin, just as the pope remembered: "We prayed in the dormitories, we did our first meditation there and began the day in this way".

After quickly washing up, all the novices made their way to the chapel in silence. "The general atmosphere was one of silence –Fr. Cravenna explains—; 'speak quickly and in few words' as the ignatian rule says". And also, as Lescano recalled, "always in Latin. Only once in a while we could speak in Spanish. This was useful; by the end of the year we were able to dominate almost perfectly the language of the Church".

They said the community prayers in the chapel and at 7:30 participated in Mass that a priest celebrated with his back to the novices and in Latin, according to the pre-conciliar rite, since it was prior to Vatican Council II that renewed the liturgy and admitted the use of the vernacular in the ceremonies.[16]

After Mass, at 8:15, the novices and almost all the members of the community went to the dining room for breakfast which was always frugal and in absolute silence.

After breakfast they began the "humble duties" that were part of their formation in humility so no one would be "inflated" with pride. The different jobs were written on a chalkboard where the more daring and clever novices would scribble jokes about the different jobs. Sooner or later everyone had to clean the bathrooms, sweep the stairwells or hallways, and help in the kitchen scrubbing pots and pans or the dishes or peeling potatoes.

After working at these jobs an hour came the intellectual work. Fr. Swinnen pointed out that the first year novices took Latin while the second year took Latin and Greek. Lescano also remembered that the first year took lessons in "tones", that is, in rhetoric. "They taught us how to speak, how to express ourselves well, to interpret what we wanted to say

---

[15] An ancient Christian prayer of thanksgiving: *Te Deum laudamus: te Dominum confitemur.Te aeternum Patrem omnis terra veneratur. Tibi omnes Angeli; tibi caeli et universae Potestates; Tibi Cherubim et Seraphim incessabili voce proclamant: Sanctus, Sanctus, Sanctus, Dominus Deus Sabaoth. Pleni sunt caeli et terra maiestatis gloriae tuae...*

[16] The second Ecumenical Vatican Council was announced by Pope John XXIII in January 1959, but its first session began in 1962. When John XXIII died, it was his successor Paul VI who presided the other three sessions until its end in 1965, which motivated a strong renovation in the Church.

so as to be able to preach to a lot of people.

Then, they received the "talks" in which the Novice Master explained in detail to the young men the rules and Constitutions of the Company of Jesus that had to be known and respected.

At twelve noon the talks ended and the students had fifteen minutes in which the Novice Master was at their disposition in case anyone had to ask for a special permission. Swinnen remembers that he used this time and this possibility to ask to be excused from using the study book "Exercise of perfection and Christian virtues" of Fr. Rodriguez[17], because it was "very dense and difficult", and he considered it was counterproductive for his spiritual life.

Then they had between thirty and forty five minutes to individually make the first examination of conscience of the day and pray the litany of the Saints.

During these examinations of conscience, that the Pope still does today, the novices asked themselves in what way they may have offended God, their brothers or themselves. Then they asked God forgiveness and the grace never again to fall into sin.

At one o'clock lunch began in the enormous refectory of the house. Fr. Swinnen remembered: "We prepared well for the midday dinner, which had its well established rules; some had to help serving the food and others sat down. There was no talking since one of the novices was assigned to read a spiritual book which we listened to as we ate. This changed on feast days, such as Sunday, when the Novice Master would stand and say "*Deo gratias*" ("Thanks be to God"), and then we could all speak".

Mondays, Wednesdays and Fridays were "penitential" days for the novices; days in which they would take a closer look at their life and their sins, as well as the sins of the whole world and do penance for them, as a

---

[17] The book *Ejercicio de perfección y virtudes cristianas* was written by Fr. Alonso Rodríguez (not to be confused with Br. St. Alonso Rodríguez) around the year 1550. It is a compendium of Christian ascetics and mysticism that inspired great saints of the Church such as John Mary Vianney, the Curé of Ars. St. Alfonsus Maria de Liguori considered it essential for holiness and St. Anthony Mary Claret considered that the book had brought more souls to heaven than there are stars in the heavens.

sign of their repentance and conversion before God and their brothers and sisters. The larger penitential acts were publically expressed at the noon meal. Fr. Swinnen and Horacio Lescano remember very well the details: some of the novices would beg to eat, that is, eat that which was given to them from others. In this case they would wait until all were served and then begin to ask for a little food from those that sat around him. "Since everyone gave you something, the plate ended up full, and so we usually wound up eating more than usual on that day", Swinnen told us with a smile. There was another exercise in humility that consisted in kissing the feet of the brothers and priests that were seated at the table. Bergoglio never stopped making this gesture at least once a year when, as a priest, bishop and now as Pope, he presides the Mass of the Lord's Supper on Holy Thursday, during which the humble service of Jesus to His disciples at the Last Supper is remembered.

Another of the "public" penances was to eat kneeling instead of comfortably seated. No one was surprised or bothered by this, it was a normal penitential exercise that everyone did at some point during their formation. They were so accustomed to it, that once it was an occasion of a prank by Bergoglio as a novice. "When Bergoglio was doing his second year of novitiate and I my first year of the scholastic period – Swinnen told us—we would play some pranks. I remember one day we told a first year novice that they were supposed to eat the mid afternoon snack on their knees. So before the dining hall filled I got on my knees and invited the novice to do the same. But just before the superior Fr. Zaragozi entered I got up. When he saw the novice doing a penance that was not prescribed he was roundly scolded, as we also were when we later confessed to the superior and asked forgiveness for our little joke".

Two or three times a week, the whole group of novices met with the Novice Master for what was called the "Exercise of Faults". It consisted in fraternal correction, during which each one would express what bothered them of the other brothers, but always with some reason. One would hear phrases like: "it seems to me so and so speaks with pride"; or "brother such and such is too sensitive and gets angry too easily", and other similar things.

It was a sharing session that permitted fraternal correction, which is a Christian practice that requires a lot of charity, whether it is to express the faults of others or to receive the correction that others have expressed. It was also a way for the novices to increase the quality of community life.

At 2:00 p.m., when the midday meal was finished, the whole community filed out in order to the Novitiate chapel to make a brief visit to the Blessed Sacrament. A few minutes later they were permitted recreation in which they could speak their native tongue. Swinnen, Cravenna, Lescano and even the Pope himself underline the fact that during these fifteen minutes they could speak Spanish instead of Latin. Even so, the "freedom" was not absolute, since there were norms also for recreation: a group of three novices had to walk in front of another three. "the *Costumbrero* said that recreation had to be done in this way and this was the way we did it: while the group of three novices walked forward, the other three in front of them walked backward until they ran into something", remembered Swinnen. And Lescano added: "In this way we walked forward and backward speaking of edifying things, nothing about television or soccer". Fr. Cravenna emphasized the fact that, in spite of its severity, those fifteen minutes were treasured by the novices.

After recreation they had a half hour to sleep a siesta. Bergoglio learned there the habit of resting twenty-five to thirty minutes that he still does to recuperate his strength. Then came the "*Oficio parvo*"[18], prayed in community with which they were once more recollected and ready to continue their intellectual work for two hours, advancing in their learning of the Constitutions of the Company, the Rules, religious life, etc...when they finished these hours of class, the novices moved to the refectory for a snack and (prepared two or three days a week) to play soccer or basketball. They removed their cassocks, put on long pants and over everything they put on a dust jacket that Swinnen remembers was "the color of a rat, dark but faded from use".

---

[18] The "Little Office of the Immaculate Virgin" is an expression of praise to Our Lady, a prayer that was prayed in all the religious communities by those who were not yet bound to pray the Liturgy of the Hours, with its prayers that are specific for different times of the day. The Second Vatican Council would later promote praying this latter for all religious and the faithful.

Bergoglio participated in these games with certain measure. "I do not remember him as great in sports –Fr. Swinnen says of Pope Francis—; since he had this serious lung problem some years earlier, he was careful".

Fr. Cravenna remembers very well that they enjoyed great soccer games in the dirt field and bounced the ball off the side of the church. The land that that field once occupied now is a supermarket.

"Go and wash". The shout of the porter put an end to the game and signaled the beginning of the next activity. It was never good news, in the summertime because they did not want to end the game and in the wintertime because they had to shower with cold water. "It was not freezing water –Swinnen explained— but it was almost always cold because the water heater was small, you had to heat it with a wood fire and it was never enough. Winter was a challenge… but you had to put up with it and we did".

Saturday afternoons and Sunday mornings the routine changes a little to leave room for one of the activities that he Pope most remembers: to go look for children in the neighborhood and nearby slum to give them catechism, a snack and recreation. Francis remembers it with a detail to names and places that reveal a remarkable memory and love: "We taught catechism Saturdays in the afternoon and Sundays in the morning. We went to look for the kids, boys and girls of the area, near the Tránsito Cáceres hospital. I remember we were able to get a lot of kids together and it was really nice. I remember a pair of brothers named Napoli, who were very lively and lived with their family on Pringles street. I remember as well the Zanotte family, very humble, but really very religious".

With the help of God and perseverance those brothers that the Pope remembered were found and interviewed for this book. The journalist Federico Papa was able to do it once he was asked by the authors and went through the long list of families named Napoli in the phone book. One by one he called them, quickly explain who he was looking for and why, hope the people on the other end of the phone understood and believed what he was saying, and move on to the next.

When Daniel Napoli heard what this unknown caller was saying he remembered that his dad, Antonio José, talked about being a "friend of the Pope", and he didn't believe him. But his dad was not lying.

Antonio José –whom everyone calls by his second name– and his brother Pedro today are 69 and 66 years old respectively (see picture n. 9). The older one is a happily retired metalworker. Pedro still works each day in a workshop for automobile electronics that he opened in the same house on Pringles Street that a half century earlier Bergoglio gave them catechism. They were thrilled when they were told that Pope Francis still remembers them with affection. It was the same thrill they felt when they saw him on television come out on the balcony of St. Peter's on March 13, 2013, moments after hearing the traditional announcement of the *"habemus papam"*. It is no wonder. The most famous man in the world, who today moves many with his messages and gestures is the same man who every Sunday during 1959, at 9 in the morning, would knock on the door of their house to teach them catechism. José and Pedro remember it as though it was yesterday: "I was nine or ten and my brother twelve or thirteen when we met Bergoglio in the street –Pedro recalled. He was walking around out there and we asked him for a holy card, he gave us one and asked us if we wanted to prepare to receive Holy Communion".

Picture 9 - Antonio José (69) and Pedro Nápoli (66) in the patio of their home: 1163 Pringles St. where Bergoglio taught them cathechism *Picture by kind permission of Nicolás Papa.*

The Jesuit novices had as part of their formation the obligation to give catechism, so this is what Bergoglio was looking for when he came across the Napoli brothers. Without hesitation, the boys brought the novice to speak with their mother.

Amanda Luisa Espinosa, who today with her ninety-one years has only a vague memory of that "seminarian", authorized him to give "doctrine" classes in the patio of the house.

In a few weeks, Bergoglio had seven or eight boys and girls coming to the Napoli family house. "We sat in the patio, under a paradise tree that is no longer there. Bergoglio sat on a chair and the children sat around him on the ground", the brothers remembered. They think the Pope remembered them because they were the hosts and the most attentive of the group during the Sunday class. "The others were really rascals", they explained.

They remembered him always wearing his black cassock; his hair was still dark "but with a high forehead", and always punctual. "On sunny days, rainy days, cold or hot days, he would arrive at 9 and we would be waiting for him", they added.

In order to get to Pringles street, five blocks from the novitiate, Bergoglio had to cross over the gullies that, for lack of drains, the runoff water had cut into what is now Viamonte Street. Small precarious houses and shacks stood in the area. "It was a slum, but he did not have any problem, he went walking through the weeds and the rocks to get there and everyone respected him".

Bergoglio gave them a catechism (they remember the book as being a thin one with a white cover) and he asked them if they had studied from one week to the next. The one who answered the questions well was rewarded with a holy card or a small medal of the Virgin Mary or of the Sacred Heart, which he always carried in his pocket. Sometimes he even had candy for them but it was not often since he had to buy it and he did not have the money. When "class" was over, they would play soccer in the patio until noon. "Bergoglio was a soccer player —one of the brothers assured us—; he liked it, he tucked up his cassock and played with us".

One Sunday at midday, the father of the boys, Antonio Napoli, who was a Sicilian immigrant who made a living repairing boilers, invited him to dinner and the novice accepted. Although the after-dinner conversation was not that long, it was enough time for Bergoglio to teach the boys a song in Italian that Pedro still remembers. "He was a really nice guy. You felt good being around him because of the goodness he transmitted. Just like you see today: simple, natural, and nice", says José.

The brothers remembered a funny story that looking back seems a paradox. They remember that sometimes on Sunday morning, while Bergoglio was in the middle of his class, the "Evangelists" would come knocking on the front door to proselytize; and half-jokingly, half seriously he would have his students yell "evangelical bums" so they would leave. The paradoxical part of the story is that years later, the elder of the Napoli brothers converted to the Evangelicals, and the novice that taught the brothers to drive away the "Protestants" became later one of the biggest enthusiasts of ecumenical dialogue in the Catholic Church.

The Napoli brothers made their First Communion in 1960, when Bergoglio had already left for Chile to continue his formation. Pedro remembers that celebration because he relives it each Sunday, early in the morning, when he goes to Mass and receives Communion.

Certain nostalgia takes over the older brother when he thinks about the years after Bergoglio left Córdoba, and although he received several letters to say hello, he never responded. "I didn't have money for the stamps", he said. To "repair" this oversight, Napoli sent a letter to the man who is now Pope Francis. He anxiously awaits a response that sooner or later will arrive.

Fr. Swinnen was able to give us more information about those "apostolic explorations" that the Jesuits made in the area to teach catechism. "We went to the area that we called 'the gully' as well as the areas that now are covered by the parishes of St. Raymond Nonato, St. Ignatius of Loyola and the Robles School".

Bergoglio enjoyed as a young man the experience of pastoral and educational closeness with children that would serve him well the rest of his life. In Chile also, where later he went two years as a scholastic in formation, he would spend time giving catechesis to poor children. The same as in Santa Fe Province where he did his regency; and finally also as a priest when he founded parishes and worked with the poor in the slum areas near the Jesuit house in San Miguel, Province of Buenos Aires.

Who could tell that this young enthusiastic Jesuit, who did not hesitate to join in the children's games, knowing that "of such is the Kingdom of God[19], fifty years later, as the head of the Catholic Church, he would have to beg the world's pardon for abuse committed by religious against children such as these?

Who knew that he would utter the words "you do not play with children", where he meant that children deserved the same treatment and pastoral attention that Jesus gave them? In April of 2014, the Pope said "I feel obliged to be responsible for all the evil done by some priests, enough priests. Enough in number, not in comparison with all of them. I am responsible for seeking forgiveness for the damage that they have done in the sexual abuse of children. The Church is conscious of this damage; it is a personal and moral damage inflicted on them... We are not going to retreat at all in what can be done to treat these problems and the sanctions that must be applied, on the contrary. I believe we must be severe. You do not play with children".

The novices returned happy, renewed and "with the smell of the sheep" from those pastoral experiences. This was not only because they heard themselves called "Father" due to their being dressed in a cassock, but also because in the middle of a formation period necessarily turned inward, working on their personal spiritual life, they were for a moment able to point their lives clearly toward the good of others.

It was really necessary to wash off the "smell of the sheep" after the hour of playing sports as well as after their catechism with games on Saturdays; those that shared those years with the Pope assure us with a smile. And the hot water heater in the Novitiate was not sufficient.

---

[19] Cfr. The Gospel according to Mark 10:13-16: "And people were bringing children to him that he might touch them, but the disciples rebuked them. When Jesus saw this he became indignant and said to them, "Let the children come to me; do not prevent them, for the kingdom of God belongs to such as these. Amen, I say to you, whoever does not accept the kingdom of God like a child will not enter it." Then he embraced them and blessed them, placing his hands on them".

After washing up, the novices had an hour of spiritual reading; a half hour of prayer in the chapel and another fifteen minutes to speak privately with the Novice Master or his assistant.

At 8 p.m. dinner was ready where there was always soup that the novices helped serve. Others were chosen to practice their "tones" (rhetoric) with an edifying chapter of reading which imposed a silence that was only broken by the noise of the silverware.

After dinner there were fifteen minutes of recreation. Lescano and Fr. Cravenna remember that it consisted in walking in the patio or in the hallways of the Novitiate (it depended on the time of the year) speaking with one another. At 9:30 p.m. the bell sounded to signal it was time for the second examination of conscience of the day.

The last half hour of the daily routine was divided into two: fifteen minutes to prepare the meditation for the following day and another fifteen to make a final visit to the chapel to pray. Around 10 p.m. all the religious went to bed. The novices went exhausted but most of them very happy. The Pope remembered that he always gave thanks to God for that time of his life that was difficult, yes, certainly, but he liked it. "I felt good and I thanked Providence" Francis said, from his room in Santa Marta, in the Vatican where Providence took him. So far and yet so close. So far in time and in distance from that Jesuit novitiate, but so close in as much as, in essence, the demanding routine of the young novice has not changed: it continues to be the path upon which he moves each day seeking to find God continually in prayer; in himself in meditation and in the examinations of conscience that the Pope never omits; and in his brothers in close dialogue and service, "man to man" as he will later say. On this path the Pope now has added visits and audiences with people of all parts of the world and of all walks of life: from prisoners and homeless to Heads of State; but Francis sees in each one of them what he saw in those children of Pueyrredon; what they have or seek in their heart.

The "papal" trees of Villa Carlos Paz

Summer begins to fade after this very hot Sunday in March 2014. Evening Mass is about to begin in the parish church of La Quinta del Niño Dios, in the town of Villa Carlos Paz. Two young families are serving the last round of mate in their picnic that has lasted over two hours in the park near the entrance of the church. The trees allow for some shade and there is space for the children to play. One of the more active of the little ones, who must behave awfully in school, is trying once again to climb one of the old trees. The rascal perseveres and climbs up, branch after branch. The parents who are absorbed in their conversation still do not see him. The child has climbed up too far and is in a precarious situation and yet he reaches for still another branch. When his mother sees him, she yells but it is too late. The child hits the ground hard and he lets his pain be known with his crying. The accident draws the attention of the people arriving for Mass. One elderly gentleman draws closer to the child still crying in the arms of his mother. He saw from where the child fell and offers his help. "It is not necessary, but thanks", the parents of the child respond to him a little more tranquil now. And the man, ventures an explanation that surprises all who hear him: "He took a big blow but did not get hurt. It must be a miracle of Pope Francis because he planted these trees".

Thursdays were different for the novices. After the morning prayers, they waited in the receiving room until they heard the horn blowing on the truck outside. The Br. John Ribicich (of Croatian descent) or Br. Cassatti, who were the "chauffeurs", honked the horn of the truck when they had parked them on Buchardo Street. The novice Master, Fr. Zaragozí, got in the cabin with the driver. The rest had to get in the back as though they were cattle. The Pope remembers with a laugh that adventure that today would be impossible since traffic laws would prohibit it: "Yes, yes, that's the way it was –the Pope said, apparently enjoying the memory—. We got into the back of the truck like livestock and we went to the *Quinta del Niño Dios* in Villa Carlos Paz. This is the way we went every Thursday, and in the summertime we lived there for a few weeks".

"La Quinta" began as a family farming ranch in the second half of the 19th century, and was given to the Society of Jesus in 1906 through the generosity of its last owner, Eugenia Gastañaga, who was devoted to St. Ignatius of Loyola.

The donation of the 741 acres with everything that it contained was completed on December 17, 1906, and as soon as the religious took charge, they began to work on it. Fr. Antonio Ortells ordered the construction of a dam and a pipeline to bring drinkable water to the house, improved the access road to the ranch and built a few bridges to span the river. In 1920, Villa Carlos Paz was still a very small village, but the Jesuit property already had electricity. They began also to construct rooms for the religious that would begin to come, especially in summer time, to rest or to recover their health.

When Br. Antonio Font arrived, who was of Spanish origin, and who had already managed estates of the Society in the province of Santa Fe, the construction and growth in the estate in Villa Carlos Paz grew enormously. With the resources that the sale of meat, milk and vegetables that were sold in the city of Córdoba (some was sent to the novitiate in Pueyrredon) provided, Font began to build the church that was blessed on January 6, 1933 by the then Archbishop of Córdoba, the most Rev. Fermin Lafitte.

After the death of Br. Font in 1941, the Jesuit superiors had difficulty finding an administrator with his capacity to run the ranch. This meant that in the following years there was a decrease in the ranch's production, while the area became a recreation center for the novices that came from Córdoba almost every Thursday during the school year and for vacation in the summer months of January and February.

The decline in the production and the increased costs led the Jesuits to decide to sell 642 acres of the original ranch. Later subdivisions helped the area grow in the measure that tourism was promoted in this mountain villa.

When the novice Jorge Bergoglio arrived for the first time to the

Quinta Del Niño Dios, one Thursday in April in 1958, the estate no longer sold fruit commercially but there was enough for their own use. The novices helped in some of the work involved.

If to plant a tree is one of the things one must do to be a man, the land of this estate gave plenty of room for the Head of the Catholic Church to move ahead in this activity. Some of the enormous trees that give shade today at the *Quinta Del Niño Dios* were planted by the novice Bergoglio.

The Pope remembers it: "Fr. Zaragozí had us plant pines and other types of trees in the *Quinta Del Niño Dios*. A large part of the forestation that is there today is because of Zaragozí, who worked on this a great deal for many years together with the novices".

Fr. Swinnen and Cravenna remember having spent long hours "drilling holes into the rock" on the land to plant the trees. "We made holes in the rock, we filled each hole with dirt and planted the trees that today are huge locust trees, thorn trees, chañares, pines, eucalyptus, and other species of trees that later became the woods that today is a Municipal Reserve", said Cravenna.

They did not only plant trees. Fresh in the memory of Pope Francis are days full of recreation that tired the body but rested the minds of the novices and predisposed them for prayer and the spiritual life. The long awaited "large vacations" began a couple of days before Christmas. "We had a pool where we would go swimming; we would go to the river and we made hikes to different places in the mountains: to Condorito (on the road that crosses the higher sierras), to the San Roque reservoir, to the locality of Cabalango. We had a really healthy and austere life", remembers the Holy Father.

Swinnen pointed out that one of the longest hikes they made was to the dam on the San Roque reservoir. We would get there hiking up the 100 Curve Road, which at that time was not paved. "We returned exhausted but very happy", the companion of the Pope pointed out.

Cravenna added that during this time the novices received different responsibilities. For example he was assigned to take care of the bee hives that gave a lot of good quality honey. His brothers, among them Bergoglio, were assigned to the garden, to pick fruit, retrieve the eggs, help in the kitchen, set up and serve Mass, etc.

Horacio Lescano recalled that during these summer months the novices could receive visitors. He showed us pictures of himself, dressed in a cassock, with his family near the church of the Quinta in December of 1958.

Thursdays –and the summer vacations— went by quickly and at dinner time, after returning home in Br. Rubicich's truck they returned to the normal routine of the residence in Pueyrredon. When they returned from the summer vacation, everyone in the community made their eight day retreat of spiritual exercises.

The last time that Bergoglio went to the Quinta as a novice was in February of 1960, when he was preparing to make his first vows as a Jesuit. A month later he left for Chile to do his years as a Scholastic. There was less and less Jesuit activity in Carlos Paz and some years later, together with the decision to move the novitiate to Buenos Aires, the Quinta was handed over to the Archdiocese of Córdoba. Now the building where Pope Francis lived and worked during his novitiate is part of the Nino Dios parish.[20]

In 1996 the municipality of Villa Carlos Paz bought the park of twelve and a half acres with the trees that were planted by Bergoglio, that surround the Jesuit constructions, the church and school. In July of the year 2000 the whole area was declared "Historical/cultural patrimony of the city of Villa Carlos Paz and called it La Quinta Ranch Park. Each year there are more visitors. There are guided visits to the park to explain the historical significance of the buildings, a history that, since March of 2013, has been greatly embellished by one of the human actors who lived and worked there.

---

[20] The "Niño Dios" parish is located on Assumption Street in the neighborhood of La Quinta, in the city of Villa Carlos Paz, presently under the care of the diocesan priest Hugo Gerardo Villagra. The Margarita Avanzzatto de Paz Parish center for Education and Culture also is located there (which contains the Niño Dios Kindergarten; the Margarita A. Paz Grammar School; and Bernardo D'Elía High School) named after the wife of Mr. Carlos Paz , who inherited the Santa Leocadia Estate, the origin of the mountain village that today bears his name.

The Jesuit formation and the Month of Exercises

"It is not easy to be a Jesuit". The phrase of the Novice Master had been a warning to Bergoglio and his companions. The Conference room, on the first floor of the Novitiate, was a box of surprises. Just knowing the different stages of the Jesuit formation process was enough to convince the young men that only with the grace of God would they be able to complete it.

They were in their period of *first probation*, a short period, between two weeks and a month, during which those entering the novitiate begin to understand the reality of what they will live, grow into and become as priests or brothers in the service of God and men. The academics during this period were orientated toward the study of the Constitutions, the History of the Society of Jesus and of its General Congregations; the autobiography of St. Ignatius of Loyola; the Apostolic plan of the Order, the vows and some basic knowledge of Church History.

At the end of this month, after a brief retreat, the novices are inscribed officially in the book of Novitiate. Then, after this symbolic event, the "second probation" begins that will take up the next two years. These years will be decisive for the novices because it will permit them to deepen their vocation and their knowledge of the Society by means of a series of tests that will mark them forever: the month of the Spiritual Exercises, the hospital month, the month of pilgrimage and the month of humble services.

Jorge Bergoglio undertook these tests in Córdoba and lived them with such intensity that half a century later he still remembers them with incredible detail.

In September of 1958, the man who today is Pope made his first month long retreat, in the Novitiate house but in absolute silence. In this his most important work, St. Ignatius of Loyola defines the Spiritual Exercises in this way: "by this name of Spiritual Exercises is meant every way of examining one's conscience, of meditating, of contemplating, of praying vocally and mentally, and of performing other spiritual actions, (...) For as strolling, walking and running are bodily exercises, so every way of preparing and disposing the soul to rid itself of all the disordered tendencies, and, after it is rid, to seek and find the Divine Will as to the management of one's life for the salvation of the soul, is called a Spiritual Exercise".[21]

As is usually the case in ignatian retreats made in groups, the Jesuit novices also received the meditations communally, that is, the preaching of each of the themes to reflect upon, in a group and not individually. In the Novitiate of Pueyrredon, these were done in the Conference room and preached by Fr. Zaragozí, the one who was responsible to guide the novices through the four "weeks" that Saint Ignatius himself had organized for its structure. The four weeks do not correspond so much to the calendar, but rather to four stages of the whole process that St. Ignatius proposed. In the first week everything is ordered to generate a contemplation of one's own disorders and to recognize them in order to ask the grace necessary to change them. In the second week, the person making the retreat meditates on his Christian vocation and the "life of Jesus Christ Our Lord up to Palm Sunday". The third stage centers on the meditation of the Eucharist and "the Passion of Jesus"; and in the fourth week one places his attention and heart in "the Resurrection and Ascension" of Jesus.

After the meditations were preached to the group by Fr. Zaragozí, each novice found a place to make his reflection and personal prayer. There were days of fasting, of penance, of consolation and of desolation as is normally the case in this type of retreat. Several Jesuits that we consulted agree that this month of retreat helps one to discover the source of the spiritual gifts that God gives each us in a process that can help transform the soul, making it more like Jesus. A thought of Fr. Arrupe, Superior of the Order until 1983, is well known in the Society: "A Jesuit really begins his novitiate after doing the Exercises". In his own experience, the Pope seems to agree with the idea of Arrupe: "the month

---

[21] St. Ignatius of Loyola, *Ejercicios Espirituales*, Autógrafo Español, Tenth Edition. Editorial Apostolado de la Prensa, Madrid, Spain, 1962.

of Exercises was, perhaps, the best part of my novitiate. This spiritual experience marked me, the month of exercises is really the best thing the novitiate had, and does a lot of good; it leads you to prayer, this is where one learns prayer seriously".

In March of 2014, as Pope, Bergoglio said of the Exercises: "Whoever lives the Spiritual Exercises in an authentic way experiments the attraction, the enchantment of God, and one returns renewed and transfigured to ordinary life, to the ministry, to daily relationships, bringing with you the perfume of God".

That vital experience also helped Jorge Bergoglio grow closer to the man who guided them spiritual during those days, Fr. Zaragozí; and it also permitted the Society, through this priest, to understand what they had in their hands: a young man full of faith, with an excellent formation, with strong convictions, with character, but at the same time always seeking to serve others. Fr. Zaragozí's opinion was taken into account by the Jesuit superiors when, in 1973, Bergoglio was elected Provincial of the Order in Argentina.

The "hospital month" and a painful experience

After the month of the Exercises, the novices returned for a few weeks to their habitual routine until the superiors decided it was time for their next trial: the hospital month. The Novice Master had to organize several different operative questions. In the meantime, between one trial and another, the novices took advantage of the time to do some personal things. Fr. Cravenna remembers for example, that to go to the dentist that was in the center of the city, not only was it necessary to coordinate a community visit to the doctor (three or four went on the same day) but also ask for permission and for "two coins" from the doorman, Brother Cirilo Rodriguez, to pay for the trolley car to and from the center. "We did not handle money, we had everything we needed", the priest clarified.

The test that the Jesuits call the "hospital month" had –and still has in almost all the novitiates of the Society of Jesus in the world— the goal that the young novice come in close contact with those "beloved of God" that are the sick and the suffering. This contact should be done with an attitude of humble and fraternal service, to accompany and console those brothers and sisters that suffer as Jesus himself did.

The location of the novitiate in Pueyrredon facilitated this work: only two blocks away, on the same Buchardo Street, stood (and still stands today) Tránsito Cáceres de Allende Hospital. Six blocks in the opposite direction is Córdoba Hospital, on Patria Avenue, where the trolley n. 2 passed. Both are public health centers, administrated by the Provincial Government.

Bergoglio was sent to the Córdoba hospital. Each morning, the man who now leads the Catholic Church from the Chair of St. Peter, left the Novitiate and walked the six blocks that separated the hospital from the Jesuit residence. To treat the sick was for the young novice the same as to touch Jesus, but there was also the human condition. The Pope himself revealed to us in one of our conversations, a painful experience that helped him become more deeply aware of what he calls "one of the worst social wounds".

"In Córdoba hospital –Francis recounted– we visited and attended the sick, giving them shaves, we washed them and this sort of thing. I remember that there I felt one of the hardest blows I received from the reality of life, in spite of being pretty familiar with these things; I never thought I would see this: we were taking care of and visiting with a man that had a terminal illness; he was an older man, but he was married with a woman who was considerably younger than he. I remember that they were not Argentines. At the time we accompanied this man that was dying, I realized that while we were talking and helping this man, his wife was "socializing" with some doctor there. When I finally realized this it gave me so much pain, that I still remember it. I felt as though I had touched one of the worst social wounds, infidelity. It pained me a great deal".

After this first experience in a hospital, that was helpful in teaching Bergoglio how to take care and accompany the sick (a service that he will repeat years later in the Major Residence of the Society in

Córdoba, with the priests and brother's that were sick and bedridden), other visits to the two hospitals mentioned were frequent.

Francis remembered a humorous story about one of his times visiting the Tránsito Cáceres de Allende Hospital: "We would often go to 'Tránsito' –the Pope said calling the hospital by the name commonly used in Córdoba— to take care of the sick. I remember that I had to go several times to take care of Fr. Antonio Aznar who lived with us at the Novitiate, but had a health problem that made it necessary to hospitalize him. In Tránsito the Capuchin Sisters of Mother Rubatto[22] were the ones that did their apostolate and service to the sick, and one of the sisters had a mustache; so every time Fr. Aznar would see this poor sister he would say: 'you can tell that you sisters are Capuchins... you have a beard... just like the friars'. Fr. Aznar was rough", recalled Francis smiling.

The "Pilgrimage month": "man to man" priests and popular religiosity

For those who have faith, life is a pilgrimage toward the Father. The meaning of the trial that the Jesuit novices still do during what is called "Pilgrimage month" is to experience how God sustains those who seek to know His will and put it into practice in service to others while abandoning themselves to Divine Providence.

In the first days of September of 1959, and in front of the anxious novices among whom was the future pope, Fr. Zaragozí drew lots to choose the three companions and their pilgrimage routes: a young man named Pautasso who months later left the Company was chosen to accompany Bergoglio, as well as Santiago Frank (see picture n. 10) who as was pointed out earlier, had entered the Novitiate already a priest, with the intention of becoming a Jesuit. They were to travel in a southeast

---

[22] Ana María Rubatto was born in Carmagnola (Turin) on February 14, 1844. She became a religious and took the name Mary Francis of Jesus. She founded the Institute of the Capuchin Sisters on January 23, 1885, a Congregation that spread throughout the world, including Uruguay and Argentina, countries that were visited by this religious. She died in Montevideo, Uruguay, on August 6, 1904. Pope John Paul II beatified her on October 10, 1993.

direction, through the towns and cities that were along Route 9 that unites the city of Córdoba with the city of Rosario.

Picture 10 – Fr Frank, one of Bergoglio's companions during the *pilgrimage month.*

Other groups received different destinations such as the south of the Province, with routes that led them through the towns of Alta Gracia, Santa Rosa de Calamuchita and Río Tercero; or the east, by Route 19, to Santa Fe.

To each group, Zaragozí gave letters of recommendation for the pastors that eventually would receive them, in order to "ease" the way for the novices.

They travelled walking or hitchhiking, waiting for some kindhearted driver to take them to the next town. It was not hard to get there, not only because of the prayers offered as they walked: at that time there was more confidence among people. On top of this, the pilgrims wore cassocks, so they appeared to be poor priests asking for a favor. When they reached the towns they would go to the parish and ask permission of the pastor to stay there in exchange for doing any work that needed to be done: whether it be organizing a patronal feast or cleaning the church or painting walls. They did not bring money and ate what was given to them. The Pope did not consider the experience so dramatic: "It was not a big deal for us to go in Providence's hands because the pastors of the towns and cities we went to knew we were coming and prepared for us with a place and with work. No one died of hunger or was left in the cold".

When the day arrived, Bergoglio and his two companions left the Novitiate early. "We left walking and went toward the city of Rosario in an attempt to reach the town of Rio Segundo. I remember some very, very nice things during this experience", the Pope pointed out. At the time the highway between Córdoba and Rosario that passes very close to Rio Segundo did not exist. Bergoglio and company hitchhiked the 30 miles that separate this town from the capital city of Córdoba and when they arrived they went straight to the parish of Our Lady of Lourdes. There they met the pastor who would mark Bergoglio's life.

"From our trip to Rio Segundo the figure of who was then the pastor, Fr. Marcos David Bustos (see picture n. 11) is deeply engrained in me. I remember that he lived in the parish house with his father, mother and a sister. When we were there –Francis added—, Fr. Zambrano's dad was104 years old and was very healthy".

Picture 11 – Fr Marcos David Bustos Zambrano, the pastor of Río Segundo for many years. *Picture by kind permission of Ángela Tabares de Granja.*

The description that the Pope gave us of this priest, who was pastor of Rio Segundo for thirty three years, reminds one of the rough but always faithful and committed figure of Blessed "Cura" Brochero. "I remember that Bustos Zambrano smoked a lot —the Pope added—. He was a good man, very good, and was one of those priest leaders of Córdoba. He was a "spiritual chief" of his town, a real father figure. He knew the life of everyone, but he didn't gossip; he knew everyone's situation and he accompanied them. You should have seen the piety with which he prayed! And he was not afraid of anything".

As soon as the novices arrived, Bustos Zambrano told them to get settled in a room of the rectory and then he asked them to do something that surprised the man who today is the Pope: "He sent us to work in the cemetery, to write down the names of everyone buried there, because he was not certain where all of his faithful were buried and he wanted all this to be clear; he wanted to know where everyone was, whether living or dead. He really was a priest who was "man to man" with his faithful and he gave us great advice".

Knowing the life (and death) of Bustos Zambrano helps us to understand why his personality, his actions, his pastoral style impressed so much this young novice. A half a century before Pope Francis asked the Catholics of the world "to go out of the church, to the 'existential outskirts'", this country priest already did it.

Two years before his death, in a written letter recovered by the professor Ángela Tabares de Granja, Fr. Bustos Zambrano described himself in this way: "I am called David in my family, and here Father or 'Fader'; I am a native Argentinean, priest with a small p and I have always ministered in the countryside. For thirty one years I have been in this parish, a little old, but with some updates: I use a long cassock... I am a man of heaven and earth who seeks peace, the fruit of justice and love, and of the long awaited message of our Heavenly Father through Christ incarnate".

Pope Francis recalled one story of Bustos Zambrano that paints a good picture of him: "While we were in Rio Segundo we heard this story: there was a very old priest whose name was Visca, I think he was pastor of the town of Oliva, that now pertains to the diocese of Villa María. He was a neighbor of Bustos Zambrano. The bishop at that time, Alberto Deane, had asked him his resignation and had taken him out of the parish because some said that Fr. Visca was losing his mind, that he wanted to beatify his mother who had died, or things like that; but the priest was not really that bad and was very bitter when they took him away from his parish. So —the Pope added— Fr. Bustos Zambrano invited him to come and say funeral Masses for fictitious people, that Fr. Bustos Zambrano would invent, although in the end the Masses were for souls in Purgatory; but it was all so he could give a little money to Fr. Visca. It was a very nice gesture of charity that impressed us who were young novices in formation".

Pope Francis told another story about Fr. Visca that the young novice heard and loved: "The town of James Craik that was under the jurisdiction of Oliva was celebrating its patronal feast. The pastor named to replace Fr. Visca was named Trinidad or something like that[23]. He was from Spain, and had told the faithful that for the procession in the afternoon they should take out only the statue of Christ and the patron St. Roque, and not all the statues as they were accustomed to do. So they took out the two statues and the pastor locked up the church. But since they were not happy with the decision, the faithful found a way to get in; I don't know if they got in through the windows or where, but the fact is they got in and in the afternoon when the pastor returned for the procession, he found all the saints outside. The priest yelled at the people, got back in his car and returned home very angry. The faithful began to ask themselves how they were going to do the procession without a priest, and decided to look for Fr. Visca, who lived in Oliva, to lead their procession. The old priest accepted. He went to James Craik, did the procession and at the end prepared to give a homily. He began with a scolding that no one forgot: 'You sons of b%$es, you threw me out of the parish and now you had to come get me...' and he continued with the sermon where he reminded them that they did not defend him when the bishop took him out of the parish, and that now God was punishing them because they had to look for him to do the procession. And he dedicated

---

[23] It was the Spanish priest Trinidad Salto Herraiz, who replaced Fr. Visca as pastor of Oliva.

the whole homily on the importance of fidelity to the priest".

As is clear from the clarity and details of the story, the Pope never forgot the episode. "I remember these things very well because they helped me see the reality of the life of priests, of the older priests, of the elderly... all in the light of the great example of Fr. David Bustos Zambrano".

The Pope is not the only one who remembers the words, gestures and ideas of the historical pastor of Rio Segundo. During the investigation for this book another story in which Bustos Zambrano took part, which is still known and enjoyed among the older clergy of Córdoba. It is a story the Pope must know since he was in Rio Segundo just a year after it happened.

In the year 1957, Archbishop Lafitte visited Río Segundo for its patronal feast; it was also to say goodbye to this community since he had already been named Apostolic Administrator of Buenos Aires. After the festivities, Fr. Bustos Zambrano thanked Lafitte for his visit and the following dialogue ensued:

— Well, Monsignor; thank you a lot for coming. I hope the next time I see you, you will be red – said Bustos Zambrano alluding to the fact that as the next Archbishop of Buenos Aires, he would be made a cardinal, who wear red.

Lafitte, who was of noble heritage, replied:

—Thank you, Father. Then I hope to see you purple— referring to the color that "monsignors" wear when given that title.

Fr. Bustos Zambrano responded:

— I already have purple.

Lafitte, surprised by this, asked him:

— What? Father, have you already been made a Monsignor?

— No, I am not a Monsignor— shot back the pastor. Then added, causing some embarrassment to the bishop: —You see I am dark skinned and we dark skinned people have purple butts!"

The story quickly spread through all of Rio Segundo and even today produces a smile on the faces of some of the priests and bishops that remember Bustos Zambrano for what he was: a man of God but close in everything to the people that God had entrusted to him —including their way of speaking and their humor. This is the way Prof. Ángela Tabares remembers him. She is a distinguished resident of Rio Segundo today and knew very well Fr. Bustos and she was moved to tears when she found out that the Pope remembered that beloved pastor.

"Fr. Bustos –Tabares told us—, as his parishioners called him, was a 'native' priest, 'one who used the long cassock' as he defined himself; with good jokes, his tone of voice that was so ours, in his conversations; the shawl over his shoulders, his impressive presence and his gift for great preaching".

Deeply moved, the historian added: "Remembering Fr. Bustos in this way we think, how would Pope Francis not remember him in a special way? For our community this remembrance that the Pope made is extremely important and we experience it with amazement and joy: the man who today is Pope was here in our town! He walked our streets, helped our pastor, and prayed in our church, he knew us!"

The archbishop of Córdoba today, Carlos Ñañez, also remembers Fr. Bustos Zambrano: "He was already very elderly the day I greeted him and asked how he was. He looked at me and said: 'I am here, playing out my last cards... but you have no idea with what joy I am playing them!' These words always fill me with consolation".

That "pilgrimage month" left other impressions on Jorge Bergoglio as well, things that he still remembers. He remembers for example very well something that happened in the small town of Impira, Province of Córdoba, which will undoubtedly be a source of pride for its one hundred and seventy inhabitants. With his memory that does not cease to amaze, Francis called to mind this small town in the Rio Segundo County, which is about forty five miles from the provincial capital city of Córdoba and about fourteen miles from the town of Laguna Larga. Impira was the first town in the county of Rio Segundo; it was founded in 1639 as a resting spot for the horse and carriages moving along the Royal Road;

for this reason it is referred to as the "Mother of towns", as those with good memory may remember.[24]

The young Bergoglio with his two companions Pautasso and Frank passed through Impira on September 24, 1959, on their patronal feast day. "In Impira –the Pope said— what impressed me was seeing the first expression of popular piety I had witnessed outside of Buenos Aires. I was impressed with the piety of the people –he added—. I remember the ceremony very well; after so many years, I can still hear the hymn 'oh Virgin of Impira, glorious mother of the Savior...' that the people sang with such devotion". The Pope left the interviewers with their mouths open. His memory and sensibility are astounding. Over a half century later and after hearing it only once, Bergoglio remembers the hymn of Impira and the devotion of the people that touched him. The verses still resound in his pious memory: Oh glorious Virgin of Impira/mother of the Savior. /From your highest throne/keep us in your loving gaze//Blessed Mother of God/pray for me to the Lord. / Allow me during all my life/to follow quickly in your virtue.// Show your great love/ to the sinner that is sorrowful. / Under your white mantle/ each will find forgiveness, / ever confident to see you/ in the joyful Mansion of heaven.

The current Mayor of the town, Susana Canalis, can't believe it either. She was deeply moved when the story and words of the Holy Father about the town and its people were told to her. She responded "surprised, happy and shocked" by the news. When she kindly sent us pictures of the church and the complete version of the Hymn, Canalis confessed to having told the news to many in the town and the whole town is "very happy"; they are talking about sending a letter to the Holy Father with pictures and an invitation to come back "whenever he wants".

The experience of popular piety always impressed and still impresses Bergoglio because it brings him back to the feast days and processions that he lived as a boy with his Grandma Rosa. These simple experiences of faith were sowed in his heart as a child, an adolescent and as a young man and they grew into becoming a firm foundation of his

---

[24] The church in Impira, Our Lady of the Merced, was built in 1880, with the economic help and labor of the faithful, whose descendants every year express their special devotion to Our Lady.

conviction that will remain with him through his philosophical and theological formation as a pastor. Decades later, these "convictions" were converted into "doctrine" for the whole Church particularly with the Fifth General Conference of the Episcopacy of Latin America and the Caribbean that took place in Aparecida, Brazil. At that Conference in May of 2007, with the help of Cardinal Bergoglio, all the bishops of Latin America and the Caribbean, in communion with the then Pope Benedict XVI, underlined the importance of these expressions of spirituality as privileged spaces of encountering Jesus Christ, and they invited all to promote them. In the final document, that had Bergoglio as the president of the commission for its composition, this was noted: "Popular piety is worthy of our respect and love, because it reflects the thirst of God that only the poor and simple can know".

In this document that would become the "guiding letter" of Pope Francis, the Latin-American Church underscores "the patronal feast days, the novenas, rosaries, Way of the Cross, processions, the dances and songs of religious folklore, the love toward the saints and angels, the promises and family prayer". It assures us that these expressions should not be "undervalued" or considered "a secondary way of living Christian life, because it would be to forget the primacy of the action of the Holy Spirit and gratuitous nature of the love of God".

During his first apostolic visit to Brazil, during the World Youth Day celebration, the Pope said that popular piety "is a legitimate way of living the faith... a way of living our missionary spirit, where the deepest vibrations of the profound American Spirit are gathered". The Pope knew what he was talking about. He had lived it in Córdoba.

The first vows

For centuries, in the long periods of formation of the Jesuits, the first stage, the novitiate of two years, ends with the professing of first vows. It is a promise to live in poverty, chastity and obedience that the novices offer to God, in a ceremony that is presided over generally by the

Master of Novices, and that is done after they have lived and experienced the "trials" of the evangelic life. They are perpetual vows, but not solemn ones, that is to say they can be dissolved by the Provincial Father. The other vows, the "final ones", as is often said among the Jesuits, are made after many years of formation and even the exercise of ministry as is the case of the priests. Only then does the Jesuit make his final vows, the solemn ones, which do not really replace the first vows (since these were already perpetual) but rather imply the definitive membership in the Society of Jesus. At the same time, while he makes his final vows, each Jesuit religious makes a fourth vow of obedience and availability to the Pope for the jobs that the Holy Father, directly or through the Fr. General- needs and wills, as well as other commitments that seek the "self-abasement" and humility of the Jesuit.

According to the Constitutions of the Company of Jesus, aside from the obedience and availability to the Pope, the fourth vow made by the Jesuits implies the commitment to reject honorific titles, to teach children and people without education and to report to the Fr. General if anyone of the members is seeking or pursuing a title. It is also established that if any Jesuit were to be named bishop (as happened in the case of Bergoglio) he must maintain a cordial relationship with the Fr. General and allow himself to be advised by him. Only the Holy See can dispense the religious of the ignatian order from these final vows.

The novice Jorge Bergoglio professed his first vows on March 12, 1960, the memory of the canonization of St. Ignatius of Loyola, in the church of the Holy Family. In the previous months, together with his companions, he underwent a special discernment on this commitment that was about to shape his life. He has discovered that he was willing to live, with the help of God and of the Virgin, evangelical poverty, obedience to his superiors and chastity. He understood that the option he was choosing implied denial. But he also knew that this denial would afford him a greater freedom, as he had experienced during the two years before.

Evangelical poverty frees one from the attachment to material things and encourages generosity with others; obedience predisposes the religious to have an absolute availability to the will of God that can be expressed through the assignments of the superiors and it stimulates humility which is the underlying virtue of the saints. When chastity is lived well, that is to say, as a gift of God, it implies the denial of the practice of sexuality in favor of an absolute love of Jesus and presenting oneself selflessly in the service of others.

On that Saturday morning, March 12, the whole community of the Novitiate of Pueyrredon was present in Holy Family church. Fr. Zaragozi presided the Mass and after the reading of the Gospel, each of the novices expressed their vows. Jorge Bergoglio was one of them. When it was his turn, he advanced in the line that his brothers had formed until he reached the stairs at the foot of the altar. He knelt and began to read in Latin[25] in a loud and solemn voice:

All powerful and eternal God:

I, Jorge Bergoglio, even though in every way unworthy in your presence, and yet full of confidence in your infinite piety and mercy, and motivated by the desire to serve you, offer, before the Most sacred Virgin Mary and the whole celestial court of your Majesty, perpetual Poverty, Chastity and Obedience in the Society of Jesus: and I promise having entered the Society to continue my life in it forever; according to the Constitutions of the Society. For such, I ask of your immense goodness and clemency, through the Blood of Jesus Christ, that you allow this sacrifice of sweet perfume; and having granted me this desire and offering, I ask also that you give me abundant grace to fulfill it.

In silence, without losing the solemnity of the moment, the now

---

[25] The original text in Latin of the first vows of Jorge Bergoglio: *Omnipotens sempiterne Deus: Ego, Jorge Mario Bergoglio, licet undecumque Divino tuo conspectus indignissimus, fretus tamen pietate ac misericordia tua infinita, et impulsus tibi serviendi desiderio, voveo, coram sagratissima Virgine Maria, et curia tua caelesti universa Divinae Maiestati tuae Paupertatem, Castitatem, et Obedientiam perpetuam in Societate Iesu: et promitto eamdem Societatem me ingressurum, ut vitam in ea perpetuo degan;Omnia intelligendo iuxta ipsius Societatis Constitutiones. A tua ergo immensa bonitate et clementia per Iesu Christi sanguinem, peto suppliciter, ut hoc holocaustum in odorem suavitatis admittere digneris; et in largitus es ad hoc desiderandum et offerendum sic etiam ad explendum gratiam uberem largiaris.*

"professed" Bergoglio got up and returned to his place to continue participating in Mass. No one could imagine that that grace the young man had asked for on his knees would accompany him for the rest of his life with such abundance. How could one know it? He was simply one more young man, among many others, where in a Novitiate at "the end of the world" a religious vocation was awakening to the Society of Jesus, where no one has an ecclesiastical career, where no one prepares to be a bishop, nor a cardinal and much less Pope.

After the ceremony there was a "party" in the community of Pueyrredon: during lunch that began as usual in silence, one of the older fathers announced the *"Deo gratia"* and everyone could speak to exchange greetings and good wishes. The last two years' experience had changed the life of many of them and now they were prepared to advance in their formation. They were still eating lunch when Fr. Zaragosí took Bergoglio aside and told him: "Go and prepare your things. In a few days you will be going to Chile to begin your scholastic period".

CHAPTER 3
PATH TO THE PRIESTHOOD

The profession of first religious vows (the commitment to obedience, poverty and chastity) was the high point of the two years of rigorous and intense spiritual and pastoral formation of Jorge Bergoglio's two years in Córdoba. His companions attest to the fact that he was an excellent student. His vocation had matured and he assumed each of the characteristics of the Jesuit charism. In daily discernment, he had made his own the Ignatian method of the Spiritual Exercises; he had experienced the value of prayer, of community life and of austerity; he had "gone out of himself" in order to share the Gospel with the poor and learned that he could find the face of Christ in the sick and suffering. He was a young man who had changed from the time he came to Córdoba two years earlier. He was ready to begin the long "trip" of 31 years outside of the Province that would take him to places and experiences that would put to test all that he had learned in the novitiate.

At the door of the large building on Buchardo Street –that would never be his home again—, Bergoglio said good-bye to Br. Cirilo Rogriguez. He asked him for the two cents to take the trolley n. 2, then he smiled and left.

Scholastic in Chile

He still felt the emotion of the first vows when, dressed in his black cassock, typical of the Jesuits, he left for Chile, to the small locality of Padre Hurtado, some 18 miles from the city of Santiago. He travelled together with Andrés Swinnen and Juan Carlos Constable, who as priests would also return to Córdoba. Today, Fr. Constable resides in San José del Boqueron, in the province of Santiago del Estero, with some health difficulties.

In Chile they met with the argentine Jesuits Miguel Ángel Moreno and Carlos Hardoy and with other Jesuit students from different Latin-American countries. (See picture n. 12).

Picture 12 – From the Scholastic in Chile: in the middle, stand, Bergoglio and Swinnen, smiling.
Picture pubblished by Jorge González Manent.

All had to advance in the next stage of formation of the Society of Jesus, the "scholastic". This period, that the Jesuits still do today, includes classic humanistic studies. This is what the scholastics from Argentina — and other Chilean students— began with during their long twelve month period, between March of 1960 and March of 1961.

They lived in the Loyola Spirituality Center that had been constructed through the initiative of Fr. Hurtado in 1938. In the pre-conciliar tradition, the rules were very strict and they still reflected the almost military discipline of the founder of the Jesuits.

The experience allowed them to see the immense work of the late Alberto Hurtado and the devotion that his memory and work awoke in all of Chile. As was said earlier, Hurtado had done his novitiate also in Córdoba but the argentine novices had not recalled the coincidence.

When Bergoglio arrived at this house of formation as a young scholastic, only eight years had passed since the death of Hurtado and both the people and the bishop already spoke of his holiness. The Church would confirm this fame on October 23, 2005, when the newly elected Pope Benedict XVI declared him a saint. When Pope Francis was asked about Fr. Hurtado he replied: "Hurtado is a model of work with the poor and of prayer. Fundamentally it is this: prayer and work with the most needy".

It was in this climate of admiration for priestly work that Bergoglio committed himself to his first year of strictly speaking intellectual formation.

The impact of that charismatic Chilean Jesuit's message was still present in the air. He was so moved by "a poor man, with severe strep throat, shaking in a short sleeved shirt", he decided to create hospice for street people. He filled it personally by driving through the streets of Santiago in his green van looking for the dispossessed that he referred to as his "little bosses". His biographers say that looking for volunteers to staff his *Christ's Home*, he used to say: "Christ walks through the streets in so many suffering poor, and sick, evicted from their miserable apartments. Christ, crouching under the bridges, in the person of so many children who have no one to call father, who have lacked for so many years the kiss of a mother on their forehead... Christ is homeless!"

This holy priest that Bergoglio came to know as a role model also created the Chilean Union Association. This allowed an option for all the workers who had been obliged to join the only union that existed until then. Hurtado understood that "the workers, even though almost all were Catholic, were obliged to obey Marxist doctrine", and he began to teach the social doctrine of the Church attempting to defend human work above and beyond any ideology. The initiative generated a lot of strong criticism but he responded calmly: "Of course there are many dangers and the going is rough... Who does not see that? Of course! Would it not be more of a mistake out of cowardice, not to do what one can?"

Bergoglio absorbed all of this in the land of Fr. Hurtado. For this reason, that young scholastic will say, fifty three years later, as head of the Catholic Church that he prefers a "Church with mistakes" before one that is closed in its own security"; that he "never shared Marxist thought because it is false" even though he met "good people who did"; and that he dreamt with "a poor Church with the poor".

In Chile the routine began at 6 in the morning, with Mass in Latin and Gregorian chant. They spent hours studying Greek, literature and the History of Art, without neglecting the household chores of serving tables and washing dishes. They spent a lot of time in prayer and never crossed paths with the students who were further along in their formation. They did not share patios, classrooms or conversation with them. Just as in the novitiate, the meals were in silence, with a student reading from scripture or some reflection. Some days of the week they would include a cold shower; an exercise of corporal more than spiritual penance, that helped temper their character and feel the effects of austerity.

On May 5, 1960, only two months after arriving in Chile, Jorge wrote a letter to his younger sister, Maria Elena —who still lives in Buenos Aires—, which shows the impact that his serving the poor was having on him. In the letter he tells her that he was giving religion classes to very poor children of the third and fourth grades. "Some were even coming without shoes to school. Many do not have anything to eat and in the winter they feel the cold with all its crudeness", wrote the young seminarian for whom "the worse was that they did not know Jesus". In the letter he tells his sister that he wished she were a "little saint" so that, she could help him in his apostolate with the poor children with her prayers and good works.

His return to Argentina

After his brief but intense year in Chile, Bergoglio returned to

Buenos Aires to study three years of philosophy at the Faculty of Philosophy and Theology in the Colegio Maximo of San José, located in the city of San Miguel. The priest Ignacio Garcia-Mata SJ, quoted in the book by the journalist Mariano Vedia *Francisco. El Papa del pueblo*, explained that the dynamics of the classes there was scholastic, and Bergoglio was very good in the reflection and debate circles. At twenty six, he now had to accustom himself to a formation that was not encyclopedic but rather combined teaching, discipline and example. All in Latin: the exams and even the hallway chats had to be in the "dead" language that the Church used as its universal language, precisely because the meaning of its words did not change with the continual use of those who spoke it.

On September 24, 1961 Mario Francisco Bergoglio, the father of Jorge, died. It was a big blow to the family and even for the young religious that was seeking answers in philosophy and theology; answers that, as he points out every chance he gets, he found in prayer. Jorge Bergoglio's father had been a man of deep Christian faith, a committed Catholic, "spiritual son" of Fr. Pozzoli who also had a decisive role in the life of the Holy Father. In a letter that the Pope wrote during his second period spent in Córdoba, he remembered that during the wake of his father, Fr. Pozzoli arrived and at one point asked the five children to gather around the casket to take a picture that would be a souvenir for him. Bergoglio says that "with the smugness of youth" he managed to avoid the picture being taken, because he was ashamed. With time he regretted that refusal, most of all because Fr. Pozzoli died less than a month later. Although these two sad events happened very quickly one after the other, Francis's faith turned them into reasons for thanksgiving, because even today the Pope remembers in his prayer these two men who guided him in life.

By the end of 1963 Bergoglio had done half of the extensive and demanding formation of the Jesuits. This included two years of novitiate in the city of Córdoba with an activity centered more on the "tests" of his priestly vocation than in his intellectual formation; a year as a scholastic with intense academic activity and the practice of catechesis in Chile; and three more years of rigorous studies of philosophy in Buenos Aires. Now he interrupted his studies again to dedicate himself to teaching.

Regency in Santa Fe

At twenty-eight, Bergoglio became "*Carucha*". This was the nickname he was given by his students in the Immaculate Conception High School in Santa Fe. Since he had studies in an industrial technical school, he thought that they would ask him to teach chemistry or physics, but they gave him a class in literature, art and psychology. This meant he had to spend the summer preparing classes. The result was a mix of academic rigor, humor and creativity in order to attract the attention of his new adolescent audience. He brought to his class renowned authors, among them even the biggest name in Argentine literature, Jorge Luis Borges. He also organized a literature contest that ended in the publication of the book "*Original Stories*" that included the best fourteen texts written by the junior and senior students. The prologue is signed by Borges himself.

He would have liked to have brought in another of his preferred authors, Leopoldo Marechal, author of the novels *Adán Buenosayres, El banquete de Severo Arcángelo* and *Megafón o la guerra*. But Marechal was an openly declared peronist and had been put under the shroud of suspicion for his political affiliation.

Immaculate Conception High School is one of the most prestigious institutions of the Jesuits in Argentina. It is an all-boys school; they went to Mass every day, they wore a crisp blue suit and tie or a brown dustcoat as a uniform. They played a lot of sports and once a week brought food and help to the poorer neighborhoods of Santa Fe. The school sought to instill love of neighbor and an interest in the poor and marginalized. The chapel of the school even contained the original image of the patroness of the Argentine Province of the Society of Jesus. Our Lady of Miracles is an oil painting of Mary that on May 9, 1636, began to shed tears of water. The liquid that was shed was gathered into pieces of cotton and many miraculous cures have been attributed to them that were recognized by Pius XI, three centuries later.

Within these walls of an almost military tradition, the young teacher –this tall thin professor dressed in a black cassock and sash, with rubber soled shoes and always smiling, won the respect of his students. "*Carucha*" was demanding in the classroom and severe in his exams, but it is clear years later that he won their hearts as well. Forty-five years later almost none of them missed the Mass that the then Cardinal Bergoglio celebrated to pray for them and for the twelve who graduated of "the class of 65" that are no longer with us.

Bergoglio was in Santa Fe only two years. The second year was particularly intense. On December 8, 1965, Vatican II ended and the High School received the visit of Fr. Pedro Arrupe, the new Superior General of the Society of Jesus (head of the Order in the world). This Basque Jesuit had his own interesting history, since he had been Novice Master in Hiroshima, Japan, during World War II. Fr. Arrupe was there the day the United States dropped the atomic bomb; he assisted hundreds of people and gave the sacrament of the anointing to thousands. Leaving a mark that is still visible today, he governed the Society of Jesus during twenty six years, between 1965 and 1983, a time of upheaval for the whole Church.

Once, in a reunion of students of different Jesuit schools, Bergoglio who was already elected Pope, revealed that during that year he had written to Arrupe to ask him to be sent as a missionary to Japan. The answer was no, but the Pope today says he is grateful: "It was good of Fr. Arrupe because he said to me: 'you are not holy enough to be a missionary'". It was a hard blow for the young seminarian since one of his motives for becoming a Jesuit was its missionary spirit; or as Francis himself would say "to go out, to announce Jesus Christ, and not to remain closed in our structures".

The two years teaching experience were spent between a very strict style of classical teaching and the winds of change and renewal that were blowing from the Council in Rome. The Church was not redefining its dogma but it did propose, not without controversy, a return to the sources of the Christian tradition and a profound updating of many of its practices.

The airs of change reached Latin America as a breeze and in some Jesuit institutions, such as the Immaculate Conception High School, it took on the force of a hurricane.

Vatican II opened an intense theological debate that gave rise to a new line of Latin-American thought: Liberation Theology, that affected particularly the ignatian order and even more so in the institution of Santa Fe. Many seminarians and religious abandoned the congregation, and former students became leaders in the political group of *Montoneros*, in which they made an option in favor of armed revolution and political violence that, together with other factors, led to the tragedy of the last military dictatorship.

In the middle of all this ideological convulsion and violence, Bergoglio strengthened his evangelical outlook on reality, which was not naïve, and without imagining that a few years later he would be given the responsibility of guiding the ship of the Jesuit argentine province through the storm.

Student in Buenos Aires

In 1966 he returned to his province to complete his teaching experience in the Del Salvador High School, and in 1967 he left teaching and returned to the life of a student in the Colegio Maximo of San Miguel.

"These were intense years", Bergoglio told us of that last stage of his extensive formation. The years were intense for the Latin-American church also. In the light of Vatican II, the bishops met in Columbia to celebrate the Second General Council of the Latin-American Episcopacy. The conclusions of that meeting are summarized in the Medellin Document that spoke of a "preferential option for the poor" and the renewal of the Church under the methodology of "look, judge, and act". Many think that this document published at the end of 1968 strengthened the so-called "liberation theologies", while others point out that the document eliminates any possibility of validating a theology united to Marxism.

"It was the result of different interpretations of Vatican II, which, as is the case when the Church changes course, it had its better results and its worse ones, its moderation and its excesses", Bergoglio said in an interview with the journalists Sergio Rubín and Francesca Ambrogetti in a series of interviews that were published in *El Jesuita*. In that book, the then archbishop of Buenos Aires recalled that, on behalf of John Paul II, Cardinal Ratzinger, at that time the prefect for the Congregation for the Doctrine of the Faith, studied Liberation Theology and published two Pastoral Instructions.   According to Bergoglio, in those documents "(Liberation Theology) is described, its limits are pointed out (one of which is the use of a Marxist hermeneutics of society) but it also points out its positive aspects". For the future Pope, the position of the Church is open since it did not condemn it entirely but denounced its deviations. He added that the preferential option for the poor was a strong post conciliar message but it was not new. "The increased preoccupation for the poor that came out in the 60s created a climate where any ideology could grow. This was capable of distorting something that the Church asked for in Vatican II and has been repeating since then: to embrace it the right way in order to respond to an unavoidable and central evangelical demand, such as concern for the poor".

Priest

There is no doubt that Bergoglio is a man who perseveres. The first "call" to the priesthood was felt when he was just a child. It was during his sixth grade of grammar school, as a student in the boarding school the Salesians had in Ramos Mejía, near the city of Buenos Aires that becoming a priest crossed his mind. He was able to keep that call alive – "with the help of God, as he says"— for twenty years. It was December 13, 1969, after finishing all of Middle and High School, a year and a half as a diocesan seminarian, two years as a novice in Córdoba, a year as a scholastic in Chile and three more studying philosophy in Buenos Aires, after two more years as a teacher in Santa Fe and three years of theological studies, Bergoglio was at last ordained a priest.

It was four days before his thirty-third birthday. The ceremony took place in the Colegio Maximo of San José, in San Miguel, Buenos Aires. As Providence would have it, the ordination was presided by the then archbishop *emeritus* of Córdoba, Bishop Ramón Castellano.[26] It is not certain if Castellano was invited to preside the ordination for some special reason, or if it was simply by chance. It is often the case –even today– for the superiors of religious congregations and orders to ask retired (*emeritus*) bishops to preside these celebrations since they often have more time at their disposal than the titular bishops of dioceses.

The whole family of Jorge came to the ordination, except his father who had passed away eight years earlier.

Grandma Rosa, who was key in the early formation of the faith of the man who will one day become Pope, and to whom Francis owes his ability to speak Italian with a Piedmont's accent, gave him a letter that day that the Holy Father still keeps. "My grandma Rosa was very important for me. In my breviary I carry her testament and I read it frequently. For me it is like a prayer", Francis explained to Fr. Antonio Spadaro.

Grandma Rosa's letter, divulged in 2013, reads: "May my grandchildren, to whom I have given the best I have, live a long and happy life. But if pain, sickness or the loss of a loved one should one day fill them with sadness, let them not forget that one sigh toward the Tabernacle, where there is the One who is greater and holier than the martyrs, and one look toward Mary at the foot of the Cross can release a drop of balm capable of healing the deepest and most painful wounds".

While in most of the religious orders and Congregations the ordination to the priesthood is normally the end of the formal formation stage, in the Society of Jesus it is another step, important to be sure, but not the final one. After ordination, the Jesuits begin the "third probation" or tertianship, a time of reflection and prayer that is done in a more spiritual and pastoral context (different than the stages done in an

---

[26] Bishop Ramon Castellano was the 27th bishop of Córdoba (and the second archbishop). He was born in Villa Dolores, Province of Córdoba on February 15, 1903, and was consecrated bishop by Pius XII on March 26, 1958. He was archbishop until January 22, 1965 when his resignation for health reasons was accepted. Having retired to a Benedictine monastery, he was replaced by Raúl Francisco Primatesta, who later would also have a good relationship with Bergoglio. The remains of Castellano, who died in Córdoba on February 27, 1979, rest in the Cathedral of this city where Jorge Bergoglio as a Cardinal returned, incidentally, upon the death of Primatesta, in May of 2006.

atmosphere of study), that is known as "a school of the heart" or "a school of affections".

Fr. Cravenna cites St. Ignatius to explain what tertianship is about. "St. Ignatius said that after the period of study, 'the spirit tends to get cold or cool down', so it is important to 'return to the oven of affections'. For this reason they do the Spiritual Exercises of one month and return to visiting hospitals".

After ordination –Pope Francis recalled in a recent conversation— they told me I had to go, in August of 1970 to do my "tertianship" in Spain, to St. Ignatius of Loyola High School in Acalá de Henares".

His next assignment was given to him before he had received his License diploma in Philosophy and Theology. "I still had to take some exams and for this reason those months before leaving were ones of very intense study and work", recalled the Pope speaking of the months before travelling to Spain.

On his way to Madrid, Bergoglio visited the novitiates in Columbia, Mexico and Canada. After finishing his year of tertianship, he spent a few days in the novitiate of the Spanish Jesuits.

The future Pope returned to Argentina in February of 1971 and shortly thereafter received his License title in Philosophy and Theology. Just a few months later the then provincial Fr. O'Farrell assigned him as vice-rector and Novice Master in the house that the Jesuits had in Villa Barilari, Buenos Aires. Two years earlier, in 1969, they had transferred there the novitiate that for many years had been in Córdoba.

In 1972 another assignment was added: that of being professor of theology in the Colegio Maximo. In 1973 he was elected "consulter" for the Provincial Government of the Argentine Jesuits that was headed by Fr. O'Farrell. By then, although he was a priest for less than four years, Bergoglio was much respected among the Jesuits.

I was doing this when the time came to make my fourth vow. "I professed the fourth vow of April 22, 1973 in San Miguel, in the Novitiate, when I was Novice Master", Francis said of this exceptional commitment that distinguishes the Jesuits from the rest of the religious orders. It is a commitment for life that now is difficult for him to fulfill, simply because in it he is to obey the Pope in all the tasks that are asked from him.

"These days the vow of obedience seems a little special ¿no?", the Pope told us laughing. There is, however, a small detail in his vows that help him keep it: "there is a simple vow we take as Jesuits that says we are always disposed, or better said, 'I make a vow to listen always to the opinion of the Superior General of the Society and to at all times follow his opinion if it seems better than my own'. This vow I can certainly keep perfectly now as a counsel. It means to listen, because the counsels of others can always be prudent, especially that of a General of the Society". The words of the Holy Father are in part a sign of "reconciliation" with the ignatian order that is the result of his election to the throne of Peter. Why? Because from the years he was called upon to govern the Jesuit Province, turbulent years in every sense of the word, some wounds will remain that will take decades to heal.

.

CHAPTER 4
A VERY DIFFICULT GOVERNING EXPERIENCE

The youngest Jesuit provincial

The natural similarity between man and God consists in the gift of power, in his capacity to use it and in the dominion that springs from it (...) A man cannot be a man and at the same time exercise or not exercise power; it is essential for him to use it. The Creator of his being has destined him to it (...). It is only when the phenomenon of power is recognized that it acquires all its importance –that is to say all its importance and seriousness. Its seriousness consists in its responsibility. Human power and the dominion that comes from it have its basis in the likeness of man to God; for this reason, man does not have power in his own right, autonomously, but rather as a fief. Man is lord by the grace of God, and must exercise his dominion responding to the One who is by His own essence Lord. Dominion in this way is converted into obedience, into service. This is the first thing, in the sense that it should be exercised according to the truth".[27]

Romano Guardini, the Italian German theologian who was preferred and studied by Jorge Bergoglio (and on whom he would write his never published doctoral thesis), described power and how it should be exercised in this way in a book that was published for the first time in 1951. Years later, the young Bergoglio would complement his theological studies and this idea of power with spiritual and moral reading that

---

[27] Guardini, Romano. *El Poder*, cuarta edición, Wurzburg, 1957. Page 27.

104

would give that concept a Christian praxis. Already in his novitiate, reading the book *The Exercise of Perfection and Christian Virtues* of Fr. Rodriguez, Bergoglio will come to understand that in the exercise of power one becomes like God, but always under the observance of a superior virtue: humility.

The young Jesuit knew very well that humility is the foundation of magnanimity and that whether it be of high office or great responsibilities, to be humble is the condition *sine qua non* in order that the exercise of power might reflect the will of God.

In the modern and Machiavellian concept of power, this may seem to be absurd, a utopia or something unreachable. Humility allows people to see that they are unworthy of practically everything, including high office. To the humble, receiving or assuming these responsibilities and "honors" might appear be a sign of pride and arrogance. And yet, as St. Thomas of Aquinas taught, to take on great things is something magnanimous and not only is it not contrary to humility, but it is a sign of it. Only a humble person can do great things because he distrusts himself and all human means and puts his confidence entirely in God.

Bergoglio took to heart in the practice of power from the book of Fr. Rodriguez and he memorized the biblical and evangelical teachings on power that are found there: "By the grace of God I am what I am"[28]. "I have the strength for everything through Him who empowers me"[29]. "We will triumph with the help of God, who will trample down our foes"[30].

Bergoglio was elected Provincial of the Society of Jesus in Argentina on July 31, 1973. He resided in Buenos Aires but travelled almost every week to different parts of the country to make canonical visits, so as to be close to those who were in the Society in Argentina: 166 priests, 32 brothers, about 20 novices and 15 communities between seminaries, residences, parishes, schools and universities.

He went often to Córdoba, where he was "born" as a Jesuit, not

[28] First Letter of St. Paul to the Corinthians, chapter 15, verse 10.
[29] Letter of St. Paul to the Philippians, chapter 4, verse 13.
[30] Psalm 60, verse 14.

only because he had to resolve several serious institutional problems, but also because he stopped there on the way to Mendoza, La Rioja and Salta among other provinces where the Society had communities.

The Superior General of the Jesuits in Rome, Fr. Arrupe, had elected Bergoglio from a list of three candidates that had been proposed by his companions. This great responsibility came to the future Pope only four years after finishing his initial formation. He was a young man, but a mature priest who was recognized by his peers.

When Fr. Andrés Swinnen was asked why Bergoglio was elected, this Jesuit who was born in Buenos Aires —but today resides in Córdoba—, responded: "Because he was very intelligent, because he had been excellent in his studies; because he was bold, capable of making decisions and he had authority over the others".

Some members of the Society think that in the early election of Fr. Jorge there was also a providential intervention in some way. They point out that another priest, Joaquin Ruis Escribano[31], was the "favorite" to replace O'Farrell; but he died in a car accident in Juncal, province of Santa Fe, when he was travelling from Córdoba to Buenos Aires.

For one reason or another, Bergoglio became provincial and he had to face a very difficult experience that marked him forever. It was an experience that some years later, because of quarrels and misunderstandings, would lead him to a forced exile in Córdoba, an experience that not only left marks on the Pope but also in the Society of Jesus.

Bergoglio always says that one has "to prefer time over space". This privileged time played a role in healing wounds in Bergoglio in a place he could not have imagined. It was much hoped for reconciliation, in which the Pope surprised many with a profound self-criticism on his time as Provincial.

---

[31] Fr. Joaquin Ruiz Escribano, "Kino" Ruiz, as his fellow Jesuits called him, was born in Corralito, province of Córdoba, on June 8, 1934. He was ordained a priest on December 16, 1967 and died in an accident on July 19, 1971. His remains were viewed in the Domestic Chapel and his Jesuit colleagues remember that that the mother of the deceased, with a profound Christian faith and consolation, said during the burial: "I give thanks to God that my son died a priest of the Society".

"My provincial government as a Jesuit had its defects. I was 36 years old: it was crazy. We had to face difficult situations, and I made decisions in an abrupt and unipersonal way. My authority and quick way of reaching decisions led me into serious problems and I was accused of being an ultraconservative. I certainly was not Blessed Imelda (an Italian blessed born in 1322 who died before reaching adolescence and because of her religious angelic devotion, was declared patroness of girls that are about to receive their First Communion), but I was never a conservative. It was my authoritarian way of making decisions that created problems for me", Francis pointed out in an interview given to the Jesuit magazine *La Civiltá Católica*.

It was not an easy time to exercise government and even less so to learn how to do it. Throughout all of Latin-America there were political coups, political violence, guerilla wars and terrorism.

"When Peron returned to the country in 1973 and there was a shootout in Ezeiza, I did not understand anything", Bergoglio admitted in the book *El Jesuita*. I had to face a difficult financial situation in the Society and a terrible political reality in Argentina. "At that time I didn't have the political information necessary to understand what was going on. We slowly came to understand better the guerilla war, its attempt to get a foothold in the province of Tucuman, the terrorist actions".

While Argentina was beginning an awful civil crisis, the Society was facing its own divisions. After Vatican II, the Society lost ten thousand members. There were desertions in Argentina as well as intense theological debates over different currents of thought that at times reached extreme levels. On top of this, over the Jesuit province hung a multi-million dollar debt.

During those years many priests, seminarians and lay people left religious life as well as devotional practices of the faith, and they sought a preferential option for the poor through political means. In Argentina, just as in other parts of Latin-America, some embraced extreme ideologies of Marxist extraction and even resorted to weapons. The new provincial never accepted this way of acting, he put order in the Society and that also provoked differences and rumors that will accompany him for many years.

"There was a great deal of confusion, and one of the most appetizing targets were the Jesuits", Carlos Velasco Suarez pointed out, who was a friend of Bergoglio and founder of the Humanist Movement and who died in 2013. Before he died, the journalist Elisabetta Piqué was able to obtain his accounting of those times in the book *Francisco, Vida y Revolución.*

Velasco Suarez was a university professor but also a psychiatrist and knew well the intimate problems of priests and seminarians of that time since, as provincial, Bergoglio sent religious with difficulties to him.

"They aimed in different ways at Jesuit seminarians and priests: indoctrinating them with liberation theology or drawing them from their vocation with women", and according to the psychiatrist, Bergoglio combatted this vigorously. He moved the novices closer to him (to the Colegio Maximo of San Miguel), he personally followed each of the priests and he imposed a strict spiritual life. "I have no doubt that Bergoglio saved the Society of Jesus" concluded the doctor. But that which was for him a virtue, in others it produced "hatred". "I can assure you that he was very firm in his convictions and for this reason he was slapped down and punished by transferring him to Córdoba", Velasco assured Piqué.

The fact that some became angry which lead to his being transferred to Córdoba will be seen in another chapter, but it was suggested by Bergoglio himself, while living in Córdoba, in a letter in 1990 to his Salesian friend Cayetano Bruno. In it Bergoglio recounts that in 1976 he had decided to move the Jesuit provincial curia to San Miguel, in the province of Buenos Aires. In the midst of so much ideological and political commotion, the Provincial wanted to be "man to man" with the young men who were preparing to be Jesuits. "New vocations began to arrive and it seemed convenient for the Provincial to be close to the Formation House", Fr. Jorge wrote at the time. He was not only worried about the seminarians but also about the professors and what they were teaching. "The study program was again restructured: two years of scholastic period (that had disappeared), he separated philosophy from theology replacing the "mix" of philosophy with theology that was called 'curriculum' which began by studying Hegel'".

He defended as well the pastoral changes that he had begun and the questioning he received because of it. "I saw the large neighborhoods without pastoral attention", he wrote. "This bothered me and so we began to meet with the children (...); I realized that we professors had vows to teach the doctrine to the poor and to children, and I began to do it myself with the students. It began to grow: five large churches were built, the children were mobilized in an organized way in the area (...), then the accusation came that this was not an appropriate apostolate for Jesuits; that I had "salesianized" the formation. I was accused of being a pro-Salesian Jesuit".

Fr. Andrés Swinnen, who at that time was novice master and later replaced Bergoglio as Provincial, told us for this book: "After the Council, at that time, there was tremendous chaos; Pope John XXIII had opened a window to let in air as he said, but instead, some took advantage of it just to run away". And he added: in the Society we had priests that assigned themselves, people that said 'I am going to live over there', 'I am going this way', and things like that. We needed someone with character, with the authority to put things in order and, in this way, Bergoglio was a very good provincial".

Time and events in the Church supported the decisions of Bergoglio. In 1975, Paul VI published the Apostolic Exhortation *Evangelii Nuntiandi* (Announcing the Gospel) which points out clearly that "violence is neither Christian nor is it of the Gospel", and that "abrupt or violent changes in structures will be deceiving, inefficient in themselves and certainly not in accordance with the dignity of the people".

Later John Paul II, with the support of his prefect for the Doctrine of the Faith, Joseph Ratzinger (future Pope Benedict XVI), will speak even more directly on the doctrinal virtues and errors of that time. In the *Instruction on some aspects of Liberation Theology*, the Church confirmed its criticism of totalitarian systems, the tyranny of the modern technological processes, the demands for justice and the preferential option for the poor, which the ecclesial base communities that are in true union with the Church embody. It also clarified that "one should not restrict sin to so-called 'social sin'". It reminded us that "it is not possible to locate evil only or principally in 'structures'"; it rejected "the self-redemption of man through class struggle" that the Marxist hermeneutic proposes and that supposes "there is only truth in and through the party". It also condemns the idea of a society that is founded on violence: "the systematic and deliberate resorting to violence, from where ever it may come, must be condemned". The document also adds that "violence breeds violence and degrades man", it teaches that "it is a deadly illusion to believe that structures in and of themselves will give rise to a new man", and finally it asserts that "class warfare (...) aggravates poverty and injustice".

In the *Instruction on Christian liberty and liberation* there is an affirmation that in the light of history has become prophetic. Those who promote "the myth of revolution, not only feed into the illusion that the elimination of a sinful situation is sufficient in itself to create a more humane society, but that it even favors the arrival of totalitarian regimes". The polish Pope and the future German Pope ratified that, for the Church, "liberation can never refer principally nor exclusively to political liberation", but it has to do with "redemption", and they concluded by adding that there is a "morality of the means".

This theological and philosophical reading permitted the healing of some wounds but also opened others, and in its imposition ran the risk of seeming "too European", and removed from some of the very peculiar Latin-American realities that have to do with the life of faith and the commitment to the Gospel.

As the journalist and writer Alver Metalli who was a correspondent of the Italian paper *La Stampa*, wrote: "there had formed in Argentina a group, a theological line, which put the emphasis on the existential, in the religious and in the popular culture, that is to say, more in history than in sociology. This group included among others, the Argentines Lucio Gera, Gerardo Farrell and Juan Carlos Scannone, people that were as well known by Bergoglio as they were to the Uruguayan philosopher Alberto Methol Ferré. They all had in common the idea of considering the popular religiosity, the poor, the culture, the Latin-

American history, and they developed a focus that was much more inclusive of the national realities that consequently came into conflict with liberation theology and its Marxist interpretation. Bergoglio identified with this line of theological thought".

In the book Pope Francis: *Our Brother Our Friend,* by the director of the Catholic Agency *ACI Prensa,* Alejandro Bermudez, the witness of Fr. Scannone was published. Scannone was one of the teachers and companions of Bergoglio during his theological, spiritual and philosophical formation. In the book, Scannone recalls that Cardinal Quarancino (Cardinal Bergoglio's predecessor as Archbishop of Buenos Aires) presented in the *L'Osservatore Romano* the first document on Liberation Theology of the Congregation of the Doctrine of the Faith, and he cited, without going into detail, an article Scannone had written years earlier. The Jesuit professor added: "In the Argentine Liberation theology the Marxist social analysis in not used, but preferably a historical-cultural analysis, without leaving out the social-structural, but not based on the struggle of the classes as the defining principle of interpreting society and history". According to Scannone, "this line of thinking, that some call 'theology of the people' helps one to understand the pastoral decisions of Bergoglio as a bishop; as well as many of his statements and teachings". This type of theology, without Marxist categories, was part "of the climate in which he did his pastoral work. In fact, the difficulties raised by popular piety, the evangelization of the culture and enculturation of the Gospel are key in this theological line".

His conclusion: "there are things that mark Cardinal Bergoglio in a special way, particularly the evangelization of the culture and the theme of popular piety. It is very typical of Bergoglio to speak of the faithful people. When he came out on the balcony (of St. Peter's, the night he was elected Pope), the first thing he did was ask the people to pray for him so that God might bless him, before blessing the people. That is typical of him."

With Bishop Angelelli

When he was provincial, and even some months before his appointment, Bergoglio several times passed through Córdoba. He remembered it himself for this book: "At that time, I returned or came through Córdoba many times: I stayed at the *Residencia Mayor* (in the Society of Jesus, on Caseros Street) or in the residence on Ituzaingó Street, a block away from the Ferreyra Palace, where the community of the Catholic University lived. I went back to make visits and also I stayed there on my way to make the canonical visits to the communities of Mendoza, La Rioja and Salta. Córdoba was generally a required stop when I travelled by land".

The Pope remembers very well June 13, 1973. He was not yet provincial but had travelled to La Rioja, from Córdoba, to accompany the Provincial Superior Ricardo O'Farrell and other Jesuits. The reason was to consult with members of the Society that were in that province matters which concerned the upcoming election of the new provincial.

This visit allowed him to meet a Cordobese who would end up being very important for the Church in Argentina: Bishop Enrique Ángel Angelelli, or the "Gringo" Angelelli, who had been auxiliary bishop of Córdoba, Rector of Our Lady of Loreto Major Seminary, and then bishop of La Rioja. Angelelli died on August 4, 1976 presumably in a car accident, which according to the Justice Department, was really an assassination orchestrated by hit men hired by the military dictatorship. On July 4, 2014, the Criminal Federal Oral Tribunal of La Rioja condemned the former general Luciano Benjamin Menéndez and the former commodore Luis Fernando Estrella to life in prison as the intellectual authors of the murder of Angelelli.

In June of 1973 Bergoglio was a direct witness to something that would later be important in the history of the murdered bishop. "Our visit coincided with the day that bishop Angelelli had rocks thrown at him in La Costa", the Pope remembered. The area of La Costa in La Rioja, or Costa de Arauco, is a region that crosses the mountains of Velasco, which had a lot of vineyards, olive oil and nuts, but also, at that time, was full of landowners and powerful businessmen that formed a strong opposition to the pastoral work of the bishop of La Rioja who was close to the very poor.

Two months after his first visit to bishop Angelelli, Bergoglio returned to that province, this time as provincial and with the Superior General, Fr. Pedro Arrupe. Bergoglio recalled that the visit of Arrupe to Argentina moved up the election which ended making him the provincial.

"I returned to Córdoba with Fr. Arrupe in August of 1973, and we took an entire day in La Rioja to see the missionaries there, and to meet with Bishop Angelelli who received us. The day was very oppressive; the situation with some people of the area of La Costa was very tense".

In one of our telephone conversations, Pope Francis told us: "At that time, Angelelli was really splattered with political gossip, but he was a great pastor. Angelelli was a great pastor and I continue to say it. Evidently there were strong interests and people were dying. The murders of the priests Gabriel Longueville and Carlos de Dios Murias and the catechist Pedernera, that happened shortly before the bishop's assassination, was a sign that those who opposed Angelelli were not, precisely, tolerant and pious people. Some, Francis added, criticized Angelelli that he had gone overboard; I don't think so. In fact, his position was quite balanced compared to what was going on at the time. These were difficult moments that were in preparation for the military coup of 1976, although already in 1973 they had thrown rocks at Angelelli because there they were planning the worst for him".

Once someone asked the Pope if the human, religious and political discernment of that time in Argentina was really that difficult and he responded: "Yes, of course. And more so for someone without experience such as myself".

In a Mass concelebrated in La Rioja on August 4, 2006, the thirtieth anniversary of the death of Angelelli, the then president of the Argentine Episcopal Conference, Cardinal Jorge Bergoglio, exclaimed: "Angelelli was stoned for preaching the Gospel and shed his blood for it". He assured all that the memory of the assassinated cordobese bishop of La Rioja "is not an isolated memory, but rather a challenge". And he underscored "the loving dialogue that existed between the pastor and his people", which he attributed to the fact that "he was a man who sought people out, a man of the outskirts, one who could understand the drama playing out in the country". With words like this coming from the mouth of the man who today is Pope it is not difficult to imagine that the Cause for Canonization may advance in Rome and make another a saint from Córdoba. In this regard, another man who was bishop of La Rioja and also from Córdoba, Roberto Rodriguez (today bishop emeritus), spoke of Angelelli in 2009: "Over time and in some cases, Angelelli's figure has been used to defend many ideologies by taking only some aspects of his life. I exhort all that we try to take his whole life, to study the testimonies we have, and there is a lot, to find the real image of this pastor, recover the whole Angelelli, who, even in the most controversial moments, had an attitude of exhortation, that is, an attitude seeking understanding of the apostolic work he was doing. (...) So we have to rediscover bishop Angelelli, so that he not seem to be of a different church, this is what we want to underline. We want to take up and point out the episcopal service of Angelelli as bishop of La Rioja".

Difficult decisions

Aside from the doctrinal debate, there were other more earthly urgencies in the Society of Jesus. Various institutions of the order founded by St. Ignatius in Argentina were in financial debt. To deal with the problem, the then Fr. Provincial decided to sell the property of Pueyrredon where the novitiate and Holy Family church were located. These were the places where Bergoglio had lived, studied and prayed. He had to sell also the properties of the *Quinta del Niño Dios* in Villa Carlos Paz, as well as the hotel with its land and everything that the Jesuits had in Parque Siquiman, a small locality on the San Roque reservoir, some 45 miles from Córdoba. This building of Parque Siquiman, where retreats and meetings of the teachers who taught in Holy Family School were held, had been bought years earlier by the Worker Association that Fr. Raggi had founded.

The Pope explained his decision: "It was up to me as provincial to sell these properties. The argentine province had a very large debt, in spite of the fact that the previous provincial (O'Farrell) with a great effort had reduced it a lot. But still there remained a debt of 1.5 million dollars of that time, and there was no way other than selling the properties".

The Pope recalled that the Jesuit Robert Pihale SJ, a north American economist had arrived from Wisconsin, USA, to help out in the founding of the Catholic University of Salta.[32]

"Fr. Pihale was very good with numbers –recalled Francis—, and he helped me in selling these properties. With the sale of what was in Córdoba and a property that was on an important corner in the city of Mendoza, we were able to pay all the debts and could hand over the University Del Salvador to the laypeople without debt as Fr. Arrupe wanted".

The pope admits today that there may have been alternatives to the sales, but he underscores the fact that the decision had its reasons. "A long time has passed since then and one can analyze the decision – Francis pointed out, in a conversation on the matter—; it is possible that we could have sought an alternative solution. In any case the church (Holy Family) was 'monstrously large' and could not be finished and already at that time it was deteriorated which would have been another problem. So I decided to change it for a smaller parish church that was built some time later".

The few pictures that remain of that church show that the Pope was right about the condition of the building structure. The building had never been finished; the roof was temporary and in very poor condition; and it was an enormous church designed as the heart of what was intended as the largest house of formation of the Society of Jesus in Argentina, but that was no longer the case.

Still, the process was very painful for the community and for Bergoglio himself that was at the head of it. He took care of negotiating a

---

[32] On March 19, 1963 the then Archbishop of Salta, Bishop Roberto Jose Tavella, signed the archdiocesan decree n. 9 in which the Catholic University of Salta was created, which began to function regularly, with the different faculties opened in 1966, led by Jesuit priests from the diocese of Wisconsin (United States). Fr. Pihale was the first administrative vice-rector.

loan contract with the Congregation of the "Daughters of the Immaculate Conception of Buenos Aires", so that Holy Family parish could use the chapel that these religious sisters had (and still have) in Sacred Heart School. This school is located on the corner of Buchardo and Roma Streets, a block away from the land and church that was sold.

In this contract, Father Provincial Jorge Bergoglio promises a series of conditions for the "provisional" and "pastoral" use of the chapel of the school "while we seek the means necessary for the definitive installment of the parish in its own headquarters".

The contract was for five years which could be extended and Bergoglio expressed his gratitude to the sisters, for the important help that they give to the People of God in the Pueyrredon neighborhood, assuring the sisters of his fraternal collaboration and constant prayers that the Lord bless them for this special generous service". The religious sisters of this congregation, who also have the administration of Our Lady of the Snow Institute, located on the corner of San Juan and Ayacucho Boulevards, in the city of Córdoba, treasure this contract that was signed on March 29, 1976 by the man who is now Pope.

The statues of the old parish church were put temporarily elsewhere. A beautiful image of the Holy Family was placed in a chapel of another area school, Bishop Caixal School, of the Sisters of the Holy Family of Urgel. By historical coincidence, the High School of this institution opened its doors in March 1958; at the same time Bergoglio arrived in Córdoba to begin his Jesuit formation as a novice, just two blocks away.

Fr. Andrés Swinnen today lives in Holy Family parish that suffered these changes. When he was asked about this time, smiling and with some exaggeration he pointed out: "Here in the neighborhood there were some people who were very upset about what happened.... people that if they could have gotten a hold of Bergoglio, they would have lynched him. Even today I think there are people who are still upset."

Swinnen had to deal with these matters as the top authority of the Jesuit Province in Argentina, since he succeeded Bergoglio as provincial. "When I assumed the responsibility after Bergoglio, things had calmed down a bit, although I had to listen to some complaints and make some decisions, among them I had to transfer Fr. Mansilla who had spent his whole life here (referring to Holy Family parish), suffering all of this, and also Br. Pamich, a Slovene, who was a very good man and who also suffered greatly with the demolition and sale. I transferred Mansilla to Posadas (Misiones Province) and Pamich to Corrientes, and they were grateful", Swinnen recalled.

Today, Holy Family parish has a more modern church, of a size proportionate to the community, but that was also difficult to finish and to maintain. Fr. Aldo Scotto had an important role in the construction. He was a Jesuit that was also an engineer and who had shared some years of his formation with Bergoglio. From his place of residence today in Holy Martyrs parish in Posadas, Province of Misiones, Scotto told a radio station from Buenos Aires that Jorge Bergoglio was always a "brilliant man". He emphasized "two very great virtues: a great love for evangelical poverty, living a life without anything very extraordinary thus sharing the life of the people. This was his life in the Society of Jesus. The other was his great love for the Virgin Mary, the Undoer of Knots[33], who now will have many knots to untie".

Fr. Aldo Scotto and the entire community began construction of the new church on the corner of General Deheza and Buchardo Streets, and it took some years to build. Today's pastor, Walter Obregón, had to seek funds from other areas and the community worked hard up to the end of 2013 to obtain the funds necessary, for example, to repair the roof. Behind the altar of the parish are the three statues that make up the Holy Family; the smallest of the Child Jesus; one of Blessed Mother and one of St. Joseph. They are the same statues that were in the old church that stood in the novitiate where the Pope was a young novice. Before them Jorge Bergoglio prayed and meditated. Anyone can go to visit them today and be a part of this history.

---

[33] "Mary, the Undoer of Knots", was an image and devotion that the Holy Father came across while studying in Germany and brought to Argentina in the 80s. As a bishop, he had a replica of the image placed in San José del Talar parish in Buenos Aires. This devotion spread rapidly throughout all Argentina, in which Mary is seen as one who intercedes for her children "undoing the knots" or difficulties in their life.

Witnesses and protagonists

Two people who still live in Córdoba were witnesses and, in some way, protagonists of those difficult decisions that Bergoglio had to make. They are the diocesan priest Juan Etulain and Dr. Margarita Schweizer. Both agree, even if with some differences, in an assessment of Bergoglio that is important for understanding why the then Fr. Jorge made the decisions he did and for understanding as well what he has done and will do as Pope Francis.

"Bergoglio is a martyr of duty", Fr. Etulain says, sitting behind his humble desk where he attends the parish office in the Divine Providence and Our Lady of the Valley chapel, in the Providence neighborhood in Córdoba. In 1974, when Fr. Etulain left the Salesian order to incardinate into the Archdiocese of Córdoba, he was put in charge of the San Roque parish in Villa Corina, in the northeast part of the city of Córdoba, and he began to look for work as a teacher in one of the area schools. The Jesuit César Azúa, who was at that time the legal representative of the Holy Family Institute, called on him to give some classes. Etulain accepted and elaborated a plan of studies in Catechesis and Human and Christian formation for High School students. Fr. Azua and Margarita Schweizer (the Principal of the institution) brought the plan to Bergoglio so that he could study it and see about the possibility of implementing it in the other high schools the Society had in the country.

The Provincial Father liked the idea and began to meet with Etulain two or three times during the year, or whenever his schedule would permit it as he passed through Córdoba.

According to Etulain, at that time Bergoglio faced the difficulty that many priests come across which is "the psychological and spiritual tension of those who seek their vocational identity in the *pastoral* priest and in the fullness of youth find themselves wrapped up in administrative or academic conflicts".

For this priest, who is four years younger than Francis, this tension was evident in Bergoglio and "he exposed it every time we met with Fr. Azúa and he commented on the options he had to resolve the debts of the Order, to sell the old novitiate building or not, with the church and the land, all administrative things which he faced with sadness but with responsibility", Etulain pointed out. He remembered that Bergoglio was worried because "he knew that the people of the parish and neighborhood would be very upset if he sold the church", which is what in the end happened. "In the light of all that –he added— I can say that if there is anything that marks Bergoglio it is his martyrdom for duty; Bergoglio is a martyr of duty because if he sees something in prayer, if he sees it clearly as the Will of God, he will give his whole body and soul to accomplish it".

Even though he has not seen him again since 1980, Etulain never forgot the characteristics, the attitudes and words of that young Fr. Jorge; memories that help one to understand the how and from where Pope Francis says and does things today.

"I remember that at that time he began to speak of the 'pastoral peripheries', of the marginalized, of those who suffer; and he was very interested in the 'pastoral journalism' of bishop Vicente Zaspe[34]. He even had us tape the Sunday homilies of Zaspe and buy the leaflets that came out with his preaching".

Etulain assured us that already in 1975, Bergoglio had a firm "no" to four questions: "no restorationism (with this he referred to turning back the *aggiornamiento* that Vatican II had desired); no socialized reductionism; no functionalism ('it is not enough that something works', he clarified); and no clericalism. From what it appears until now, Francis has not changed his opinion". He added: "when we speak of difficulties and challenges, he always said, citing Marechal, that 'you can get out of every labyrinth going upward'[35]. And I would complete the idea: 'or through the door or window of laughter'".

---

[34] Vicente Zaspe (1020-1984) priest from Buenos Aires, first bishop of Rafaela, later archbishop of Santa Fe (Argentina) and vice-president of the Argentine Episcopal Conference. One of the bishops who spoke out with the most courage for the "disappeared" during the military dictatorship and demanded respect for human rights. In 2009, the then Cardinal Bergoglio said of him: "He was a worker of the Kingdom, a prophetic bishop who was not deceived by any political messianism of his time because in that messianism there were hidden lies, corruption, shady deals".
[35] Fragment of the poem *Laberinto de Amor*.

Could this have anything to do with the contagious joy that the world so admires in the Pope today?

"Probably", responds Margarita Schweizer, who also shared time, work and challenges with Bergoglio. To speak with her is to enjoy a personalized class of human education. Doctor in philosophy with a specialty in pedagogy, Margarita has been a member of the National Academy of Education since 2010. She has many of degrees and academic achievements. Today, with surprising vitality, she is the Academic secretary of the National University of Villa María, the city she commutes to each day from her home in the capital city of Córdoba. She lives there with her husband, an architect and ex-professor, as she is of the University of Córdoba. It is not easy to find her at home. Once or twice a year she travels to Europe to give courses and seminars in Germany and Italy. Margarita is this and much more. Since I am a son and husband of teachers I can give witness to the fact that she is exactly that: a Teacher.

It is probably for this reason that in October of 1973 she became the first woman in the history of the Society of Jesus in Argentina to be named Principal of a Jesuit institution –and an all-boys school at that—; she was given the responsibility by the man who today is Pope.

Francis remembers her fondly, and underlines the circumstances of her assignment. It's logical, since in order to name her Principal of the Holy Family Institute, the then Provincial had to ask permission of the Superior General of the Society.

Schweizer entered the school in Pueyrredon for the first time as a professor of language, literature, Latin and Greek on March 15, 1960. She had no idea that days earlier, in the large church of the novitiate that stood at the time in front of the school, a future Pope had professed his first vows as a Jesuit religious. Without knowing one another, Bergoglio left in those days for Chile to start his scholastic period while Margarita began to teach class at the newly founded high school for boys. Thirteen years later their paths would cross again.

"I met Bergoglio in the middle of October in 1973 –she told us—. Two months earlier, on September 27, 1973, the then Principal of the

School, Fr. Carlos Carranza (today a chaplain for the Reina Fabiola Clinic, of the Catholic University of Córdoba), handed me the responsibility because he had come down with hepatitis and could not go on. He said to me 'here are the keys to my office, take charge'".

It was an informal transferal of responsibility that had to be confirmed by the Fr. Provincial. "I did not know that there had been changes in the Society and I did not know Bergoglio", Margarita explained. And she added a story: "That day in October, I was in the Principal's office, among papers and all that, when the then Fr. Osvaldo Bueno SJ (who would later leave the Society) entered together with another priest a little taller, very serious and formal, who greeted me cordially. It was Bergoglio, the new Provincial".

Schweizer tells it as though she were still living it: "He asked me if I could speak with him the next day, in the Residence of the Society in the center of the city. I said yes and the next day we met. It was a long conversation. He received me with great courtesy and he asked me to give him a report on the state of the school and I was very honest with him; I told him that the buildings were in terrible condition, there were economic problems and some other problems that were common at that time. I had little information that would help me understand the political problems that were going on nationally, and affected the school. I don't know what the impression wasthat he took of me but after listening to me he asked one of those questions that –I learned later— he often asked to get his bearings and to understand the person he was talking to:

— Tell me, Madame, after everything you have told me, do you think there is anything we can do to save the school?

— Yes, of course, sure– I responded.

— Very well. Perfect –he said and he thanked me.

Margarita Schweizer left the Holy Family Institute thirty years after that conversation. In three decades, the school that she began to administer with less than two hundred students became an educational community with more than one thousand five hundred children, adolescents and young people. Margarita left the Institute that was her home in 2002, after forty two years of fruitful work, in which Bergoglio had an important part.

"Of the relationship that we had, he as provincial and I as principal, I can underline two aspects: on the one hand, his attitude, always open and understanding every time I spoke with him about something that had come up in the school, in order to seek counsel and orientation from him; he was always disposed, no matter where he was. And, on the other hand, the unconditional support he always gave to our administration. He supported the teachers a lot and even the parents who were there and who worked a great deal, with enormous educational idealism, vocation and openness for the school, at a time that was very complicated".

On October 11, 1976, Margarita Schweizer was named dean of the faculties of Philosophy and Humanities of the Catholic University of Córdoba by Bergoglio. She had entered this house of higher studies in 1963 and left on December 23, 2005.

Bergoglian Pedagogy

The memories of Dr. Schweizer, the detailed accounts of her experience also help us to outline some pieces of Bergoglio's thought when he was not yet forty years old. They are thoughts that he still thinks and expresses today.

The academic support Bergoglio offered was also at times spiritual. "When I started as principal, I had the possibility to work in a Mexican University because they accepted my application. When I mentioned it to Bergoglio and asked him to help me discern what to do, he told me: 'How nice Madame, congratulations'. But added, 'I think this is an achievement, but it seems to me you should look also at your roots; remember this means an uprooting, have you thought about the uprooting aspect? Remember that you will be far from your loved ones, and when one leaves his country where his or her loved ones are, it is difficult to put down roots anywhere else in the same way. Think about what it means to be uprooted'. This was the first sharp reflection that I received on a personal level from him; and between the thousand dollars monthly salary they offered me in Mexico and the 350 *pesos ley* that I was making here, if that much, I decided to stay. I was not mistaken".

Another time, when as a young principal she complained that there were problems and some people were putting obstacles in the way of the educational project they were creating, Bergoglio told her, in Schweizer's own words: "my dear lady, let the weeds grow, remember the Gospel; let them grow until the harvest and then you will keep what is worthwhile".

Margarita becomes emotional when she remembers some things: "Another time, when I was complaining that there so much to do in the school and we had so little resources, he told me: 'Madame, always favor time over space'. At first I didn't know what he meant; time and life had to be lived and spent to understand it: one has to live time in hope, because time will put things in their place. Life is a construction in time and the Pope always knew it".

With a meticulous precision, Schweizer remembers another teaching of that Jesuit provincial: "I was worried because what we were doing with so much work did not seem to produce fruit. So I told him that it was like working in that rocky soil of the Parable of the Sower[36]. Then, seeing my worry, Bergoglio told me: 'It seems good that you have as a guide the Parable of the Sower, but you should realize that the parable only shows the end; before the parable begins, the sower has prepared the soil, he has chosen the seed, before he sows there is a lot of work that you and the community are doing'".

On June 8, 2013, Pope Francis said during a homily in the morning Mass in St. Martha residence: "Caring for the Word of God means opening our hearts to it, like the earth opens itself to receive the

---

[36] In the Gospel of Saint Mark, chapter 4, 1-20, Jesus tell the parable: "A sower went out to sow. And as he sowed, some seed fell on the path, and the birds came and ate it up. Other seed fell on rocky ground where it had little soil. It sprang up at once because the soil was not deep. And when the sun rose, it was scorched and it withered for lack of roots. Some seed fell among thorns, and the thorns grew up and choked it and it produced no grain. And some seed fell on rich soil and produced fruit. It came up and grew and yielded thirty, sixty, and a hundredfold."

seed. The Word of God is the seed and it is sowed. Jesus told us what happens to the seed. Some falls by the wayside and the birds come to eat it. This is what happens when one does not take care of the Word. It means some hearts do not know how to receive it. It also happens that some of the seed falls on rocky ground and the seed is not able to put down roots and it dies, that is when we cannot care for the Word because we are not constant; and when tribulation comes we do not remember it. The Word also falls on unprepared ground, where there are thorns, and in the end it dies because it is not cared for. But, what are the thorns? Jesus himself tells us: 'the attachment to riches, to vices, all these things'. To take care of the Word of God is to receive it in our hearts. But it is necessary to prepare our heart to receive it. Meditate always on what the Word says today, looking at what happens in your life".

What then is the Bergoglian pedagogy?

Margarita Schweizer responds: "Bergoglio is a hinge-man; he was for the Society of Jesus in Argentina, in which he created a link between one time and another. His reflections and ideas helped me understand an expression of Fr. Arrupe: 'School yes, but not like this'. Or what is the same thing: the educational institution goes on with its values and mission but adapting to the times. Bergoglio is discipline, order, respect, morality; and he is also education in values, trying to do what can be done from the human condition, to draw a horizon of good, of love of others. Is he a 'martyr of duty'? The word 'martyr' might be a bit exaggerated, but yes, he definitely was one who suffered for duty. But one has to say that while he suffered doing what he had to do, at the same time he has gathered good fruits in the basket of his life as well as bitter and painful fruits. It is the act of living." She added: "Bergoglio has a structure in his personality that defines him; there is an idea of order, of discipline, of keeping his word, of being with others, of committing himself to the human person and his dignity. To this structure of his personality one can add his Jesuit formation, in which nothing was light, nothing easy, and where there is a profound discernment of things. Uniting all these elements into one, one can understand why that young provincial made the decisions he did in the middle of difficult situations".

For Schweizer, the decisions that Bergoglio takes "are taken after putting them to prayer, to deep reflection, discern them and deal with them from his formation; all of this allows him to take on the risk and bear with the responsibility and judgment that is made on the decision. He was always well positioned to make decisions and to accept the results and the judgments".

When Bergoglio ended his term as provincial in 1979, he no longer came to Córdoba. If it were not for one or another telephone call, he lost contact with the majority of people with which he had worked. For this reason, Margarita would see him again only in 1991, twelve years later, when Bergoglio lived in the Major Residence of the Society in the center of Córdoba. "I remember that together with Fr. Petty (ex-rector of the Catholic University of Córdoba) we were showing a group of German professors that were visiting the 'Jesuit Block Patrimony of Humanity'. When we entered the Domestic Chapel everything was dark, with the lights off. I asked for the lights to be turned on and before anyone was able to do it, I distinguished a human figure that was praying, he got up, and left the chapel quickly. It was Bergoglio. I called him and he did not hear me. I should mention that those were complicated times especially for him". It is true. And yet, twenty two years later, this man would become Pope.

Del Salvador University

Another decision that Bergoglio faced as provincial and that did not have a unanimous positive reception in the Society, was that of handing over the administration of the Del Salvador University, which had a lot of debt and problems, to a Civil Association of laypeople. Bergoglio really was attempting to fulfill the will of the Superior General. Fr. Arrupe thought that it made no sense to maintain a second Catholic university in Buenos Aires, where there already is the Pontifical Catholic University of Argentina, which depends on the Archdiocese of Buenos Aires. Many questioned the wisdom of the Society letting go of one of its most influential and symbolic institutions.

The Pope knows that the decision to hand over the Del Salvador University to laypeople was a difficult one. "It was a decision that some people never understood, because for some Jesuits that had worked there for many years it was very painful".

Others opposed the idea that the university would be in the hands of the "Iron Guard", a Peronist political group that arose in 1962 and about which there are numerous debates and positions, as there almost always is when you move in the area of ideas and of political action.

While some (linked to the political left) think that the Iron Guard took its name from the ultra-nationalistic and Romanian fascist movement *Garda de Fier*, that took place in Rumania in the 1930s, others opine that the "Iron Guard of Peron" united militants of the younger generation that "tried to articulate their personal projects with the revolutionary longings of social change of the populist sectors of Argentina and Latin-American". There were sectors of the Peronist resistance that was critical and opposed the armed fighting that other sectors of Peronism supported, such as "La Tendencia y Montoneros", as well as the guerilla warfare of the Marxist left.

In 1973, the directors and militants of the Iron Guard, among them one of the founders, Alejandro "Gallego" Álvarez, supported the candidacy of Hector Cámpora and then of Peron, but they did not have an organic link with José López Rega, promoter of the rightwing police group known as the Triple A (*Alianza Anticomunista Argentina*). People associated with the group affirm that they did not participate in the structure of political, business or Union power, and the majority of them did not accept public office in 1973.

Although it is certain that he knew and met several of its directors and militants, as he did with other groups with political concerns, Bergoglio never was part of the Iron Guard, nor was he a member of any party. To clarify these associations, recently the Pope explained the following to the authors of this book: "I knew Alejandro Álvarez when I was provincial (of the Society of Jesus), because there were meetings of intellectuals in the Del Salvador University and I participated in these meetings because the process of giving the University to lay people had begun. Alejandro Álvarez was in one of these meetings. Later I met him again in a conference with Alberto Methol Ferré. I met several of the people of the Iron Guard, just as I knew people of other sectors of peronism, but most of it in the meetings we had in the Del Salvador University".

Among those that participated in these meetings at the Del Salvador University was Francisco José Piñon, who is now rector of the De Congreso University, Mendoza, Argentina. Piñon was the first layman to be named rector of this house of studies now separated from the Society of Jesus. In the book *Francisco, vida y revolución*, Piñon told the author that Bergoglio decided to leave the university in the hands of laypeople in order to allow the Jesuits to return to the poorer neighborhoods. The Jesuits remained on the pastoral staff and continued to play a role in the Faculty of Theology". Piñon himself clarified in this book a polemic episode that some still today use to criticize Pope Francis. On November 25, 1977, in the middle of the military dictatorship, the Del Salvador University gave a doctorate *honoris causa* to Admiral Emilio Massera, a member of the Military Junta who crushed terrorism with an even greater and abominable terror from the State itself. Massera died in November of 2010, condemned by the Argentine justice system for Human Rights violations. Piñon told Piqué what happened at that time: "Massera was invited to give a conference as an exchange to save lives. Bergoglio was not at the conference. It was an important decision in order to save lives; lives of people of the University, of peronists, of many".

The controversial changes that involved handing over the University Del Salvador from the Society also responded to the mark that Fr. Arrupe had left on the Society since 1974. In that year, the Superior General had called for the General Congregation n.32, in which the Society would make a historic turn: the Society was to leave the security of academic formation that had linked it to the most influential families of society and which permitted them to form hundreds of political leaders, in order to concentrate on the poor. A document released from that large Jesuit assembly, read that proclaiming faith in God ought "to be unavoidably united to the tireless struggle to abolish all injustices that still weigh on humanity". At the same time it asked its members to unite themselves to the poor with the practice of a life of austerity: "The Society of Jesus will not be able to hear 'the cry of the poor' if its members do not acquire the direct personal experience of the misery and limitations of the poor". We must make a serious effort to reduce consumerism, to feel the real effects of poverty" the document continued, and at the same time it invited the members to examine their meals, their dress, the rooms where the Jesuits slept, trips and vacations.

"It is absolutely unthinkable that the Society could effectively promote justice and human dignity everywhere if the better part of the apostolate is concerned with the rich and powerful or is rooted in the security of property, of knowledge or power". Bergoglio, with his austere life, showed how to apply this teaching.

A future Pope in the Catholic University of Córdoba

It is true that Jorge Bergoglio, Pope Francis, was never a student or a professor in the Catholic University of Córdoba (CUC). As father provincial of the Society of Jesus in Argentina however, he was in charge of it for six years. This is not insignificant, and should be a point of pride for this house of higher studies, the first private university in the country, that soon will have completed sixty years of service.

Veritas liberabit vos ("the Truth will set you free") is the motto in Latin of the seal of the CUC. The author of the words is Jesus Christ. The man who today "represents" Him on earth, the Pope, participated actively in the history of this house of knowledge.

Although many do not notice it, documents and some witnesses show that Fr. Bergoglio was really involved in the direction of the CUC according to the institutional responsibilities of his office. The academic rules of the CUC require that the highest authority of the University be the archbishop of Córdoba, who puts it under the care of the Society of Jesus "in the person of the provincial". The provincial, as vice chancellor delegates the immediate exercise of his authority to the person assigned as rector.

Between 1973 and 1979, the chancellor of the CUC was Cardinal Raúl Francisco Primatesta, archbishop of Córdoba, and Bergoglio was the vice chancellor,. Although it is clear that he delegated the operative jobs to the different rectors that were in office, and to the organisms of direction of the CUC, Bergoglio took charge of the ideological direction and established through a consensus, the lines of conduction that helped this house of higher learning get out of the rut that the whole country was suffering at the time.

During Bergoglio's time as provincial, the following Jesuits were rectors of the CUC: Fernando Storni (1965-1975), Hipólito Salvo (1975-1979) and Jorge Fourcade (1979-1985). The following laymen were academic vice-rectors: Arturo Granillo (1969-1974) and Carlos Luis Diamanti (1975-2000).

One has to remember that these were complicated times. When Bergoglio took charge of the Jesuit Province, in July of 1973, there were still echoes of the massacre that took place in Ezeiza, on June 20 of the same year, as factions of the extreme right and left struggled for control of peronism in violent infighting while they awaited the "triumphant" return of Juan Domingo Peron. While Bergoglio assumed the office of provincial, the then president Hector José Cámpora, "el Tío", announced his resignation in order to allow Peron to return to power through new elections. The campaign slogan "Cámpora in government, Peron in power" was becoming a reality.

The difficulty of ideological conflicts, of the political violence, and the mix of these things with the Christian commitment to the poor, had been discussed by the authorities of the Society and of the CUC already since 1970, after a series of violent outbreaks rocked Córdoba and the country and that had effects on the life of the "*la Católica*". Bergoglio also had to attend to and resolve these types of problems, in order to neutralize any attempt by students or faculty influenced by these violent political groups to interfere with the life of the university.

In the book "A history with meaning" edited by the CUC itself in 2006, on the occasion of its fiftieth anniversary, it is chronicled that in 1971 the University "seeks to combat" the "social context of confusion about the intentions and activities of the Church in social-economic problems (...) clarifying and affirming its objectives and the ordering of its plans and actions to the ends for which they are established".

For this reason, when Bergoglio came into contact with the University in his authority as provincial, the ideological thinking was not so much the problem —but rather the political guidelines of the leadership and the governance of the University generally (academic, financial and religious questions as well as future projects, etc.).

In February of 1975, Bergoglio designated a new rector, Fr. Hipólito Salvo, who took charge however, a little later, on December 2, due to health reasons. The book cited above goes on to say that the assumption of the new rector came "at a special moment, in that the Society of Jesus had decided to concentrate all its university focus in Córdoba, after handing over the Del Salvador University to the laypeople"

During the canonical visit that Fr. Bergoglio realized to the CUC on October 13, 1976, he directed a message to the Honorable Academic Council, where he pointed out that growth is possible "if the university is faithful to the inheritance and the conditions that brought it about in its origins". He added that "even if there are conditions that limit it, it is an unavoidable fact that every authentic growth must find its roots in the originality that conceived it and must be a reflection of what identifies it".[37]

This image that identifies the CUC is stated in article 4 of the Statutes of the University, that state "the CUC has as its end the profound seeking of the Truth and the total promotion of the person through a humanistic, social, scientific and professional formation of the students, through teaching and the highest forms of investigation and the cultivation of the arts. As a witness to this it will give out academic and/or professional titles and/or diplomas. It will serve the community according to its capacity. It does not seek profit and will not discriminate against any student for religious beliefs, but it will reflect in its investigation and teaching the Christian message as taught by the Catholic

---

[37] A quote from a document from the CUC Archives.

Church, in an ecumenical search for the Truth. It will carry out its activities in harmony with the principles that are contained in the National Constitution and with the republican and democratic institutions of the Nation". Effectively, in union with Bergoglio, the rector Salvo showed himself to be "willing to keep the Society of Jesus in control of the governing body of the University so as to establish how and with what content the students would be formed at a time when a cruel military dictatorship had taken control of the country".[38]

In the same message dated October of 1976, Bergoglio stated: "the mission of the Catholic University is not founded on division, or on the sector of society that is in style, nor in ideological reductionisms of whatever type. Its mission is to construct; its image is the whole Body of Christ that is the Church, its reality is the young people —with their own personality— that are being incorporated into this body. Paul VI says that the world today is characterized by the 'virtiginousness of evolution'. And, what is opposed to the vertiginous, that is to say what passes dominatingly, is the organic, which is like a formula that unites wholeness with identity".

In this same opportunity, with a religious and transcendent look at the complicated reality of Argentina, Bergoglio called for all to "have before our eyes that which makes and identifies us so as to go forward with the steps that the concrete historical situation demands of us. Remembering the past and openness to creating new spaces for God".

In this line of action the vice-rectorate of formation was created and Fr. Salvo designated for this responsibility Fr. José Regis Álvarez, who developed a great pastoral work which was crowned in May of 1979, with the celebration of daily Mass in the chapel of the Campus on the Camino a Alta Gracia Highway.

---

[38] Universidad Católica de Córdoba, *Una historia con sentido*, page 151.

A step forward

When Pope Francis is asked today about his experience in the CUC, he summarizes all of it in a sentence: "I remember that there were serious problems in the Catholic University of Córdoba, where I again made a rapid decision; only this time the decision was the right one, since even today I can see that there was really no other way, and thanks to the decisions made, the University was able to take a step forward".

The Pope realizes and is thankful that those decisions were not made alone but with valuable people who he still remembers very much. "There are people that helped me a lot there. I remember with gratitude the Accountant Nestor Giraudo, a person who was good with numbers and who clarified the financial-economic situation. The academic Vice-rector, the engineer Carlos Diamanti, also helped me greatly, aside from being very intelligent and carrying out well his duties, he did it from his wheel chair which was an important witness and a very nice thing for that time".

Giraudo and Diamanti are friends. Now retired, they share a good portion of the past. A past that both, with their families included, were consecrated to "the Catholic", as they call the University where they studied, grew, where they taught, where they worked and even where one of them –Diamanti– got married. "I was married in the Chapel of the University –recalls the ex-academic vice-rector, who was the second metal engineer in the history of Córdoba— because it was practically my home".

When told by the authors of this book that Pope Francis had remembered them, recalling his relationship with the CUC, Diamanti and Giraudo got together to give their testimony. They wanted to since, as can be noted in their faces and their voices, the ascension of "Fr. Jorge" to the Chair of Peter not only renewed the value of those past memories, but it has given them a transcendent vital relevance.

Both knew Bergoglio in 1975, when they were authorities of the CUC: Diamanti was the dean of the Faculty of Engineering and was academic vice-rector and Giraudo was Economics vice-rector. (See pictures n. 13 and n. 14).

Picture 13 – April 3, 1979. Fr Bergoglio, vice-chancellor of the CUC, appoints Carlos Diamanti as vice-rector. *Picture by kind permission of the Diamanti family.*

Picture 14 - Néstor Giraudo is appointed as vice-rector of Economics by Fr Bergoglio, April 1979. *Picture by kind permission of the Giraudo family.*

The two of them were confirmed in their posts by Bergoglio (Diamanti even had to assume the post of interim rector until Fr. Salvo assumed the position), and they agree in their impression that this priest who was only a couple of years older, left them: "he was extremely intelligent, lucid, very agile, quick to make decisions and turning them into action. He was sure of himself, expeditious and had authority. The impression he gave was of a Father provincial that really had authority, but he exercised it with simplicity, with humility and after creating consensus".

Just as forty years ago, in an attitude that the Pope himself underscores, with good humor and serenity Diamanti continues to face the paralysis and ill health that was caused by a traffic accident in the United States, where he had gone to study on a scholarship that was given him by the CUC. Without losing his good humor, he assured us that Bergoglio's objective "was to consolidate a very Jesuit university, very catholic and orthodox, and that the greatest importance to the problems of Córdoba were given while helping to form high quality professionals, people of science and conscience". He has no doubt in his mind that the work of the then Fr. Provincial produced "a straightening out of the CUC".

This "straightening out", Giraudo also assures us, was not only with regards to the mission. But the economic situation of the CUC was similar to that of Del Salvador (that was separated from the Society) in its difficulties. It had a large debt, a serious operative deficit and in its organization it was not clear of the need to "ground it" economically. "When Bergoglio assumed control of the University –Giraudo, who was in charge of the economic administration, explained— the CUC had a large debt with IBM, close to 300 thousand dollars, for equipment that was bought; as well as other debts due to construction, and the interest on loans that had to be paid. As well, there was an imbalance between the administration and teaching structure and the number of students that accentuated the operative deficit".

Diamanti and Giraudo also mentioned that the University paid a lot "simply to cancel the interests on the debt", and it got to the point where "for some years, many professors were not paid anything, but taught classes *ad honorem*".

It is true that the majority of those professors did not live from what they earned in teaching, because they were important professionals in the private sector and taught in the CUC from their own personal commitment. But there were some who did need the money. "Thus there were difficult decisions to make —Giraudo remembered, throwing light on what the Pope already had mentioned—; they were difficult decisions, but were agreed upon. Some were paid a little and others nothing".

Giraudo said that on Bergoglio's instructions agreements were signed with providers and even a condoning of interests on the capital of the debt was obtained with IBM. "The provincial said that the objective of the University was to heal itself economically so as to be able to grow and support the academic needs. To have the best Professors it was important to pay them, and to pay them resources are necessary. Bergoglio didn't want financial risks and a lot of common sense was used", the Accountant explained.

With Diamanti he remembered another "hard decision" of the man who now as head of the Vatican State, is applying reforms to aim the financial administration of the Church toward its primary goal: evangelization. "Since there were many years during which the professors did not receive a salary or received very little, one of the instructions that Bergoglio gave was that this entire salary amount that was not paid should at least be paid in their retirement amount. The objective was that when the professors reached retirement age, they could do so without any problem and be paid", said Giraudo. And he added: "The University little by little took advantage of all the facilities that the government offered to get up to date on the back liabilities and thus was able to pay all the retirements of everyone from the beginning of the CUC. Today there is no one who has not been able to retire due to lack of back payments. Even today there are people that come looking for the certificates and they are there. Everyone can retire. This was an important decision of Fr. Bergoglio".

Margarita Schweizer who, as was pointed out, was named by Bergoglio as dean of a faculty in the CUC, agrees with the vision of Diamanti and Giraudo, and adds to it a theological-pastoral dimension as well as a conclusion: "Because of the respect Bergoglio always had for history, in some way he recovered the efforts and dreams of those Jesuits

that came to Córdoba in the 16th and 17th centuries and founded a
university that later became the National University of Córdoba. From a
theological-pastoral-pedagogical point of view, he realized that the CUC
had to assume the continuation or re-foundation of those dreams and
efforts, to start them, according to the mission and tradition of the Society,
in the 20th century and for the future". And she added: "The work of
Bergoglio in *La Catolica* was very important. He encouraged unity,
generated consensus in the administration and concentrated his efforts to
create a unique and strong Jesuit university in Argentina. The division,
the antithetical game of Bergoglianos and anti-bergoglianos that came
later on, in some way obscured the work he did, but the CUC owes a lot to
the man who today is Pope".

By the time Fr. Jorge left office as provincial, the CUC was
completely healed financially and ready to begin a period of growth that
continues to this day. Today, it is one of the principal universities of the
country, with thousands of students, with a high level of academic
achievement, with an important percentage of its budget given to
investigation, with a strong social commitment, and recognized
technological services... and with an ex-collaborator that sits on the chair
of Peter.

The kidnapping of Yorio and Jalics

Bergoglio also had to deal with problems that involved Jesuits in
very delicate matters (in some cases, life or death) related to the military
dictatorship.

The worst case was that of the priests Francisco Jalics and Orlando
Yorio, who in 1976 were kidnapped and tortured during five months. For
years, several members of the Society of Jesus accused Bergoglio of having
"handed over" these two priests. They were living in a very poor section
of the barrio Rivadavia, in Bajo Flores (Buenos Aires), with the idea of
forming a new religious community, separate from the Society of which
they were members. Two years later both left the country.

The journalist Marcelo Larraquy in his book *Recen por él, la historia jamás contada del hombre que desafía los secretos del Vaticano* (Pray for him, the untold story of the man that challenges the secrets of the Vatican), delves seriously into the details of this story, even if the title of his book appears to be that of a Dan Brown novel. He tells of the political and ideological positions held by members of this problematic community, of the contacts some of them had with the group *Juventud Peronista* and others even with the *Montoneros*. He assures us though that neither Yorio nor Jalics agreed with the armed resistance —as Bergoglio himself would also clarify— and he researches the warnings that the then provincial gave them of the dangers they were facing, and about the orders from Fr, Arrupe that they were to make a decision: either leave that community or leave the Society.

Larraquy shows that the relationship between Yorio and Bergoglio was not a good one. But he never directly accuses the provincial for the kidnapping of the priests. And even if he does describe the management of Bergoglio as rigorous in ideological control and firm in his struggle against those that mix their religious commitments with political contacts and action, he concedes the fact that the now Pope Francis permitted "pastoral" work with the most poor. Even more, he underscores the fact that with "a moderate approach with regards to the priests of the Third World" Bergoglio "sent students out on weekends for pastoral work with the poor. He wanted them to roll up their sleeves and personally work with them, but without their getting politically involved".

As well, he maintains that during Bergoglio's time in office, the Colegio Maximo, which was also his Jesuit headquarters, "served as a refuge of the Society of Jesus in the Province", where several of those persecuted by the dictatorship and repression were housed.

In one of the few times Bergoglio answered questions in this matter, when he was interviewed by the authors of the book *El Jesuita*, he pointed out that the then superior general of the Society, Fr. Pedro Arrupe, said that they had to choose between the community where they were living or the Society of Jesus. "Since they persisted in their project and the group was dissolved, they asked to leave the Society". Bergoglio explained that the resignation of Yorio was accepted on March 19, 1976 and that "among the rumors of an imminent coup" he told them they should be very careful. "I remember having offered to them, if it were convenient for their security, that they come and live in the provincial house of the Society", said Bergoglio, who clarified also that he never thought that Yorio or Jalics were involved in subversive activity. "But because of their relationship with some of the priests in the slums, they were too exposed to the paranoia of the witch hunt that was going on. Since they remained in the slum, Yorio and Jalics were kidnapped during a raid".

In March 2013, when due to the election of Cardinal Bergoglio as Pope, a section of "kirchernism" and the anticlerical Argentine left brought up the accusation again, Fr. Jalics, from his home in Germany, indicated the following: "These are the facts: Fr. Bergoglio did not turn in Orlando Yorio or myself".

When Fr. Swinnen was asked about the truth of the suspicions and accusations against Bergoglio, the response was severe: "In no way did Bergoglio hand over any one. I deny it absolutely. I was a Consulter for the province while Bergoglio was provincial, and I remember very well in a meeting with all the consulters and superiors he told us what was happening, he told us he had gone to speak with (Admiral Emilio) Massera, to intercede for Yorio, Jalics and (Luis) Dourrón. I know very well what went on, no one had to tell me, and I know very well that Bergoglio did not hand over anyone, that he had very good information and for this reason he asked them to come and live in the Colegio Maximo where they would have been protected". But neither Yorio nor Jalics accepted to go "because of solidarity with the people, although they had a vow of obedience", Swinnen added that he thinks the theme was utilized politically and in the media to discredit the Pope".

The priest said that the situation "was very delicate", to the point that when he was Novice Master, and Bergoglio provincial, they raided the house of formation twice at midnight. "I knew that there were some Jesuits that were threatened –Swinnen pointed out—. I remember one that was in Jujuy who, a little naïve, put up a couple of guerrilla warriors and the police began to persecute him; Bergoglio took him to San Miguel to protect him, although in the records he still figured as being in the Province of Jujuy".

In his book *La Lista de Bergoglio* (editorial Claretiana), the Italian journalist Nello Scavo cited the diocesan priest Miguel La Civita, who worked with Bishop Angelelli in La Rioja, and now is pastor in a town near the city of Rosario in Argentina, who affirmed that he had seen Bergoglio "help many people who were persecuted" by the military, not only priests and seminarians. La Civita was a witness in the trials for the assassinations of the priests Carlos Murias and Gabriel Longueville during the dictatorship, and he stated that Bergoglio was far from a collaborator with the repression. It is more, he even pointed out that he had a kind of organization set up with collaborators "to help people that were persecuted" by the military. "No one told me this, I lived it. After the assassination of Angelelli, it was Bergoglio who occupied the place of a father for those of us young people who saw in the Church a commitment to the poor. He took us under his wing and protection until our ordination, at a time when we too were very much observed", the priest recalled, when interviewed by the *La Capital* newspaper of Rosario.

"In the Colegio Maximo –La Civita remembers— some mysterious people would appear, alone or in small groups, they stayed around for a few days and then left. Bergoglio would say 'they have come for a spiritual retreat'. The retreat lasted for a week. I understood that they were laypeople that Fr. Jorge helped escape. How? Any way he could, and always with much risk involved".

His witness coincides with that of Fr. Ángel Rossi: "When I entered the Society in 1976, I asked admission from Bergoglio who was the provincial, and in the Colegio Maximo where he lived there were three or four seminarians from the province of La Rioja, that Bishop Angelelli had sent to study. I remember Enrique Martinez Ossola and Carlos Gonzalez because they were Cordobese and my mother knew their mothers because by chance they had been companions in teaching school. I can't say for sure that they were there for their protection but in fact they were".

Scavo presents some examples of people "saved" by the then Jesuit superior, for example, Sergio and Ana Gobulin, a couple that worked in a slum of Buenos Aires and was persecuted by the repressors...

It is certain that in political discussions and debates, just as in times of war, the truth can lose its strength and even fall by the wayside. For this reason, to judge the administration of that young Jesuit provincial and his life by the political and ideological criteria of some people, could take us to a reductionism that would result in uncertainty. Especially since Bergoglio —one must remember— was not a bishop or archbishop, not a monsignor, nor a cardinal. He was a provincial of the Society of Jesus, the youngest the Order had had up till then.

In this context, Fr. Swinnen prefers to judge that which was really the responsibility of Bergoglio: "His administration was excellent: he was the provincial we needed at that moment. He put order; he gave each Jesuit a mission and ended the internal dispersion".

Thinking about what went on at that time, Francis recently recalled: "We had to make some hard decisions, the ordering of the small base communities according to the directives that came from Rome. It is true that I made decisions with some authority. I think that, with age, one learns to consult a bit more, to open the doors of possibility more widely and be a little more harmonious in how we make decisions".

When the Pope is told that from some sectors of the Society and also on a political level he is accused of being "ultra conservative", he attributes it to his love of discipline: "That I am an ultraconservative? Maybe because of the discipline... I always demanded discipline".

Swinnen adds his own version: "No one can say Bergoglio is of the right or of the left: he is himself, he cannot be qualified in these parameters. This is because for some things he appears conservative, for others, he appears progressive. You cannot box him in".

The descent

The administration of Bergoglio as provincial ended on December 8, 1979. In six very intense years the Society of Jesus in Argentina had made it through a true "perfect storm", the meeting of a national social-political crisis, an ideological-theological crisis that had affected the whole Church with an enormous loss of vocations, and an internal economic-financial crisis.

By the end of Bergoglio's term of office, the loss of vocations not only had stopped but on the contrary there was a considerable increase of them. In a letter that Bergoglio sent in 1986 to the well-known Salesian historian, Cayetano Bruno, to speak of his devotion to Artémides Zatti (the Italian-Argentine who was beatified by John Paul II on April 14, 2002), he recounts that in September of 1979 the Society had 35 novices. In thanksgiving for this "divine gift", Bergoglio took all of them in pilgrimage to the province of Salta for the feast of Our Lady of the Miracle.

He was also able to economically improve the situation in both the Jesuit province and its institutions, among them the University of Córdoba. But the time had come to leave the office of provincial.

The now ex-provincial began then a slow "decline". From the position of "power to govern", he would go on to other responsibilities each one of less authority in the Society, until he reached the "ground level" of room n. 5 of the Jesuit residence in Córdoba.

His first step of this long pilgrimage was as rector of the Colegio Maximo of San Miguel. Faithful to his style, he imposed a strict discipline. Everyone had to get up at 6 in the morning and a half hour later participate in the first Mass. The routine included intense study but also household chores such as washing dishes, cooking, taking care of the farm animals there (when Bergoglio was elected Pope, Fr. Rafael Velasco, then rector of the CUC said: "He sent us out to take care of the pigs"), and he even made them repeat the experience he had lived as a novice in Córdoba. He sent them out in groups to look for children in the slums that were beginning to grow in the area, to take them to Mass.

It was hard for the students not to obey, since they habitually found Fr. Jorge with his sleeves rolled up, feeding the pigs or cleaning the pigpen, hanging clothes to dry or cooking tasty *paellas*.

In 1980, he had another painful experience similar to the one he had during his youth, before entering the Society. Gangrene infected his gallbladder, which put him again close to death. The Pope himself attributes his healing to Dr. Juan Carlos Parodi, who today is a renown surgeon and who when interviewed by a radio of Buenos Aires recently, remembered that "very sick humble priest" that he attended, operated on and with time became Pope.

According to Parodi, at the time, he was called by another doctor who told him he was attending a very sick humble priest. "He was a Jesuit who had taken the vows of poverty, chastity and obedience and did not have money", Parodi remembers. His colleague asked him if he could take his case and he did. The surgery went well and when the patient got better he gifted him a book. The doctor refused to charge him even though the Jesuit tried to pay him. In April, 2013, Pope Francis received Parodi in his residence in Santa Marta: "As soon as he entered, radiant, he told me —the surgeon recalled—: 'Juan Carlos, you look the same as when I saw you the night I thought I was going to die. You saved my life', he told me. 'How?' I asked, 'Yes, you saved my life because I had gallbladder gangrene, which everyone knows is deadly. That same night you operated on me; I will never forget your face, because when I saw your face I began to feel better, I got better'".

When he recovered, Bergoglio continued as rector until 1985. During that time, he reorganized the study plan proposing a clearer separation between humanities, philosophy and theology, a classic schema that permitted the students to receive a civil diploma and to better the quality of teaching. He was able to visit all the families in the area as well.

He sent the students to investigate what the necessities of each of the families and organized the help that was to be given from soup kitchens to soccer tournaments. In October he opened the doors of the college to celebrate the Children's Day and each year he organized camping trips to Chapadmalal.

As a rector, Bergoglio was an example of someone who sought the "evangelization of the culture" and the "enculturation of the Gospel", which were paradigms of the new evangelization proposed by John Paul

II, whom Pope Francis has just canonized. He was able to bring with him all those who were around him in this mission. That "popular piety" which so impressed him in his stay in the little cordobese town of Impira during his novitiate, had matured. The image of that "spiritual chief" called David Bustos Zambrano whom he discovered in Río Segundo also grew in him as well as that of "Cura" José Gabriel del Rosario Brochero, whose beatification he would sign as Pope. He had become a "man to man" priest.

When he finished his term as rector, the new authorities of the Colegio Maximo will give him what could be called another hit to Bergoglio's "career". They put in place a series of reforms that would turn back the changes that Fr. Jorge had made.

In this context, Bergoglio decided, once again, to move from teacher to student. He traveled to Frankfurt to write his doctoral thesis on the Italian-German theologian Romano Guardini, one who sowed the seeds of the Second Vatican Council and teacher of the great theologians of the 20th century. Some see in this trip a kind of self-imposed exile. During a melancholic year in 1986 he would pass his time between the library of the Sankt Georgen Jesuit University and the parks close to the airport that made him feel a little closer to his beloved Argentina.

His stay in Germany was relatively short, although he left behind some friends with whom he remains in contact. He returned knowing a new language, with a couple of books under his arm and an image of Our Lady of *Knotenlöserin* (undoer of knots). In this image, the Virgin Mary is dressed in red with a blue tunic, surrounded by angels and in an attitude of prayer. This devotion has its origin in the church of St. Peter *am Perlach*, in Augsberg. When it was brought to Argentina by Bergoglio it had an unexpected popularity. Our Lady the Undoer of Knots will be from then on a companion of Bergoglio with an easily recognizable message. "God, who pours his grace abundantly upon his children, wants us to confide in her, that we confide the knots of our sins to her so that she can bring them to Jesus", he will say on December 8, 2011, while presiding the Eucharist in the sanctuary that was built, with his support, in the church of St. Joseph of Talar, in Buenos Aires. A replica of this picture hangs today on the walls of the Santa Marta House, in the Vatican.

Bergoglio moved to the Del Salvador College to give classes in Pastoral Theology and at the same time, advance in his doctoral thesis in order to present it in the Colegio Maximo of San Miguel. But his presence once again provoked reactions. Eight years had passed since his leaving office as provincial, but he continued to have a large influence in a great part of the Society and this made him a nuisance. There are those who maintain that this is the reason he was again sent away from Buenos Aires: "I was elected Procurator of the province, and so had to travel to Rome. Then I passed through Japan to visit the Argentine missionaries there, making the visit that as a Procurator I had to make. When I returned, I stayed in the Del Salvador College until 1990", Francis told the authors of this book.

That June 25, 1990 was a difficult day for Bergoglio. His superiors decided to take away the only assignment he had, which was teaching Pastoral Theology, and they sent him to Córdoba in a decision that many considered really a true exile, a dark period in his life.

CHAPTER 5

HIS RETURN TO CÓRDOBA, TIME OF DARKNESS AND PURIFICATION

A time of interior purification

Although it is a very common name in all of Hispano-America, few know where the name "Carmen" comes from, and it has to do with these days that the now Pope Francis passed in Córdoba, between 1990 and 1992. The name "Carmen" comes from the avocation of the Virgin of Carmel, better known as Our Lady of Mt. Carmel. In fact the name refers to Mt. Carmel, a mountainous area in the north of what is now Israel. It received the name because of the beauty of its landscape: *Karmel, Al-Karem* or *hakkarmel* mean "garden" or "place of the garden" in the local language. In this place, which is mentioned in the Hebrew Bible as a place of religious devotion, (it appears in the Book of Isaiah and the book of Kings that recount the story of the prophet Elias, centuries before Christ), around the 12th century after Christ it was inhabited by Christian hermits and contemplatives that had arrived there in timt of the Crusades. Inspired by the devotion of Elias, being close to Nazareth where Jesus grew up, some of these monks formed a "Carmelite" community dedicated to prayer, meditation and work. This contemplative order began to spread and other communities sprang up in different parts of Europe, and reached England. There, in Cambridge, on July 16, 1251, the Virgin Mary appeared to the then superior general of the Carmelites, Simon Stock and she gave him the habit and scapular, with the promise that whoever wore it on the day of his death would be saved from eternal damnation.

Because of this apparition, the Church celebrates the feast day of Our Lady of Mt. Carmel on July 16. Pope Francis remembers that it was precisely that day in 1990 that he returned to Córdoba to live for a second time in his life. Perhaps for this reason, during his two years there, Bergoglio had the custom of weekly walking down Caseros Street to La Cañada, and along this street he reached the beautiful church of our Lady of Mt. Carmel convent located together with the Christ the Worker Church, at 160 Figueroa Alcorta Street. In this church, built between 1909 and 1912, the future pope prayed before the image of the Virgin of Mt. Carmel (see picture 15). Bergoglio contemplated the statue, work of the artist Francisco Font of Madrid, Spain, that still stands in the center of the altarpiece of metal plated oak, and asked of the Mother of God humility and help during this special moment in his life; a moment of interior purification.

Picture 15 – Retable of the Virgin of Mt. Carmel. Picture: *La Voz del Interior.*

On July 16, Fr. Jorge returned to the city that had seen him become a Jesuit thirty years earlier. In some way he was also returning to the historical origin and the spiritual center of the Argentine Province of the Society of Jesus.

The "Jesuit Province of the Paraquaria" was founded in 1608, and during this same year the novitiate in Córdoba was started to form the young missionaries of the Order, the "heart" of the evangelization of the Jesuit province. Bergoglio had also done his novitiate in Córdoba but not in this residence; but he had absorbed the passion to bring souls to God that the sons of St. Ignatius inherit from their founding father.

After a marathon "career" that led him to being a Master of Novices as soon as he was ordained, to directing the religious Province at the age of thirty six and then leading as rector of the Colegio Maximo of the Jesuits in San Miguel, suddenly he found himself in cell number five of the Major Residence of the Society of Jesus, on Caceros Street at 450 miles from his beloved Buenos Aires. He was in the historic building of the Society, a living witness to the "glory" of the Jesuits, but stripped of any office or governing responsibility; and only with the job of confessing and spiritually directing the faithful who by chance passed through. He did not even have a scheduled time for Mass in the magnificent central church, which was a symbol of religious art that marked an era in Córdoba and was declared, together with the whole Jesuit block and the Missions in the interior of the Province, Cultural Patrimony of Humanity, by UNESCO, in November of the year 2000.

The man who considered himself a missionary in search of new horizons, would have more than enough time to reach, from this kind of enclosure, the frontiers of his own existence. That is what he did. But it came with a high price, the price of abandoning himself to the will of God, just as twenty three years later he was deposited on the chair of the first apostle so that he might be a "Servant of the servants of God".

The bare white walls of the barely twelve square yards of the room that was his by chance did not bother him. He was a man accustomed to austerity as those who visited him can give witness. What bothered him were more important things, deeper things, darker things. So dark, that Pope Francis remembers his stay in Córdoba, between 1990 and 1992, as a "time of darkness, of shadows", as "a moment of interior purification". One could say it was a test of his spiritual health; something that, for a man who would end up being a religious leader of universal transcendence, is very important.

Would the Pope Francis that we know today through his gestures and decisions have existed, if that Jesuit priest of fifty four years had not been sent to Córdoba to live there for two years, with an intense spiritual life, and passing through a kind of "dark night", such as so many saints and important lives in the Church have lived? Was what Bergoglio lived in Córdoba really a "dark night of the soul", the spiritual state that is not only produced by external factors but by movement of the Holy Spirit or the lack of it?[39]

Once, when the authors of this book asked Francis himself if in Córdoba he had experienced the "dark night", his humility got the better of him: "I would not use the word "dark night" for me; it wasn't that bad. The 'dark night' is for saints. I am a poor guy. It was a time of spiritual purification".

And yet, there was a reason for the darkness, the silence and the trial. It was said that the then Fr. Bergoglio was sent to Córdoba as a "punishment" by the new superiors of the Argentine Province of the Society of Jesus, which had Fr. Victor Zorzín as provincial. Everything makes one think that Zorzín, who had been a "companion" of Bergoglio, that is, his vice-provincial, had not been in agreement with some of the decisions made by Fr. Jorge.

According to various conversations that we had with different members of the Society of Jesus, during the provincial administrations of Frs. Zorzín (1986-1991), who today lives in Mendoza, and Ignacio García-Mata (1991-1997) there was a campaign of disparagement of Bergoglio and his style of formation that went beyond the limits of the Argentine Province reaching the Jesuit provinces of other countries in South America and even to the General House in Rome.

Fr. Angel Rossi, today the superior of the Major Residence of the Society where Bergoglio lived, told a story recently that illustrates very well how far the campaign reached. The story is doubly sad for Rossi because not only does it show the poor treatment the actual Pope received but also because it occurred at the time his mother died. "People close to

---

[39] The spiritual experience of the Dark Night, was described as a mystical experience by St. John of the Cross although many saints have experienced it before and after him, including modern saints such as Mother Teresa of Calcutta. In general, it consists of a an experience which is a gift although it is a desolate of the soul through which God purifies and renews placing "the intellect in darkness, the will of the person in aridity, the memory without reminders and the affections submerged in sorrow and anguish" according to the description found in a treatise of catholic spirituality.

the community –he remembered— took it upon themselves to spread the gossip, taken from Jesuit sources that said that the man who had been provincial of the Society so young, so brilliant, had ended up in Córdoba because he was sick, crazy". And he added: "In my mother's wake, a layperson, very close to the Residence came up to me and pointed to Bergoglio who was praying by the casket, saying: 'what a shame that man is crazy!' I looked at him and replied: 'if that man is crazy, what am I?'".

Bergoglio was not the first distinguished Jesuit that had to confront a kind of punishment or internal exile because of decisions of his own religious order. At least two other notable sons of St. Ignatius faced periods of darkness in the Society before giving the best of themselves to the Catholic Church. Apart from the differences of geography and of theological production, Bergoglio faced an internal exile, from within the Society of Jesus, similar to that suffered by the Jesuits Henri de Lubac (French) and Han Urs Von Balthazar (Swiss). It is interesting to draw the similarities even if it may appear a little affected. Yet, both De Lubac and Von Balthazar, perhaps two of the five or six most important theologians of the 20th century, were misunderstood and/or punished by some of their superiors from within and from outside the Society as well as the diocesan clergy, and they lived periods of trial, of loneliness, of temptation, of painful discernment, only to later give to the Church and humanity their best fruits. De Lubac and Von Balthazar were "persecuted" or exiled for their theological work. Bergoglio, on the other hand, was for his pastoral work. Those eminent theologians would be recognized in the end by the Church; to the point of being called in as consulters of Vatican II, and later considered and admired by Popes John XXIII, Paul VI, John Paul II and Benedict XVI. The polish pope even gave the dignity of the Cardinal's hat to Von Balthazar, although he passed away a day before the ceremony.

The differences

Returning to Bergoglio, one can say that there were different motivations for the criticism that some Jesuits made against him. Among them there are ideological differences (some complain that Bergoglio was "conservative") and differences in formation and leadership style that characterized the then Fr. Jorge. His was a style of very clear rules —for some they were harsh— with a very strong pastoral sense to them. This pastoral sense was informed in the service of the poorest in the humble slum areas, but with a spiritual characteristic determined by a pastoral closeness with the people –but that was colored neither by ideology nor politics.

In this style which Bergoglio and others of his companions had has a lot to do with the figure and teaching of Miguel Angel Fiorito, for whom the preferential option for the poor must always be a pastoral commitment.

Until his death in August of 2005, Fiorito was a spiritual master and great authority in ignatian spirituality. He taught philosophy in the Colegio Maximo, in San Miguel, to many generations of Jesuits. Fr. Juan Carlos Scannone, who taught Greek and Literature to Bergoglio, but was also a student of Fiorito, remembers this Jesuit as a true master, and points out the theological and spiritual work displayed in the books he wrote.[40]

For some, the formation of Fiorito that Bergoglio also lived in his administration as provincial, freed the Society in Argentina from the radicalized ideological extremes —whether toward the right or the left— that so damaged the country at the time. For this reason, after the term of office of Fr. Jorge, in Argentina there were bergoglian Jesuits and antibergoglian Jesuits which was a real, palpable and painful dichotomy which time, the good will of some of those involved and Pope Francis himself are seeking to heal.

The information that was used maliciously to try to avoid Bergoglio's being elected Pope in the conclaves of 2005 and 2013, in maneuvers that were noticed and denounced by the press, cite witnesses

---

[40] The most important Works of Fr. Miguel Ángel Fiorito are the following: *La Ley Ignaciana de la oracion en la Compañía de Jesús* (Pellegrini impresores, Buenos Aires, 1967, 89 pages); *Discernimiento y lucha espiritual. Comentario de las reglas de discernir de la primera semana de los Ejercicios Espirituales de San Ignacio de Loyola* (Editorial Diego de Torres, Buenos Aires, 1985); and *Buscar y hallar la voluntad de Dios. Comentario practico de los Ejercicios Espirituales de San Ignacio de Loyola* (Editorial Diego de Torres, Buenos Aires, first edition 1988).

who pointed out with first and last name several Jesuits that at the time questioned the ex-Father Provincial, today successor of St. Peter.

In her book *Francisco, Vida y Revolución*, the journalist Elisabetta Piqué, correspondent of the newspaper *La Nación* in Rome, and friend of the pope, recounts the situation of the Jesuits and Bergoglio around 1990: "The Society is immersed in a hard internal battle. Bergoglio continues to have prestige among many in the Society and they elect him procurator for a meeting of the Society in Rome. But to neutralize him, or better said, 'to wipe him off the map', his superiors decide to send him as a confessor to the Major Residence of Córdoba, virtually an exile".

Piqué cites, immediately, the testimony of Ernesto Giovando, ex-student of Bergoglio in the Colegio Maximo of San José in San Miguel, Buenos Aires. Giovando, who was named auxiliary bishop of Buenos Aires by Pope Francis on March 5, 2014, recounted to the journalist Bergoglio's situation in 1990: "At the time, he was my professor of Pastoral Theology and they took him from the class. The rector said that: 'Bergoglio is not coming back to teach theology at this seminary'. The reaction was one of pain, we were dumbfounded. Bergoglio's exile represents a traumatic event for the Jesuits".

Fr. Swinnen, on the other hand, sees it in a less dramatic way. It is as though he sees the hand of God behind everything that happened, Who as the saying goes, "writes straight with crooked lines".

Seated peacefully in a chair in the rectory of Holy Family parish, on Buchardo Street, Córdoba, Swinnen explains his thesis: "Jorge (Bergoglio) had a lot of authority in the Society since he had done a lot of good as provincial as well as rector of the Colegio Maximo. But the problem is that when he was no longer rector he continued to have authority, and so he influences many of the younger Jesuits. I remember in fact that some of them left the Society".

For Swinnen, "Jorge had a way of acting that was bothersome to the superior of the house where he lived. He acted like a parallel superior. This happened to Fr. Ernesto López Rosas, who was the Novice Master, and to the rector of the Del Salvador College (Fr. Luis de Maussion) where Bergoglio was when they decided to send him to

Córdoba. Speaking plainly, they wanted to get him off their backs. This is what happened".

Until February 2014, De Maussion was rector of the Holy Family High school, of Pueyrredon, Córdoba, and lived many years in the same religious community as Swinnen. Until that time, it was normal to see both of them during Sunday afternoon Mass, occupy the two confessionals of the parish church. There is no doubt that the election of their ex-companion as Pope has renewed the memories as well as became the focus of new and long conversations. As a conclusion and with a bit of mischief that appears to be part of his character, Fr. Swinnen reflects: "Beyond what anyone says, the second time Bergoglio came to live in Córdoba, which he calls a time of purification, did not do him any harm; I would say just the opposite". It would appear Swinnen is right. The man he speaks of is today none other than the Pope.

In a telephone conversation with the authors of this book, the Holy Father said of his being sent and his stay in Córdoba: "It was a time of purification that God sometimes permits. It is a dark time, when one does not see much. I prayed a lot, I read, I wrote quite a bit and lived my life. It was something of the inner life. Beyond being a confessor or a spiritual director, what I did in Córdoba had more to do with my inner life".

The above cited book, Piqué sustains that during this time he passed in Córdoba, "about which few Jesuits want to talk about, they did not transfer all his telephone calls and controlled his correspondence". Francis questioned this affirmation: "I would not say that. I don't dare say that. Because to make such an accusation, aside from presuming that someone had bad will, you would have to have all the evidence to prove it. It may have happened, that on occasion, someone may have called me, the call was received in the central of the Residence, they called me by Morse Code as was usually the case, but I did not hear it and I didn't go to the booth we had to speak; and so they replied to the person who called me that I was not there, and the person hung up. I may have been reading, distracted and didn't hear the buzzer ring that I was assigned, that was short-long-short. So I didn't respond, and the other person thought that I had not been given the communication. This may have happened. But right now, in the presence of God and remembering that time, I cannot accuse anyone of doing that. And I always received mail. It may be that some correspondence got lost, but I was always receiving mail".

He faced this time of trial praying, reading and writing. At the time, as will be seen later on in greater detail, Bergoglio wrote and also compiled some spiritual texts that he wrote during those years for the book *Reflexiones en esperanza*. One of these texts (*El exilio de toda carne. La oracion de la carne exiliada*), is interesting because it speaks precisely of exile, of loneliness, of silence, of sadness, sentiments and experiences Fr. Jorge faced in Córdoba. Although Francis assured us that its content did not come from his own situation, (in his words: "I was not speaking of my own experience, but rather of the biblical experience of human life on its way, because I am always impressed and I like working with biblical theology, especially the part from the Promise to the Covenant, seeking the final encounter with God"), it is worth looking at a few paragraphs.

1.   (...)   *"Our flesh, on its way, feels the nostalgia of the homeland, and it becomes conscious, it makes it explicit in prayer, in the presence of the glorious Lord, Lord of the homeland that we hope for. In the meantime, between feelings and thoughtlessness, between grace and sin, between obedience and rebellion, our flesh feels the exile to which it is subject, the walk it is obliged to make, and it struggles for itself, to defend this hope. The day this nostalgia is extinguished, is the day our flesh has stopped praying, it has chosen this homeland, it has preferred the liberation of exile in exchange for deals that free it from continuing on in a foreign land. It has tired of seeking God. On that day the biggest grace that we can receive is the one given to Elijah: that an angel touch us in the midst of this sleepy depression: 'Get up and eat, else the journey will be too long for you!' (1 Kings 19:7)*

2.   *The man or woman who consciously takes charge of his exile suffers a double loneliness. On the one hand, he or she feels the solitude with respect to others; he or she is fundamentally a foreigner, a foreigner on the road. On the other hand, one is also given to taste the*

bitterness of solitude before God. It is the double solitude of the one who prays. Fundamentally the one who prays is a marginalized person, twice marginalized (from God and from men) and —at the same time— one cannot rescind from God (because he seeks Him and feels sought by Him), nor of others (because his mission puts him in the service of his brothers and sisters whom he seeks to love as himself). Jeremiah felt this experience to his bones. By announcing that which God asked of him, he ended up being the object of infighting and contradiction for the whole people (15:10). And, in the loneliness of this contradiction, he complains that God has left him alone, even going so far as to curse the day he was born, but he cannot deny the nostalgic seduction of the face of God that burns into his bones: 'you have seduced me...everyone ridicules me...' (cfr.:20:ss). It's the prayer of a man that gave everything and would like —at least— that God would be on his side... But in life, sometimes it seems as though God puts Himself on the other side (Jer. 20:7-18).

The servant of God feels as though there were a double solitude outside of himself: we are dealing with a profound experience of the exile. Reality appears to ridicule the believer. Where is the Word of God? Let it come to pass at least once (cfr. Jer. 17:15). It seems as though God has not kept the promise He made when he was chosen: I will be there to protect you (Jer. 1:8). It looks as though God has no words (cfr.: Jer. 15:18; Job 6:15-20). This ridicule that comes from around us and from people, the ridicule for having trusted in God, reaches its greatest expression on Calvary: 'Those passing by reviled him, shaking their heads and saying, "You who would destroy the temple and rebuild it in three days, save yourself, if you are the Son of God, (and) come down from the cross!" ... "He saved others; he cannot save himself. So he is the king of Israel! Let him come down from the cross now, and we will believe in him. He trusted in God; let him deliver him now if he wants him... (Mt. 27:39-44). In this silence of God our flesh is once again submitted to a change: we discover that the dialogue of obedience in prayer is not a 'deal', but rather the promise and fidelity of God is very different from what we imagined... In this way too our heart is changed.

3.   The experience of the silence of God and the silence of men is the experience of the exile in itself. We are stripped of all possessions, we are 'by the rivers of Babylon', the harps hung on the poplars and the pain do not allow us to utter the songs of Israel (Ps. 137:19. This exile in oneself also finds its culmination in the Passion of the Lord: the prayer in Gethsemane. It is the most human and the most dramatic of Jesus' prayers. There is begging, sadness, anguish and almost a disorientation (Mc. 14:33 and following). It has to do with the sadness of an exiled person far from the Lord. It is the culmination of the sadness of Jonah, who does not understand the plan of God (Jon. 4:9).

Fr. Jorge, author of these spiritual reflections, also did not have a clear idea of where the plan of God would take him. But he did not rebel. On the contrary, without ever suspecting where he would end up, he trusted in the promise and the faithfulness of God Who never abandons His children.

Weariness and the broom

During his religious life, Bergoglio had studied and taught for fourteen years; he had made his own the austerity he imagined the Basque Ignatius of Loyola intended for the Society and the "companions" and masters of obedience to the pope. He was obedient to the orders of his superiors when he was asked to be the captain of a ship in the middle of a great political, economic and theological storm; he became one with the poor, he faced with courage the risks that the political actors of Argentina invented and he bore attacks in silence. But, after living a life that humanly speaking appeared to be a continual ascent, he began to live in descent. Sometimes it is difficult to understand the plan of God. From provincial, he went on to be the rector of the Colegio Maximo, from there a teacher, then he was a student of a doctoral thesis never finished, to end up without any responsibilities of government, as a confessor in Córdoba. It was, some will say a kind of "erosion", which was the title of a book that by chance he wrote later, in the same residence where Bergoglio ended up, Fr. Sixto Castellano, a late priest that the Pope admires.

"At that time, —Pope Francis revealed remembering his days in his second stay in Córdoba— I spoke a lot with Fr. Sixto Castellano or 'el Negro' Castellano as we called him, about philosophy". Perhaps these profound dialogues with a downcast Bergoglio inspired Fr. Sixto to write "Erosion". "What is the most important thing in life —one reads in this work— is it what one does or what one suffers?" This question Castellano attributes to the mystics, who "do not know what they should give importance to, because they see and recognize that in action and in the mission that a person must assume in life there is a lot of his sanctification and his transcendence".

The Pope agrees with his admired Sixto Castellano: "What one suffers and what one does in life go together, but at times what he suffers is more important. This is in the line of the activities and passivity of Teilhard de Chardin[41], and the purification of the activities and passivity", the Pope reflected, when he was consulted on that work of Castellano.

In those old patios of the Society and even more in his austere room, the then Fr. Jorge experienced in his own flesh that confusion the Jesuit tradition describes in a story that has St. Ignatius of Loyola himself as protagonist. According to this story, told by Fr. Angel Rossi in his book Teresa de Lisieux, that Ignatius himself had the custom of asking one of his first companions of sweeping the patio of the residence where they lived with an old and ruined broom. The Jesuit swept the patio time and again, but there was always dirt that remained. With tears of anger and impotence, the novice asked himself: "What have I done that Fr. Ignatius would treat me like this?" This confused man troubled by his situation was Fr. Diego Laínez, who did not know what Ignatius knew: that he would be the next Father General of the Jesuits. Ignatius was trying him in patience. Ignatius may have thought: "If this man cannot accept now a broken broom and the fact that he cannot control a little dirt, how will he be able to govern one thousand Jesuits? If he does not learn to take with patience and a good dose of humor, this one is a sure candidate for an ulcer".

---

[41] Perre Teilhard de Chardin was a French Jesuit priest, as well as a paleontologist and philosopher who produced original and controversial scientific and theological visions of life, evolution and the cosmos. He was born in France in 1881 and died in New York, in April, 1955.

That Jesuit did not imagine the great responsibilities that awaited him in the government of the Society and the place that the Church would give him. Bergoglio didn't either.

The same priest that retold this story, whom the pope considers "a friend, a spiritual son, a great fruit of the Church in Argentina", has the feeling that that period of the life of Bergoglio "was probably something humanly unjust, excessive, but perhaps necessary in the eyes of God; a mysterious time, dark, that Bergoglio himself, helped by grace, prayer and silence, turned into a time of gestation".

The Pope, however, doubted that he had been a victim of injustice, and said this about it: "St. Teresa said to her religious 'a nun should never say 'they did me an injustice''. A religious should never say 'they did me an injustice', because they will always find in it or in the circumstances a way of God, perhaps an interior purification. For this reason I can never say it was an injustice although I know others think so".

A "weighty" community

Bergoglio arrived to live in Córdoba, for the second time in his life, thinking that he would stay several years. The Pope remembers that "in God's plan", the first to receive him was Br. Cirilo Rodriguez, the same man who thirty years earlier had opened the doors of the Holy Family Novitiate for him, in Pueyrredon, when he began his formation.

Br. Cirilo received him with a smile but the newly arrived member of the community had signs of worry on his face.

"I returned to Córdoba as a confessor and spiritual director in the Major Residence of the Society, in Caceros Street", Pope Francis remembered in a conversation. The Jesuit community that lived there was very important because the priests that formed part of it were religious "of weight", that is, distinguished, recognized for their different work and services both within and outside the Society of Jesus.

The superior of the house was Fr. José Antonio Sojo, an enormous man "inside and out", as those that knew him assure us, whose death in June of 2003 provoked a large vacuum among the friends of the Jesuit community of Córdoba. Formed in European universities, he was one of the founders —together with Fr. Alberto Camargo and other religious and laypeople— of the Catholic University of Córdoba, of which he was the first vice-rector. He also was a promotor of the cause for the beatification of the priest José Gabriel del Rosario Brochero, the first beatification signed by Francis after assuming the papacy.

However, shortly after the arrival of Bergoglio to Córdoba, Sojo was replaced as superior of the house by Fr. Fernando Boasso, a Jesuit born in Santa Fe, but who even today considers himself a "Cordobese by adoption" since he lived in this province, with his family, since he was very little. An expert in the work of Atahualpa Yupanqui, of whom he was a personal friend, today Boasso lives in the Regina Martyrum house, 65 Sarandi Street, in Buenos Aires. At 95 years of age, he faces with courage and strength difficulties in hearing and mobility and his memory recalls those years when Bergoglio was his student and later his companion in the community in the Major Residence in Córdoba.

He gave us this testimony in the days following the canonization of John Paul II and John XIII that Pope Francis presided; Boasso was particularly happy of that event since he had written a book about John XXIII and shared a house and vocation with today's pope. Also, Boasso recalled, Francis had the kindness to write a prologue for a book on Cura Brochero. And last year, months after the election of the new Pope, Francis himself called him to say hello.

"Truly the Church, as Pope Francis is leading it, is a jewel and has the whole world admiring it; Bergoglio is a man who has unsuspected qualities, a tremendous courage, he doesn't fear the truth, he is able to support himself on the truth and live accordingly. He had the kindness to call me, he wrote the prologue to my little book on Cura Brochero, and he responded with a beautiful letter. God has helped me assist a little these extraordinary men, these protagonists". Still, he preferred not to speak about the time Fr. Jorge lived on Caceros Street. It's that, as has been said, those were complicated times and Boasso prefers not to wound susceptibilities.

According to the official catalogue of the Society, as well as Boasso, in the community the following priests lived at the time: Fr. Alfredo Estrella (who was in charge of the economy of the Residence and who the Pope describes as "a great guy"), Fr. Manuel Beltrán (who lived there in the community but who was in charge of the parish in the Zumarán neighborhood, today administered by the archdiocese of Córdoba); the already mentioned Fr. Sixto Castellano (Professor of Philosophy in the CUC and advisor to the Christian Family Movement and to the Marriage Encounter group); Fr. Buenaventura Di Filippis (writer, historian, Retreat director, and room "neighbor" of Bergoglio); Fr. Deolindo Dosso (confessor); Fr. Jorge Mario Hardoy (who was chaplain of the General Paz Military School); Fr. Leopoldo Martínez Novillo (confessor, who many remember because he was a ham radio operator and worked in the La Salle High School); Fr. Osvaldo Pol (renown author, poet, who is still professor in the CUC and in the Colegio Maximo in Buenso Aires, who at that time worked in the library of the Residence where he lived and wrote); Fr. Guillermo Randle (who was a confessor in the main church and directed retreats); and Fr. Enrique Tagliaferri (worker), remembered by the Pope.

There were also five coadjutor brothers who lived and worked there: Cirilo Rodriguez (doorman), José Bustamante (Sacristan and Special minister of Holy Communion), Julio Córdoba (who gave catechism in several schools), Miguel Ángel Maradiaga (Minister of the Eucharist, nurse and in charge of the Domestic Chapel) and Fortunato Murri (Minister of the Eucharist and sacristan of the main church).

At that time Fr. Ignacio Garaigorta passed through the community for a while who is a priest originally from the Basque area and today resides in Spain.   Garaigorta told us that, as much as he remembers, "Bergoglio led a very discrete life; you hardly saw him because he was by himself."   After excusing himself for not remembering more "because with old age comes forgetfulness, and one begins not to give importance to anything", he added that since he did not know Bergoglio before coming to Córdoba, he had very little interaction with him.

In fact, the members of that community —as happens with the majority of the religious communities that are not monastic— not many activities are shared, except breakfast and some meals. As is the case today, there were so many activities at that time that there remained little time for long chats as one might imagine.

Although not as a religious, the layman Ricardo Spinassi also lived in the Residence, an employee of the Society for the many jobs that spring up all the time in a house like the one where the Pope lived. As well, each day Irma Irene Peralta, cousin of Spinassi (see picture n. 16), and Lucila Tejeda, came in to work during the day as a cook and to attend the door.

Picture 16 - Ricardo Spinassi and Irma Peralta.

Each one of them has stories with and about Bergoglio that until now kept to themselves like a personal treasure; surprising actions and sayings of the then Fr. Jorge that speak to his goodness and generosity. Things that were sowed in Córdoba, in silence, by that priest who was undergoing a moment of trial, like seeds that history made sure would germinate with time.

In the room number 5

Bergoglio arrived Monday July 16 to the capital city of the province[42]. In the streets there was sadness similar to the sensation that overcame the priest, although for very different reasons. Two weeks earlier, the Argentine National soccer team had lost the final of the World Cup in Italy to their rival German team. An uncertain penalty foul, charged a few minutes before the end of the game, had turned the triumphant argentine elation into anguish. There is no argentine soccer fan more than thirty years old that does not remember that televised picture of Diego Maradona weeping over the loss.

But the Jesuit from Buenos Aires was more concerned about things that were brewing in his conscience and that were developing in the country, which was complicating the lives of millions of Argentines. President Menem had not yet launched the Plan of Convertability[43]; the national currency was the Austral, whose value was agonizing because of the runaway inflation, and threatened the future of the Economy Minister of the time, Erman González.

The privatizations were being carried out and with them, the internal quarrels and charges of corruption that menemism fomented. The president himself was faced during that time with a large family scandal, since he had thrown out of the presidential residence in Olivos his first wife Zulema Yoma, in a divorce that was on the front page of all the newspapers.

The world also was in upheaval. The echoes of the fall of the Berlin Wall were spreading throughout the world. The day before Bergoglio arrived in Córdoba, more than a hundred thousand protesters had come together in front of the Kremlin in Moscow to protest the Communist Party leadership.

---

[42] In 1990, the Province of Córdoba had a little more than two million eight hundred thousand inhabitants, almost half of which lived in the capital city.
[43] The plan of Convertability was established by law in 1991, proposed by the then Economy Minister Domingo Cavallo, during the presidency of Carlos Menem. The objective was to establish a fixed exchange between the argentine currency and the American dollar, in order to control the hyperinflation that, then as now, damages the economy of the Argentines.

Fr. Jorge learned of these things and much more each day from the newspaper *La Nación* that he went to pick up in the magazine kiosk on the corner of Obispo Trejo and Caseros Streets.

They assigned him room n. 5 located in the verandah that surrounds the interior patio of the Residence, which if seen from above, a bird's eye view, it appears as an oasis of green in the midst of the "desert" of stone, tile, brick and cement of the Jesuit construction and the buildings in this central area of the city.

In this small green garden there no longer stands the vine with delicious grapes that Fr. De Filippis harvested, or the immense avocado trees that lent their shade and fruit. The vine was replaced by flowering santaritas that have taken over the old pergolas of the grape vines creating a roof over the garden with its thick foliage. Where there were avocado trees now there are ornamental palms.

The grape vine afforded shade for Fr. Bergoglio when in the spring or summer, he would pray the rosary in the patio, or when he crossed it to reach the kitchen or dining room of the community.

If one stands at the corner of Caseros Street and Vélez Sarsfield Boulevard, and looks toward the Jesuit church, one can find a line of windows that break the monotony of the stone wall of the colonial Jesuit construction. The third window, counting from the one nearest the corner, is the one that was of the room that Pope Francis occupied (see picture n. 17). From the outside, it is not yet identified and people walk by ignoring the history and the one who occupied this room. But it is probable that, soon, the Holy Father's fame will convert the place into an attraction for tourists and locals who will want to see where the austere Francis lived.

Picture 17 - The corner of Caseros Street and Vélez Sarsfield Boulevard, in downtown Córdoba. The third window of the wall is Fr. Bergoglios's room between 1990 and 1992.

What does it feel like to be in the room (see picture n. 18) where the man who today is Pope lived a time of trial, of purification? What were his sensations? What memories are hidden in these walls?

Picture 18 - Room number 5 where Bergoglio slept for two years.

It is 11:20 a.m. on a day in July 2013. 23 years ago, in this seat where I am sitting, in this room, sat the man who is Pope. I imagine him in prayer, here, before this wooden desk with small drawers on each side.

He just arrived from Buenos Aires and is sorrowful, because he knows that they have sent him there as a kind of punishment. In his mind and heart he goes over his own personal history: "Do I deserve this?", he asks himself. He does not go on thinking about it because he perceives it as a temptation to pride or vainglory. The God who had looked upon him with mercy and had chosen him ("miserandi atque eligendo") so that he might follow him more closely, and had given him high pastoral and governing responsibilities, now is not showing him the way with clarity.

It is a time of shadows. Bergoglio prays, meditates, although the constant noise outside is bothersome. Caceros Street is not yet a pedestrian street. Right below the window of his room that looks out on the street there is a bus stop. All day long people are there talking; buses screech to a halt and accelerate. The murmuring is constant throughout the day and night although the window is shut and the stone walls are 32 inches thick. It is cold in this room, which was built in 1839, when the Jesuits returned to Argentina. In spite of the low temperature, Bergoglio opens the window that looks out on the patio. The window has a metal screen. "At least there will not be any mosquitos", he thinks. Outside, his vision is partially blocked by the thick break ax wood columns (see picture n. 19) that hold up the roof of the gallery, along with a rose plant among others. Fr. DeFilippis suddenly walks by. He is carrying a pail. Bergoglio follows him with his eyes. The priest, already an elderly man, gets up on a chair to prune the vines. Another priest passes praying his rosary. Bergoglio has just left his own hanging on a water handle of the hot water line that is in the wall of his room, under the window and close to the head of his bed. He's now too distracted to go on praying. "I will write a little", he thinks. He has to write a letter to one of his brothers, and continue with the meditations of the spiritual retreat that he has to preach in December. He looks for the typewriter that he keeps in the closet where his cassock and black dust jacket hang. He places it on the desk and begins to type the date: "Córdoba, July..., 1990". He stops. A question comes into his head: "How long will I be here?" Another temptation.

"Only God knows", he responds. One has to give oneself entirely to the will of God. And obedience to superiors is a guide and teacher of humility.

Picture 19 – The door of room number 5 with the sign:
"Here lived Pope Francis from June 1990 till May 1992".

He writes: "When one has received the grace he has asked for in the (Spiritual) Exercises, 'to receive insults and injury so as to imitate Him more' (as St. Ignatius himself wrote in old Spanish), and one allows oneself to be put on the cross with Jesus, aside from the normal 'thrashing about', it could happen that one falls into a kind of spiritual victimization —considering that 'they hurt me without any reason'—, and thus one feels as though he is imitating Our Lord, and one feels sorry for oneself: in this case one does not have love and of course it is a form of pride…of the worse kind. The constancy necessary to not come down from the cross is a grace that is given freely and is fed by the humble prayer of petition (since one feels himself fragile), and by the real (therefore humble) recognizing that one is in this position because he deserves it, as well as by the contemplation of the fact that He was there while innocent, and "all of this was done for me". Only in this way there is no danger of falling into morbid self-pity of being crucified in some tribulation".

Fr. Jorge leaves for a minute the noisy keyboard of the typewriter. He seeks inspiration looking through the window again at the patio. On the other side are the doors to the kitchen and the windows of the dining room of the community. Also, one can see the windows of the upper floor where there are other rooms. In this building, for many years the Noviate was located, and for this reason there are many rooms, almost none of them with bathrooms. For personal hygiene he has to leave his room and walk between thirty and forty-five feet to one of the two barrages of bathrooms located at the ends of the gallery that surrounds the patio. To take a shower there will remind him of his days as a novice, when the hot water was not enough for the enormous community in the house of Pueyrredon, in the building he had ordered sold to pay the debts of the Del Salvador University. Those difficult decisions return to his thought once in a while. Several years have passed but still there are people who are upset. "Look at me with mercy, Lord", Bergoglio prays. He is going through a period of shadows, he knows it and accepts it. If God wills, it will be for something. It is clear that he cannot write. He separates his chair from the desk and kneels on the tile floor to pray. Since the room is tiny (just nine feet wide and four feet deep), while he is kneeling before the bed, he has close to him the simple night stand. From the drawer he takes out the holy card of Our Lady Undoer of Knots that he brought from Germany. He takes his rosary and begins the prayer. In Córdoba "of the bells" there is interior silence; a future pope is praying.

The routine of a saint

With or without the noise: in heat or cold, Fr. Jorge woke up in Córdoba at 4:30 or 4:45 a.m., as he still does as Pope. "I was always pretty ordered in my routine —the Argentine pope mentioned recently— especially with the time of getting up in the morning and going to bed at night, because it is good for me. And I get up early because I have always been a "morning person" rather than a "night person": I think and write better in the morning".

At 5 a.m., you could find him washing his face in the community bathrooms, or polishing his black shoes, in which, even then, Bergoglio put a special insole to alleviate pain as he walked.

"When I began my routine, around 5 in the morning —the layman Ricardo Spinassi recounted, who worked at the time in the Residence— I would find him polishing his shoes, sitting on a black box that was there, with a discalced foot or, better said, a foot with a sock on it, with one of the two pairs of socks he owned; 'why more? —he would ask me— a clean pair to put on while the other was washed and dried'. When they gave him socks as a gift, which is one of the only things you can give a priest, he would give them away. And when at the end of the year they had a lot of holes in them, he would keep the first pair he received".

After washing up, Bergoglio would go to prayer. He prayed in the Domestic Chapel (see picture n. 20), a cordobese treasure of colonial Jesuit sacred art[44], or at the altar of the sacristy of the same chapel that is connected by means of a low hidden door cut into the imposing altar piece.

Picture 20 – Domestic Chapel of the *Residencia Mayor* in Córdoba.

---

[44] The Domestic Chapel. The specialist Carlos Maria Lopez Ramos points out in his *Estudio histórico artístico y de la técnica de ejecución de la Capilla Doméstica*: "It was built in the middle of the XVII century. It is pointed toward the east, just as the other churches of Córdoba are. It is a chapel of a single nave, built with walls of stone covered in wood. The technique of the construction of the walls can only be observed from one of its lateral sides, since inside the walls are covered in stucco. Originally the chapel was under the advocation of the Virgin Mary, the main inspiration for the decoration.

He used to spend a lot of time meditating or contemplating in the Domestic Chapel. He gives proof of this in one of the reflections he wrote in Córdoba, in which he speaks of an image painted in the vault of the Chapel with details that only one who has looked at it attentively can appreciate (see picture n. 21). He meditated there on his own situation: "In the silence of a circumstance of suffering —he wrote at the time— we are only asked to protect the wheat, and not that we go around pulling up the weeds. In the ceiling of the Domestic Chapel of the Residence of the Society in Córdoba there is an image. In it the brother novices are under the mantel of Mary, protected, and underneath there is written: '*Monstra te esse matrem*' ('Show yourself as mother'). At times of spiritual trial, when God wants to do the fighting, our place is below the mantel of the Holy Mother of God."[45]

Picture 21 - *Monstra te esse matrem*: picture of the Blessed Virgin protecting the Jesuit novices in the roof of the *Capilla Doméstica*, that recalled the attention of Fr. Jorge.

On more than one occasion during his stay there, Bergoglio was "surprised" by religious and laypeople in the Domestic Chapel, praying alone, at times in the shadows, spiritually under the mantel of the Virgin

---

[45] Jorge M. Bergoglio SJ, *Reflexiones en esperanza*, page 169 "Silencio y Palabra", December, 1990.

and in the silence of this spot so full of history and mystical beauty.

Francis remembers having "taken advantage of the time to pray" during those two years in Córdoba: "I prayed a lot, yes. I took advantage of the time to pray", the Pope said to the authors of this book. He did so almost at any hour due to the "interior work" that he mentioned before; even when he was doing manual work or when he left the Residence to do some errand or to visit one of the churches of the center of Córdoba that he still remembers. But he did these visits in the evening hours as we will see later.

After the first prayer of the morning, Bergoglio went to have breakfast in the large refectory of the Residence or in the kitchen ("it depended upon with whom he was at the time", Spinassi explained). What did not vary was the frugality: tea or coffee or some *mates*; toast or cookies with jelly or a homemade preserve that was always available in the refrigerator of the religious house, the same as now. Usually, there he met with some member of the community, with Spinassi or with Irma Peralta, cousin of Spinassi, who worked in the kitchen.

"When he saw me he asked me what I was doing and if I needed any help —Spinassi tells us— I would tell him no, but he helped me look for dirty laundry all over the house and put it in the washing machines. Other times he would help me clean the priests and brothers that were ill or bedridden because of their age; he would clean them himself, but he cleaned them all over, you know? Because these brothers and priests could not even get to the bathroom, and at times would go on themselves, and Fr. Bergoglio had no problem rolling up his sleeves and clean them up well; he was never disgusted. He would change them, take off the dirty linens and attend them".

Spinassi recalls that Bergoglio was "the only" member of the community that did these things. But that was not the only "help" that the man who had been provincial of the Society offered. He would also go into the laundry room of the Residence and take up the laundromat iron that Spinassi worked with. "He'd say: 'Look at all you have!', and he would start ironing a little", Spinassi remembered.

The Pope does not speak of any of this. He overlooks it or

minimalizes it. He only remembers that he was assigned to take care of Br. Cirilo Rodríguez, the same man who opened the doors of the Novitiate and of the Residence to him, when he was suffering his final agony. "Some nights I recall having to put a mattress down beside the bed of Br. Cirilo to accompany him, to pray with him, with this good man who was so important for me", the Pope revealed in a phone conversation. This detail that the Pope mentioned in passing reveals another story. In the friendship between Bergoglio and Br. Cirilo there is something special that to the careful observer has a symbolic significance. Those who know Jesuit history might find in this link of religious fraternity between Bergoglio and Br. Cirilo, an analogy with a "mystical" friendship between two great saints of the Society and of the Church: St. Alonso Rodríguez (also called "Alfonso" Rodríguez) and St. Peter Claver.

Apart from the obvious differences, St. Alonso had the same last name and the same vocation as Br. Cirilo, both were brother coadjutors in the Society. Alonso, as has been said, was the patron of the brothers. They were also similar in their humility and in the service that they performed: both were doormen; Alonso between the last years of the 16th century and the first of the 17th, in different Jesuit residences in Europe, and Cirilo in the Novitiate of Pueyrredon and the Mayor Residence in the center of the city, during the second half of the 20th century.

Just as what happened to Bergoglio with Br. Cirilo, St. Peter Claver met Br. Alonso when he opened the door of the formation house where he had been sent to study and prepare for the priesthood, and when the humble brother was already advanced in years. Yet, despite the difference in years, between them a friendship grew that was founded on mutual respect, humility and the love of God. The similarities are surprising.[46]

In his morning ritual in Córdoba, after the "extra" activities, Fr. Jorge had options that depended upon others: he could celebrate Mass in the main church —if the superior or Br. Bustamante, the sacristan at the time, asked him to do it— or in one of the chapels that the Residency had.

---

[46] Cfr.: www.cpalsj.org/*espiritualidad/nuestros -santos/san-alonso-rodriguez*

But he also had an obligation: which was to be available for confessions or spiritual direction to whoever asked for it in the entrance of the Residence. However, since this also was called for through the "Morse code" buzzer of the house, he could remain in the meantime in his room to read or write which is what he usually did.

Study, reading, "prophesies" and walks

"We have to go back and reevaluate seriously the problem of where our human existence is headed, that is, the problem of God. Man is not made in such a way that he is complete in himself, and as well he can enter into a relationship with God or not, according to his ideas and his tastes. On the contrary, his essence consists decisively in his relation with God. Man only exists in reference to God; and because of this he is defined according to the manner that he understands that relationship, the seriousness with which he lives it and what he does about it. This is the way it is and neither the philosophers not the politicians, nor the poets, or the psychologists can change anything about it. It is not good to act as though reality did not matter, because it will exact its revenge. When the instincts are smothered and impulses are not purified, neurosis ensues. God is the reality that grounds everything else, even the human. When justice is not done to it, our existence takes ill".[47]

The author of this phrase which gives us in a condensed way a complete cosmovision of existence is Romano Guardini, one of the best theologians of the 20th century. He is the theologian most studied by the man who is now bishop of Rome, pastor of the Church in the whole world. A couple of years before being sent to Córdoba, Fr. Bergoglio had travelled to Germany and he had settled in there to learn the original language in which Guardini had written his prolific and all-encompassing intellectual work. Born in the Italian city of Verona, in 1885, before completing a year he had moved with his family to Germany

---

[47] Guardini, Romano (1957). *El Poder.* Madrid: Ediciones Cristiandad. Page 122.

where he grew up, he received his formation and he was ordained a priest. He was a professor in several German Universities and became one of the theological precursors of Vatican II. Looking back, his theology-philosophy-psychology which can be characterized in general as a work of profound catholic humanist culture, ended up influencing the magisterium of the last three great pontificates of the Church, including the Argentine Francis.

Guardini died in the German city of Munich in 1968, but his theology was more alive than ever when Bergoglio choose it for his doctoral thesis in the 80's.

Guardini's phrase that is quoted above referring to the character of man "being defined according to the way he understands" his "relationship" with God, "the seriousness with which he takes it and what he does with it", help to understand the character of Bergoglio who lived in Córdoba at the beginning of the decade of the 90's and who today is Pope: a man who takes his relationship with God seriously and acts accordingly.

"In Córdoba —Francis remembered for this book— I continued to study to see if I could advance a little more in the thesis, but this resolution waned with the passing months. I still needed to publish the thesis, that is, to defend it and publish it. But as often happens with these things, if time passes, the work with the thesis becomes boring and harder... So either one does it all at once or it isn't done, right?".

The Pope has yet to defend his thesis and publish it as such; but the contents of that philosophical-theological work came to light in first apostolic exhortation that he signed as Pope.

"Even if I never got to defend my thesis, the study I made for it helped a lot for everything that came later. Even for writing the apostolic Exhortation *Evangelii Gaudium* ("the Joy of the Gospel"), since the whole part on the social criteria is taken from the thesis on Guardini".

Fr. Jorge looked for the books he needed in order to study in the main library of the Residence or he borrowed books from the other priests who lived there. Then he would bring them to his room where he worked at his desk. At the time, because of the thesis, he read a lot of philosophy, which provoked the attention and the curiosity of another member of the community. The Pope himself recounts the story that involved Fr. Sixto Castellano with a hint of prophesy: "One day, I had asked Fr. Castellano to borrow a book of Nietzche[48], that I wanted to read. But when he brought it to me he met me in the patio of the Residence and told me: 'don't get involved with philosophy or any of this because you are going to end up somewhere else. Your life has never been a straight line. Your life seems to go straight ahead and then it turns to one side before going ahead again, it is a zigzag. You are here in a part of your journey, but this is not the end'. He said something of this sort to me and it impressed me a lot and I have always remembered it".

Having fulfilled the "prophesy", the Pope remembers his brother priest with admiration and sincerity. "Fr. Sixto was quite direct when he said things and, in private, a little foul mouthed".

That humble cell of the chastised Jesuit was the scene of another "prophetic" circumstance. Aside from philosophical and theological texts, Bergoglio read there "without knowing why", he clarified, thirty seven of the forty volumes of the complete collection of *The History of the Popes*, of Ludwig von Pastor, a German historian who studied deeply each and every successor of the apostle St. Peter, from the end of the Middle Ages until 1900.[49]

"Why did I choose this work to read?", he asked himself, upon hearing the surprise of the authors of this book. "I don't know —he responded to himself—. It is a mystery. I felt the desire to read it and I read it quickly, so it was not hard. With an hour or two each day that I had for reading, I read the history of the Popes". And he added: "In the whole work of Von Pastor, I was impressed with the figure of Mother Church, the fidelity of the Lord with the sinful, unfaithful Church, but

---

[48] Friedrich Wilhelm Nietzche was a German philosopher, poet, musician and philologist, considered the "father" of nihilism and one of the most influential thinkers of modern times. He was born October 15, 1844, in Rocken, Germany; and died August 25, 1900, in Weimar, Germany.
[49] Ludwig von Pastor, born in Aquisgran, in January of 1854, and died Innsbruck, September 30 of 1928. *Geschichte der Papste seit dem Ausgang des Mittelters* (The History of the Popes) is his most prized and known work. The first volume was published in 1886 and the last in 1933 when the author had already died. In 1881 he had obtained a special permission from Pope Leo XIII to access the Archives of the Vatican Library.

also one with many saints. The image of the Mother Church was deeply impressed upon me. This book helped me to love the Church more".

As well, since he preached spiritual exercises and needed to prepare them, Bergoglio read books of spirituality, the exhortations and encyclicals of Pope John Paul II, and the books that at the time the German Cardinal Razinger was publishing. One can see this in the numerous citations of phrases from the one who would become Benedict XVI that are found throughout the writings that Bergoglio did in Córdoba. He would reread his favorite books, some that he found interesting and he would buy in the bookstores in the center of the city (for example, one that his friend Cayetano Bruno published in 1990: *Creo en la vida eterna. El ocaso cristiano de los próceres*, ("I believe in Eternal Life, the Christian last days of the Founding Fathers"). He would read the newspaper *La Nación* as well, and the personal letters that came in from all over the country and the world.

Around midday, he almost always went to the kitchen to see if he could "give a hand" or else he would go directly to the dining room to have lunch with the other members of the community. Irma Peralta, the cook remembers that lunch was served at 1:00 p.m. and usually lasted until 1:30 or 2:00. If he could, Fr. Bergoglio would help us in the kitchen; he would bring in a bag of fresh vegetables and when he saw what we were cooking he said 'that looks great!'". The cook added: "he always ate some chicken with some vegetables; a chicken leg or breast grilled very lightly, never very well cooked, I would say in fact he would eat it a little raw".

After a piece of fruit or crème caramel that was dessert (the Pope still loves sweets) some of the religious would go out into the little reading room where especially Fr. Pol and Fr. Castellando stopped to read the newspapers that the community received: *La Nación* and the *La Voz del Interior*. Br. Fortunato Murri used to serve tea or an herbal infusion that Bergoglio refers to as "tea of herbs".

Usually, the midday and principal meal as well as the after lunch conversation were fairly animated, with conversations on the news, or something that had to do with the Church and even jokes among some of them. When lunch was over, Bergoglio had been awake for ten hours. So then, as is the case today, a siesta of twenty five or thirty minutes was "sacred".

"At 2:30, when I was finishing washing the plates or putting things away —Spinazzi pointed out—, I would see him come out of his room before all of the other fathers would appear". Methodically, he would go to where even today there stands a statue of St. Joseph (see picture n. 22), on the upper floor of the Residence, in front of the stairwell that leads to the hallway where the rooms are.

Some of the people that lived with him at this time say that Bergoglio would stand in silence before the image, placing his hands on the glass that protects the statue and in this way he would pray to the chaste adoptive father of Jesus, virginal spouse of Mary, Patron of the universal Church, of workers and of a holy death.

Picture 22 – St. Joseph, first floor of the Major Residence. Here Bergoglio used to pray every day.

"There, in prayer before St. Joseph, he could spend a while… there still must be his fingerprints stamped on the glass", says Spinassi who would "spy" on him in admiration. "He always told me: 'Pray to St. Joseph, pray to St. Joseph to help you'", this privileged witness of the devotion of the Pope told him.

Fr. Rossi, whose room and office today are right below this image (on the ground floor), indicated another detail about his devotion: Already when he was a provincial he had a small statue of St. Joseph sleeping, lying down, under which he would place all the letters of those asking for prayers which he commended to the saint. I think this image was taken to Rome and he has it with him. It must have a pile of papers under it".

With time, he acquired a deep devotion to St. Teresa of the Child Jesus, whose teachings once in a while the Pope cites.

After this prayer time before the image of St. Joseph, Fr. Jorge went to the laundry room of the Residence, where he spoke with Irma and with Spinazzi who continued with the chores of washing and ironing. "He asked us if we needed anything, if we had everything we needed for dinner and next day's lunch, since he was the "provider" for the Residence, and as such had to attend to the provision of food".

During the afternoon the man who today is Pope spent another hour in study, an hour in reading and an hour in writing. All this while listening for the buzzer that might ring his code "short-long-short" at any time to indicate that someone was looking for spiritual guidance.

Sometimes (rarely, really, since he did not leave the Residence often), when the weather permitted it and his mental tension required it, Bergoglio took a half hour walk around the center of the city of Córdoba. His objective always had to do with his faith and devotion. Just like any other Cordobese, although he was not like any other, the future pope walked on the sidewalk of Caceros Street to the Cañada, and along the edge of this traditional rock walled stream that crosses the center of the city, and went to the church of the Discalced Carmelite fathers that is located close to Colon Avenue (see picture n. 23). There, as was mentioned at the beginning of the chapter, he would pray in front of the statue of Our Lady of Mt. Carmel, to whom he asked protection while he lived in Córdoba.

Picture 23 — Church of the Discalced Carmelites located at the *Cañada*.
Picture: La Voz del Interior.

The Pope today remembers that his sporadic walks had another destination as well: to the basilica of our Lady of Ransom, on the corner of May 25 Street and Rivadavia Avenue (see picture n. 24), which he walked to taking the pedestrian streets of Córdoba.

Picture 24 — The Basilica of our Lady of Ransom, in downtown Córdoba.
Picture: La Voz del Interior.

In this beautiful church that the Mercedarian Fathers attend, above the tabernacle where the Eucharist is kept there is a beautiful image of St. Joseph and the Child Jesus (see picture n. 25). There, on his knees, Bergoglio used to pray.

Picture 25 — St. Joseph and the Child Jesus in the Blessed Sacrament Chapel The Basilica of the Basilica of our Lady of Ransom, Córdoba.

The Superior General of the Mercedarian today, Fr. Pablo Ordoñc, who on his Facebook page has a picture of himself drinking *mate* with Francis, was surprised when we told him that the Pope used to walk to his home in Córdoba and pray in his church. "How wonderful to find this out! —Fr. Paul exclaimed from his residence now in Rome—, that St. Joseph statue gave me great consolation many times to me as well. When I was in Córdoba several years later, we would celebrate weekday Mass there".

Although Bergoglio celebrated Mass each day, he did not have a normal Mass assignment in the main church of the Society; although he did have a time set to hear Confessions in the church in the afternoon: "I did not have a fixed schedule for Mass –Francis explained, but I did have a time set to hear Confessions in the church. I sat in one of the confessionals in the middle of the four that are on the left side". Br. Luis Rausch, sacristan at the time in the church of the Society, who is a friend of the pope, with whom he speaks frequently by telephone, clarified the information: "Fr. Jorge had assigned the second confessional on the left, the one that Fr. Fernando Cervera uses today" (see picture n. 26).

Picture 26 — The confessional of the Church of the Company where Fr. Bergoglio used to hear confessions during the celebration of the afternoon Mass.

The Jesuit father Cervera thinks a moment before responding to the question of how he feels to sit in the place where years ago the Pope gave absolution. "It is a grace. Every time I sit in the confessional I think Bergoglio must have chosen it because from it you can see clearly the statue of St. Joseph with the Child Jesus that is on the inside of the chapel dedicated to Our Lady of Lourdes".

In fact, when the door that joins the chapel to the main church is open, from the confessional one can see the statue of the adoptive father of Jesus. In the years that Bergoglio used this confessional, Monica Moore, who now is a mother, professor of Sacred Sciences and doctor in semiotics, at the time had just left the Congregation of the Slaves of the Sacred Heart Sisters, where she had made an experience in religious life. Since this Congregation and she herself identify with the Jesuit spirituality, Monica went frequently to the mass at 8:00 p.m. in the Society church, and used to bring her guitar so as to accompany the liturgy with her music and voice. "I remember that the superior of the house was Fr. Fernando Boasso, with whom I had a warm friendship. He valued my participation with the guitar and singing during the Masses, which I was able to do that year and the following year, because in 1993 I got married and I didn't go that frequently". But Monica remembers very well this: "At that time, a priest that I observed always with his head down, very thin, almost emaciated and very serious, he would appear halfway through the Mass and take his place in the confessional. I never went to go to confession to him, in part because I had another confessor, and in part because I was a little afraid of him. The sacristan of the time, Br. José Bustamante, with whom I talked a lot before and after Mass, when I asked about the extreme seriousness of that priest, he told me: 'this father is a little ill and a bit depressed'. This priest, I learned later, was Bergoglio, today the Pope. And now I wonder if he remembers my voice, and if perhaps I was able to provide him with a little consolation for his heart in that time of trial; it is something that I think about and treasure". Just like Monica, many from Córdoba and elsewhere had the opportunity to confess to that unknown priest who today is the Pope. This was true whether he heard confessions in the main church confessional or in the private rooms to the side of the entrance hall of the residence, on Caceros Street, where Bergoglio also used to hear confessions for those who sought it.

Brocherian confessions

Fr. Jorge took from Córdoba a special remembrance of some of his penitents; a memory that still today unites Pope Francis to one of the most important historical figures of the church in Córdoba.

"Sometimes —the Pope revealed to the authors of this book— I also heard confessions in the Residence when they called me from the front desk, where they knew the times I would be free. I have a nice story from one of those times: the church of the Society in Córdoba is a place where people from different social sectors come to confess: university professors and students, because the Law School is close by; people that are from the center as well as people form the outskirts, because in the outskirts the priest can only confess a half hour before Mass and people are not able to get to confession. So when the people come to the center of the city, they confess in one of the churches of the different orders: for example, the Franciscans, Jesuits or Dominicans. I noticed that there were some people who confessed very, very well; who did not say a word too much; that what they said was what they should say, and they made their confessions very correctly. And they were people that were of different social levels. After a while this got my attention. One day I got up the courage to ask one where they were from. He told me they were from the other side of the Sierras of Córdoba. Later I asked another woman and she told me the same, and I came to the conclusion that people that confessed in this way were from the other side of the mountains, and that this kind of confession, well done, was fruit of the catechesis of "Cura" Brochero. Later I would confirm it. After almost a century, Brochero was still influencing the way the people lived their faith. Brochero did a lot, really a lot for the country and for Córdoba, as did the woman from Santiago del Estero Mother Antula (Venerable Maria Antonia de la Paz y Figueroa). These are persons that have been very righteous and at the same time, brought the mercy of God to the people".

In the afternoon, when the time for confessions ended, Bergoglio again returned to the concerns of the house and those who lived and worked there, without drawing attention to himself. He would ask Spinassi again if he needed anything for dinner, he would give him a hand with the laundry if there was still a lot of it, or he would go visit the priests and brothers that were ill or bedridden. He could also take the time to pray a rosary or write a letter or make a phone call to his family in Buenos Aires. During those two years some of his brothers and sisters came to visit him. These were the only times Fr. Jorge would go out to eat at some restaurant in the center of the city, when he was invited by his guest. It was not common for him to leave the residence in the evening; so rare that the Pope remembers today the times he did and for what occasion. He remembers for example, that Thursday, January 24 1991, when he took the bus at 6:30 p.m. to go to Alta Córdoba in the north of the city. He was invited to participate in a Mass in which a priest from Córdoba was ordained a bishop. The ceremony took place in a stadium – the gymnasium of the Heart of Mary High School, and Francis remembers the tremendous heat in the place. This vivid memory of the Pope surprised, recently, the archbishop of Córdoba, Carlos Ñañez, who found out in this way, from the Pope himself, that the Pontiff had participated in his episcopal consecration.

"On January 7, 2014 —Ñañez said— when we visited the Holy Father together with Bishop Pedro Torres (auxiliary bishop of Córdoba) he surprised me with the news that he had been in my episcopal ordination. It was a surprise and a joy, because I never knew until he told me". Ñañez was ordained by the then archbishop of Córdoba, Cardinal Raúl Francisco Primatesta, who presided the celebration which was concelebrated by the then apostolic nuncio in Argentina, Ubaldo Calabresi (who died in 2004), and by Bishop Adolfo Arana, who was in charge of the Curia of Río Cuarto (Córdoba) and who died in 2003. No one noticed at the time that silent Jesuit priest who wanted to be in the celebration along with the diocesan priests. Until 2014, Ñañez thought that Bergoglio had met him the year after his ordination, in the chancery of Córdoba, when Primatesta presented him and said he had just been named auxiliary bishop of Buenos Aires.

After that ceremony, Fr. Jorge returned to his house in the center of the city to take up his daily routine. Between 8:30 p.m. and 9:00 p.m. he had a frugal supper, which usually consisted in heated leftovers and other food that Irma Peralta had prepared at midday. Spinassi, who at the time lived in the residence as a "live in" employee, was in charge of heating it up; the fathers and brothers served themselves and, after a prayer, ate their supper.

When supper was over, Bergoglio might have a brief conversation with a member of the community, or he would make a brief visit to the ill in the house to see if they needed something. At times, as was the case with Br. Cirilo, he stayed to accompany during the night those that were the most ill. If not, he had a few minutes to look at the newspaper or a book in the reading room. Prayer was his obligation in the evening. Bergoglio always reserved the last forty or fifty minutes of the day for his examination of conscience, for the last prayers of the Breviary and for meditation that united his heart to God. The Pope has said in several occasions that he ends his day in prayer at 10 p.m. going to sleep "thinking about God". That is the way he ended his daily routine in Córdoba, the routine of a saint.

Giving away things, giving of himself

Bergoglio always sought to live in an austere way, without too many possessions, like a poor man. In his religious life, in silence, he sought to take on what for him is a great evangelical virtue: spiritual poverty, which is essential in the life of St. Francis of Assisi, from whom the Pope has taken his name.

To be "poor in spirit" does not mean —even if it sounds like it— to have a poor spirit. The concept does not refer to spirituality but to poverty. To be poor in spirit means to take on poverty from within, spiritually, as a grace from God. To be poor in spirit means not to be tied down with material things, riches or human "treasures" that may be large or small, but in the end make us slaves.

Having been born and raised in an Italian immigrant working family, Bergoglio learned as a boy to work to earn his living and to live a dignified life; but not earning to spend or consume, but in order to live and help others live. For this reason, Fr. Jorge chose to have little while working a lot. He had and has little, almost nothing. In the little bag he used and still uses for his trips, could fit almost all his possessions: a few family pictures and small statues of St. Joseph and the Virgin Mary. The two pairs of socks which we already mentioned. A change of clothes. A pair of shoes. His black schedule book and the breviary, the book of prayers. A rosary. A few more books. Nothing more.

Already in Córdoba he did what many of his friends now know: almost everything he received as a gift, he gave to others. For this reason, as a priest who knows him well has suggested, if some day you want to offer the Pope a personal gift, bring him something sweet to eat, but in an opened package. Bergoglio always liked sweet things but if you leave him the unopened package he will give it away. But if the package is opened, (cookies for example) at least he will eat one. The rest he will share with his collaborators or with the Swiss Guard.

Contrary to what is repeated in the media, Bergoglio always knew that it is not good to have many things. To have them will draw too much attention or will be a problem. They take away your freedom.

On June 7, 2013, in a message to students of Jesuit run schools, Pope Francis said: "Please, let no one steal your hope! Who will rob your hope? The spirit of the world, riches, the spirit of vanity, pride, arrogance. All these things rob you of hope. Where do I find hope? In Jesus the poor man, Jesus who made himself poor for our sakes...Do not let yourselves be robbed by comforts, by the spirit of comfort which in the end will lead you to be nothing in life". For Bergoglio it was always important to be able to live poverty, to know that one is not self-sufficient. He pointed it out during the first year of his pontificate when he remembered a letter written by the Jesuit General Superior Fr. Pedro Arrupe. In the letter Fr. Arrupe had written that "one cannot speak of poverty unless one experiences it with a direct insertion in the places where those that live it are". And the Pope added: "one cannot speak of poverty, of abstract poverty, it doesn't exist! Poverty is the flesh of Jesus in the poor man, in that child who is hungry, in the sick, in those social structures that are unjust".

Fr. Jorge always sought to be closely committed to the suffering of the poor as another poor man. During those years, enclosed in his small room in Córdoba, he wrote that "the lack of poverty encourages division" among men and in communities. And he remembered that St. Ignatius of Loyola, founder of the Jesuit Order, said that poverty "was 'mother' and 'wall' of contention in the religious life". St. Ignatius gave so much importance to poverty —and so too it was for Bergoglio— that in the Jesuit Constitutions the article on this "virtue" is one that can never be modified unless it is to make it more demanding.

The fact is that for Bergoglio-Francis, poverty is much more than poverty. As Fr. José "Pepe" Di Paola, a priest who works in the slums of Buenos Aires, formed in this theology by the then Cardinal Bergoglio, the commitment of Bergoglio with the poor "has to do with his faith in Jesus".

Francis himself explained it three months after his election: "To touch the flesh of Christ, to take upon ourselves this sorrow for the poor. Poverty for us Christians is not a sociological, cultural or psychological category; no, it is a theological category. I would say, perhaps the first category, because God, the Son of God, humbled himself, he made himself poor to walk with us on the way. And this is our poverty: the poverty of the flesh of Christ, the poverty that the Son of God brought us in the Incarnation. A poor Church for the poor begins with moving toward the flesh of Christ. If we go to the flesh of Christ we begin to understand something, to understand what this poverty is, the poverty of the Lord".

The life that Bergoglio has tried to live, that is poor and close to the poor has helped him understand a truth that today the Pope teaches: "The most beautiful and spontaneous joy that I have seen in my life has been in the poor people, who have little to hold on to". These beautiful and spontaneous joys Fr. Jorge Bergoglio also experienced in Córdoba during his second stay in Córdoba. And he could appreciate it in the faces and in the hard life of three cordobeses that knew him then, and today would love to hear his voice again —the voice of a friend who is now Pope.

Ricardo Spinassi was born and raised in the slum quarter of Lower Pueyrredon, located along highway n. 19 in one of the entrances to the city of Córdoba. Until thirty years ago this area was part of the Holy Family parish and, thus, under the care of the Jesuits; so much so that between 1958 and 1960, it was one of the areas where the young novice Bergoglio and his companions went to look for children in need of catechism. In that very poor area, that later became jurisdiction of St. Ignatius of Loyola parish (today attended by the Congregation of the Oblates of the Virgin Mary), the Jesuits installed a chapel where Ricardo Spinassi went as a child with his grandmother. There he met several priests and brothers of the Society of Jesus whose example generated in him interest in a religious life. After a very poor childhood, in 1981 Ricardo entered the Society of Jesus as an aspirant, and he met Fr. Bergoglio when he preached the first Spiritual Exercises to him in the Colegio Maximo in Buenos Aires. Moreover, it was Fr. Jorge himself, at the end of the retreat, who told Ricardo with great charity that he did not have a vocation to the Society but rather to some other Congregation that worked in hospitals, or served the sick, those that suffer. And Ricardo understood: "I never liked to read and the Jesuits read a lot, they are very intellectual, that is why they know so much – he said. I remember that I broke down and cried when Fr. Bergoglio told me that I would not be able to be a Jesuit. But he hugged me and said: 'Don't cry, we will see what the Lord wants'".

Days later Ricardo asked to be admitted as a novice in the Congregation founded by Don Orione that has its residence in front of the Colegio Maximo, in San Miguel. He did two years of novitiate with the Orionites, but when he returned to Córdoba he found his grandmother who was still living in the slum who asked him —weeping— that he not leave her alone. For this reason, as well as for reasons of his own heath and other difficulties, Spinassi did not return to complete his formation as a son of Don Orione. But he did go to the chapel of the Jesuits in Lower Pueyrredon to help with catechism. That is how he came to know Fr. Carlos Alberto Carranza who offered him work in the mayor Residence of the Society in Córdoba, "doing a little of everything", including living there with the religious community. Spinassi accepted, and with time and work earned the trust of the superiors of the house. Months later, Ricardo navigated the entrance of his cousin, Irma Peralta, to be in charge of the kitchen for some days of the week.

When Bergoglio came to Córdoba that Monday, July 16, 1990, he found Ricardo washing clothes and immediately he recognized him. "He remembered me because he had always been generous with me, generous in spiritual things and everything. He was always a very special man, so very special —Ricardo remarked, and he was again with me during those two years when he taught me many things".

Ricardo said that he and his cousin spent a lot of money. "When one is born poor, in a slum such as in my case, from a young age you desire to have things; then the money you make, you spend. I remember that Fr. Bergoglio helped us a lot economically but when he saw that we were big spenders, and that we desired to have a lot of things and spend too much, he helped us and told us to be careful how we spend what we made working, not to spend so much in things that were not important".

The two Christmases that they shared with the man who today is Pope were very special for Ricardo and Irma. "For Christmas he asked us what we were going to prepare to eat with our families on Christmas eve, and he would give us a little money to buy a goat or piglet".

One of the biggest surprises Fr. Jorge gave them took place when a niece of both of them, Alejandra Spinassi, got married in the summer of 1992. Today, Alejandra lives in the city of San Francisco, in the east of the province of Córdoba, with her twenty-one year old daughter. Ricardo remembers in detail what happened: "My brother, the father of the bride, had asked us to take care of the food for the celebration, which was not going to be a big affair, but certainly a reunion with some friends and family members. I didn't know what to prepare with Irma and we were worried. Fr. Jorge asked us what was the problem and we explained it to him. He said to us: 'Let's make some cold meat and a little rice for the meal'. Not only that, he began to make it himself!"

The man who was to become Pope, who was living a time of interior purification, who in the future will intervene in the world with a plea for peace, rolled up the sleeves of his black cassock, put on an apron and spent the whole early morning and the "sacred" siesta that Saturday to prepare a meal for a humble wedding of a poor family that he barely knew. "When we arrived in the morning to the Residence kitchen, Fr. Bergoglio had already prepared the meat... He had spent all the early morning hours cooking while the other priests and brothers of the community were still asleep!"

After cutting the meat in thin slices, Bergoglio, Spinassi and Irma prepared a sauce to cover the meat; they cooked the rice and put the portions on each plate with a plastic yogurt cup. Without anyone realizing it, except Irma and Ricardo, their niece's wedding turned into a renewed version of the wedding at Cana[50]. In this case, man who will be Pope permitted with his generosity the "miracle" of food, becoming an image of Jesus in the Gospel who, through the intercession of his mother,

---

[50] Cfr. Gospel of St. John 2, 1-13.

and for a celebration of conjugal love, converted water into wine.

Ricardo added that Bergoglio did not only help them with the cooking. So that they could prepare the entire celebration and they had time to spend with their niece, he would take care of everything that they would not be able to do in the Residence, from washing the dishes to assisting the sick.

Lucila Tejeda, "Lucy", is a good woman who has suffered and been buffeted in life, which only makes her good humor, faith and responsibility all the more notable. The Pope remembers her, together with her sister Blanca Tejeda, as "strong women, women of faith". From a poor family, Lucila came to work as the door-keeper at the Residence a couple of years before Bergoglio returned to Córdoba. In 1988, Lucila was forty two years old and had three very small children when her husband died tragically in a construction accident. All the faithful of the St. Joachim and St. Ann parish of the Zumarán neighborhood, where Lucila lived, heard of the tragedy. Fr. Beltrán, a Jesuit and the pastor of this community, accompanied her spiritually and offered her half-day work as a door-keeper of the Residence. The poor woman had to face life alone and raise and educate her three children. She was doing just that when she met Fr. Bergoglio, "this good man who each day at three in the afternoon, when I arrived, I found at the door of the Residence handing out food to the poor".

Lucy remembers that a few days after the arrival of Bergoglio from Buenos Aires something happened that revealed to her the vocation of service that he sustained: "Some people I knew called one day too ask me if I could get a priest to pray a Mass for a deceased relative. I could not find anyone until he appeared, and saw me a little exasperated and asked me what was happening. I told him and he responded: 'I will do it, that is what we are here for'. And he celebrated Mass for them in the Domestic chapel".

Lucila remembers also the image —often repeated— of Bergoglio entering the front door with bags of groceries that he left at the entrance for her or for those who came looking for food. "When I told him not to give me anything, that this was for the priests he replied: 'we priests have enough'". Bergoglio was moved by Lucila's story and never stopped asking about her children, what they needed, how they were doing in school. "But he didn't only ask me —Mrs. Tejeda added— he gave me money and groceries all the time".

In December of 1990, Lucy's brother—in—law had a problem. In the factory where he worked in Los Boulevares neighborhood, the workers had organized a pool of money which they asked him to organize for a "Christmas Lottery" or a "Year—end Bingo". "My brother—in—law, —Lucy explained— gathered all the money, which was a lot; I don't remember how much but it was a lot of money. He went to the center of the city to deposit it in the bank and when he was close to the bank a couple came up to him and stole the bag with the money from him". When Lucy arrived at the Residence the next day to begin work she found her sister Blanca, who also worked there cleaning the sacristy, telling Bergoglio, tearfully, what had happened to her husband.

The next day, according to Lucila, Bergoglio went to her house in the Zumarán neighborhood and left them an envelope with the same amount of money that was robbed from the brother-in-law. "He told me: 'Take this, give it to your sister and brother-in-law, and tell them if they happen to recover any of the other money, they should give it to the poor."

After Bergoglio left for Buenos Aires in 1992, Lucila and Irma went several times to visit him, including when Fr. Jorge was Cardinal. "He received us, prepared tea for us and listened to us. He never stopped being a humble, special, close and generous person. When I heard he had been elected Pope I cried like a baby, I couldn't believe it. Fr. Bergoglio is a wonderful priest; I pray to God that He may give him a long life, that He may help him a lot because he deserves it".

Bergoglio "Real Estate Agency"

A day in December of 1990, in the laundry room of the Residence, Ricardo Spinassi was washing clothes. The news that Fr. Sojo was no longer going to be superior of the community had provoked great concern. He was thinking about this when Fr. Bergoglio arrived to wash his socks. He asked Ricardo what was troubling him. Spinassi told him that he feared the new superior (he did not know yet who he was, he had heard only rumors) would fire him, and that would mean he would have to return to the slum, living with shortages of all kinds, because he did not have "even a small room" to his name.

As Spinassi tells it, Bergoglio looked at him and said, "Don't cry; calm down. We will see what we can do. You pray to St. Joseph and to sister Teresa (St. Teresa of Lisieux) and you'll see that something will come up".

Days later, before Spinassi left on vacation, Bergoglio called him and said: "there are some sisters in Germany that are going to send me some money; I am going to give you some of it, so go look for a little house, go see where you can live". Ricardo did not waste time and began to look. His brother-in-law, who was a construction worker, told him that in the neighborhood of Talleres, on Carlos III Street, there was a house on sale. The construction was old, in poor condition, almost uninhabitable, but his brother-in-law assured him that he could fix it.

"Fr. Bergoglio called me one day —Spinassi recalls— and handed me 12 thousand pesos that they had sent him from Germany. He asked me to keep it a secret and we thought it was a good idea to say I won it in the lottery, because I always played the lottery and still do".

Ricardo hid the money under the mattress of his bed at the Jesuit Residence. It would be safe there until he had to pay for the house. "His" house. A couple of weeks later the moment arrived. The house —or what looked like a house— cost him 9 thousand pesos. Ricardo was now a homeowner and with the other 3 thousand his brother-in-law bought the materials that the place needed to fix it. They worked two months to convert what was a ruin into a habitable home. When the house was almost finished, Ricardo went and sat down in the patio, still full of rubble. There he realized the importance of what had happened. He never dreamt of having his own home. If for any reason in the future he should be without a job in the Society of Jesus, he had a place to go. It was an enormous gift of God... that came to him through the immeasurable generosity of Fr. Bergoglio. But Ricardo could not say anything. And if Providence had not ordained that, twenty three years later, 115 Cardinals elected this man Pope, the story would have remained hidden in the silent and almost forgotten gratitude of Ricardo, and in the eternal memory of God.

The story did not end there between Spinassi and Francis. When Ricardo asked Fr. Jorge to bless the house something serious happened. Content to see the happiness and gratitude of Spinassi, Bergoglio went to the Talleres sector in the n. 60 bus. He walked to the house and together with the new owner, sprinkled holy water on the front of the house rebuilt with the money he had given him. But when they went out to the back patio, Fr. Jorge saw something he did not like. Ricardo retells the story, between regrets and repentance. "When I was a boy, one day I went with a friend to the pool in the Córdoba Water Co. Club, which no longer exists. They would not let me in because I was from the slum, I was a "slum kid". I always have remembered this and I onstantly wanted to have a pool of my own, but I would have been happy with one of those canvas pools that you set up and take down. When my brother-in-law was working on the house, I asked him to build me a small platform in the patio to use as a base to set up a pool. But he thought I meant a real pool, one set in the ground and made of cement and he began to build it. When I arrived a week later he had almost finished it and it was too late to undo it. When Fr. Bergoglio saw it he got really angry. He told me that those things are not of a poor or humble person. He was so angry at me that I remember that he did not speak with me for a long time".

Ricardo never went to see Bergoglio again after the day he left Córdoba, and when we interviewed him, he told us, tearfully, that he still carries with him the weight of the guilt of that mistake. And that he would like to know that the Pope has forgiven him. "I would like to know that before I die", he exclaimed.

When a Jesuit priest was asked about the incident to confirm its truth, the priest said that Spinassi's was not the only house that Bergoglio had given to poor people. He explained that in Buenos Aires as well there were similar stories but that many times the details never came to light because the people who received them had promised Fr. Jorge never to reveal who the "Real Estate Agent" was.

Irma Peralta no longer sees any reason not to reveal that her first house, in the neighborhood of Arenales, a very poor section of the far eastern part of the city of Córdoba, was also bought with money from the man who today is the Pope. Irma is a very humble woman who also has suffered a lot during her life. When she met Bergoglio, her husband was in prison, and it was Fr. Jorge who helped her pay a lawyer to get him out. After this he helped with the house, as she told us: "Some months after helping my cousin Ricardo buy his house, he gave him money so that I could buy my own. The difference is that the house he bought me came with everything in it: a stove, a washing machine, a table, chairs, everything. Why would we not tell everyone what he did for us?

Irma no longer lives in that house in Arenales. She recalled that when she bought it, she had married a widower who had other children and for this reason Bergoglio suggested to her to put the house she bought in the name of her daughter Elizabeth, Eli.

Today, surviving on a pension of only two thousand pesos, Irma spends most of her time in the house where her daughter lives, takes care of the littlest of her three grandchildren and goes often to visit her cousin Ricardo. When she spoke to us she said she felt a little depressed. "I miss Fr. Jorge", she explained. When Bergoglio left Córdoba to be auxiliary bishop in Buenos Aires and then archbishop, she continued to see him, at least once a year, until he was elected Pope. "We went with Lucy (Lucila Tejeda) to visit him, almost always in January or February —she recalled—. I always said that he would be Pope because, how could such a good, generous man not be? But he would just laugh and ask us to pray for him".

After hearing these stories, one understands where Pope Francis gets teachings such as these: "We must be concerned for the poor, be aware of their spiritual and material needs. I entrust to the young people in a special way the task of placing solidarity at the center of human culture. Faced with the old and new forms of poverty —unemployment, immigration, the different kinds of enslavements—, we have to pay attention and be vigilant, overcoming the temptation to indifference. Let us think also of those that feel unloved, those that do not have hope in the future, who refuse to get involved in life because they are discouraged, disillusioned, frightened. We have to learn to be with the poor. Let's not just fill our mouths with beautiful words about the poor. Let's get close to them, look them in the eye, and listen to them. The poor are an occasion for us to encounter Christ himself, to touch his flesh that suffers".

CHAPTER 6
THE CORDOBESE TEXTS OF A "MORNING" WRITER

"I get up early in the morning because I am more of a "morning person" than a "night person": I think and write better in the morning". With this methodology that he revealed, Jorge Mario Bergoglio wrote in his own hand seven books before becoming Pope. They are: *Meditaciones para religiosos* (Meditations for religious); *Reflexiones en esperanza* (Reflections of hope); *Corrupción y pecado* (Corruption and sin); *Educar: exigencia y pasión* (To educate: challenge and passion); *El verdadero poder es el servicio* (True power is service); *Ponerse la patria al hombro* (Putting the Country on your shoulders); and *La nación por construir* (The country that has to be built), the last three were collections of his homilies or conferences as archbishop of Buenos Aires. He is also co-author of other works, for example, *Entre cielo y la tierra* (Between heaven and earth), that contains a dialogue with the rabbi Abraham Skorka, the wise Jewish man that Pope Francis embraced in front of the Wall of Lamentations in Jerusalem during his historic visit to the holy Land in May of 2014.

Of all these texts, two were written almost entirely in Córdoba, between 1990 and 1992: *Refexiones en Esperanza* and *Corrupción y pecado*.

Pope Francis revealed to us in a conversation about this book: "In Córdoba I wrote a lot. I wrote *Reflexiones en esperanza*, a little book with a yellow cover that I edited later on when I was auxiliary bishop, but it was written in Córdoba. Also the book that people seem to like: *Corrupción y pecado*, which I wrote inspired by the tremendous case of the young woman from the province of Catamarca who was murdered, María Soledad Morales. I was inspired one day while I was reading an article about the case in the newspaper *La Nación*, signed by Octavio Frigerio, and entitled *'Corrupción, un problema político'* (Corruption, a political problem). It inspired me and I thought 'I have to write something'".

"Sinners yes, Corruption No!"

On June 3, 2013 was the first time that the world heard the phrase "sinners yes, corruption no" from the mouth of Pope Francis. Few people know that these words had been written by Jorge Bergoglio, twenty two years earlier, in a room whose window looked out at Caceros Street, in the center of the city of Córdoba.

Perhaps there were not new concepts, but they were for Cardenal Ángelo Amato (prefect of the Congregation for the Cause of the Saints) who concelebrated that Eucharist in the Saint Martha chapel; it was new also to the many priests, collaborators of this Congregation, for the Knights of His Holiness present and for the millions of people in the world who read these words in the headlines of newspapers and news broadcasts.

That morning the Pope had reflected upon "three types of Christians in the Church: sinners, the corrupt, and saints", and he exclaimed: "sinners yes, corruption, no!".

"It is not necessary to speak much about sinners, because we all are", Bergoglio pointed out. "And if anyone of us does not feel himself to be a sinner, let him go to a spiritual doctor", because, he added "something is not working".

He did stop to speak about the corrupt, those who "seek to take over the vineyard and have lost all relationship with the Owner of the vineyard". "They feel strong, the feel they do not need God".

On November 11, 2013, Francis again brought up those words

in his morning Mass. That time he spoke of the corrupt, whose "double life" makes them like "a varnished rottenness".

The ideas of the pope came out of a reading of the Gospel of St. Luke (17, 1-6) that says: "If your brother sins, rebuke him; and if he repents, forgive him". The Pope explained that in this biblical passage he sees Jesus as "one who never tires of forgiving, and he counsels us to do the same". But in the same reading there is another episode in which Jesus says "Woe to those who cause scandals to occur!", and he adds "It would be better for him if a millstone were put around his neck and he be thrown into the sea than for him to cause one of these little ones to sin. Be careful". The Pope then asked, what difference there is between sinning and giving scandal. The difference he responded, is that "the one who sins and repents, asks forgiveness, he feels weak, he feels like a son of God, he humbles himself and asks for the salvation of Jesus. But the one who provokes scandal does not repent and continues to sin pretending to be Christian". It is as though he leads "a double life, and the double life of a Christian does a lot of damage".

These thoughts had been thought out and analyzed in detail by the then Fr. Bergoglio in a long article that he typed on his typewriter on the bare desk of his room in the Mayor Residence of the Society, in March 1991.

At that time, Argentina was submerged in a heated debate over the brutal assassination of Maria Soledad Morales, a young seventeen year old student whose body appeared, on November 10, 1990, mutilated and abused in a park of the city of Catamarca. Right away the suspicions of that crime laid heavily on the "sons of power" in that Argentine province, the son of a national legislator, two nephews of the mayor and the son of a police chief. The investigation was from the start, scandalous; and people suspected a cover-up on the part of the authorities. This resulted in the reaction of family members, neighbors, school companions and even the authorities of the school who did not hesitate to organize a series of protests that had an unexpected impact. The manifestations called "Marches in silence" had an outcome that was never seen and an overwhelming power. The image of thousands of citizens holding candles, photographs of Maria Soledad, signs seeking justice and who only broke silence when they prayed the rosary, was an image that went through the country and the world.

The protests, the details of the crime and the scandalous attitude of that provincial government, revealed the semi feudal conditions in the exercise of authority and revealed the corruption in the province that lead to the intervention of the three branches of government by the then president Carlos Menem.

A first trial began only after five years; but again, an act of corruption caused its annulment. Television, which recorded every minute of the proceedings, caught the gestures and attitudes of the judges that showed a clear partiality with the defense. The trial was suspended and annulled and the president ordered the intervention of the province. Finally in 1998, after a second trial, Guillermo Luque was condemned to twenty-one years in prison for the assassination and rape of Maria Soledad, and Luis Tula to nine years, accused of being an accessory to the crime.

It was those first *Marches in Silence* and the reflection by Frigerio published in *La Nación*, which inspired Bergoglio to write about corruption.

"The action of a people has produced a moment in which the reality of corruption emerged in a special way", Bergoglio points out in the first lines. "All social corruption is nothing other than the consequence of a corrupt heart". And he added: "The human heart is a heart in as much as it is capable of referring to something other than itself, in the measure it is capable of loving or denying love (hating), and he cited Mathew (6:21) where Jesus says: "For where your treasure is, there also will your heart be".

In the text, Fr. Jorge clarifies that one should not confuse sin with corruption. "One can be very sinful and yet not have fallen into corruption. But at the same time, sin that is repeated can lead to corruption. How can this be? It is a subtle form of progression, or rather, a qualitative leap".

In another paragraph, the man who will become Pope and who will have as a motto of his pontificate an homage to the mercy of God, sustained: "Sinner, yes. How beautiful it is to feel and say this and, right now, to throw ourselves into the mercy of God Who loves us and is always waiting for us".

In the anthropological vision of the future Pope, the sinner recognizes his error, is repentant and seeks forgiveness from God. "On the other hand —he expressed—, the corrupt person has an attitude of 'it wasn't me', a 'holy card face' as my grandmother would say. The corrupt could get an honorary doctorate in social cosmetics. And the worst is that they end up believing it".

In fact, for Bergoglio, the difference between sin and corruption is abysmal: "We could say that sin is forgiven; corruption cannot be forgiven". The phrase, taken out of context could generate theological problems. Perhaps for this reason the then Jesuit priest explains it in detail in his book: "Sincerely because at the bottom of every corrupt attitude there is a weariness of transcendence: before the God Who never tires of forgiving us, the corrupt sets himself up as self-sufficient... he tires of seeking pardon".

Maybe for this reason in his first prayer of the *Angelus* as head of the Catholic Church, which he pronounced only four days after his election, the new Pope emphasized: "God never tires of forgiving us, never!... the problem is that we tire, we don't want it, we get tired of asking forgiveness". This sentence from the Pope who came "from the end of the earth" provoked an ovation from the one hundred and fifty thousand that were following his prayer that came from the small window on the third floor of the papal apartments, over sixty feet above the plaza. The powerful sound equipment and the gigantic screens reproduced clearly his last advice, with a thunderous tone: "let us never get tired!, never get tired!"

Twenty-two years before, Bergoglio had explained the basis for those words. The corrupt feel self-sufficient and do not permit any questioning. "Corruption has the smell of rot", but the corrupt person does not smell his own corruption. "It is like bad breath: it is hard for one with it to realize he has it. Others notice and have to bring his attention to it. This is why it is hard for the corrupt to get out of corruption through remorse. His good spirit is under anesthesia". And he explains that the Lord saves him through trials (sickness, loss of fortune, loss of loved ones) that crack the corrupt shell so grace can enter. This is the reason the corrupt are not forgiven, but rather "cured".

After explaining the differences between sin and corruption, Bergoglio lists the characteristics of the corrupt. He tells us that the corrupt person has a "complex of unquestionability. Before any criticism he is offended, he resorts to sophism and to nominalist-ideological equivocations to justify himself, to devalue everyone else, and responds with insults to whoever thinks differently. The corrupt person often persecutes himself unconsciously and the irritation that it produces is so great, that he projects it to others". In this way he becomes a persecutor. "While persecuting —Bergoglio explains in the text— he imposes a reign of terror to all those who contradict him and he kicks them out of social life".

The Pope makes a keen psychological observation, noticing that "the corrupt person cultivates good manners to an extreme" in order to hide his bad manners. And Bergoglio reminds us that "Jesus called whitened sepulchers to the corrupt sectors of society of his time".

In fact the columnist of *La Nación* who inspired Bergoglio with his reflections said in his article that "among these (party) leaders, there are those that like courtesans of old converted into vestal virgins, they pretend to escape the suspicions of corruption by officiating as unexpected guardians of public honesty".

Another characteristic of the corrupt person, the future Pope explains is the need "to compare themselves to others who appear coherent in their lives in order to cover up their own incoherence. For example, for one who is inconstant, the person who seeks clear moral limits and does not negotiate with them, is a fundamentalist, old-fashioned, closed minded, a person who has not kept up with the times". In this way he justifies himself.

But, moreover, comparing themselves, "the corrupt person makes himself judge of others: he is the measure of moral conduct". "Corruption leads to loss of shame which guards truth", it moves on another plain, in "shameless modesty", and the author explains it with an example: "Robbing a purse from a woman is a sin and the thief is put in jail, and the woman tells her friend what happened, and everyone agrees how bad the world has gotten, that the authorities should do more, and how 'no one can go out anymore'. And the woman in question does not even think about how her husband handles his business, who swindles the government by not paying taxes and firing his employees every three months to avoid paying benefits".

Bergoglio mentions "triumphalism" as the last characteristic of the corrupt. "The sinner awaits forgiveness...the corrupt person, on the other hand, does not, because he does not feel he has sinned: he has triumphed". And it is precisely this triumphalism that gives him the presumption to "humiliate all the rest".

Finally, he describes the corruption of the religious. These concepts that were described two decades ago, will also sound new when they are repeated during that first homily preached in the Sistine Chapel on March 14, 2013. "We can go as far as we want, we can build many new things, but if we do not announce Jesus Christ, something is wrong. We will end up being a Non-profit that gives assistance, but not the Church... When we do not announce Jesus Christ, we announce the worldliness of the devil", he said without euphemisms, in his first Mass as Bishop of Rome and Holy Father, in front of the cardinals that had just elected him and still under the seal of the conclave. That sermon ended with a radical teaching: "When we announce Christ without the cross, we are worldly".

These strong words also find their explanation, their source and origin in the ideas gestated in Córdoba; in that "time of interior purification" that Bergoglio lived between 1990 and 1992.

"Certainly there are. That there were, it is enough to read history", wrote Bergoglio about corrupt religious. "In the different orders that asked for a reform or that made a reform, there was, in a greater or lesser degree, corruption". "Blessed Fabro[51] gave a golden rule to detect the state of a soul that lives tranquilly and in peace: propose something more. If a soul is closed to generosity, it would react badly". After citing an "accumulation of resistances" that are found in the Bible, whether in the Old or New Testaments, he indicates that "the heart does not want problems. There is fear that God will lead us into situations that we cannot control". "In this supposedly realistic preference there is a subtle process of corruption: one attains mediocrity and tepidity (two forms of spiritual corruption); it is the slow but fatal sclerosis of the heart".

It is the so-called "spiritual worldliness" that constitutes for the Pope "the greatest danger, the most treacherous temptation, the one that comes back after all the others have been overcome". Worldliness "is nothing other than a radically anthropocentric attitude". "If this spiritual worldliness were to invade the Church and work to corrupt her, attacking her at the roots, it would be infinitely more disastrous than any other simply moral worldliness".

The text was turned into a humble book two years later, and in December of 2005, with Bergoglio already a Cardinal, it was re-published for a Archdiocesan Assembly[52]. It has a surprising relevance since it allows us to penetrate the profound thinking on the subject of corruption that the Pope alludes to almost constantly.

A good example is during the mass that he offered to all the Italian politicians on March 27, 2014. They had asked for months for the privilege to assist at one of his morning celebrations in Santa Marta. They finally organized one, but in the Basilica of St. Peter, so as to accommodate the five hundred parliament members and politicians that assisted that day. The meditation was inspired in the Gospel of St. Mathew, chapter 23, verse 27: "Woe to you, scribes and Pharisees, you hypocrites. You are like whitewashed tombs, which appear beautiful on the outside, but inside are full of dead men's bones and every kind of

[51] St. Peter Fabro, Jesuit saint, co-founder of the Society of Jesus, was born in France, on April 13,1506 and died in Rome on August 1, 1546; beatified by Pope Pius IX on September 5, 1872 and was canonized by Pope Francis on December 17, 2013.
[52] *Corrupción y pecado*, Editorial Claretiana, Buenos Aires, 2013.

filth". Bergoglio spoke of the "Pharisees", a kind of politician that, in the time of Jesus had "moved away from the people, enclosed in their own group, in the party and in internal divisions". In the text written in Córdoba, he had already defined the Pharisees as authors of a doctrine of fulfilling the law to the point of an exasperating nominalism, to such a point that it led them to despise sinners, whom they consider as those who broke a law that was crushing them".

"They turned their back on me", the Pope said citing Jeremiah, making a reference to the blindness to God on the part of the leaders of the people. "Their hearts are hardened, it was impossible for them to listen to the voice of the Lord... from sinful people that became corrupt".

And he added: "It is difficult for the corrupt to turn back; they are stuck in their ways".

Massimo Franco, vaticanist journalist and columnist of the *Corriere della Sera*, wrote at the time: "The homily had the same tone as the *Te Deum* that he gave in the Cathedral of Buenos Aires and that the Kirchner family did not want to hear". And he added: "In this Mass all the politicians felt like Kirchner".

Reflections of hope

The most important book that Bergoglio prepared during his stay in Córdoba is a collection of writings that are surprising because, with or without intention, they could be deep readings of the time of spiritual purification that he was undergoing at the time.

Of the thirteen articles that are part of this book only three were written integrally in Córdoba. One of them carries the title "Silence and Word", and is fruit of a reflection that Bergoglio wrote in December of 1990, "to help in discernment for a religious community that was going through difficult circumstances".

Knowing the intimate details of the situation of the Jesuits, during his government as provincial and also his peculiar relationship with many of them when he no longer was, it is quite significant that Bergoglio should have written these lines "destined to help in the discernment of a religious community that was going through difficult circumstances", as he himself clarifies when presenting the text.

Bergoglio had been in Córdoba six months, without great responsibilities and with time to think and go over his years as provincial and the circumstances that led him to his new assignment, which he accepted with obedience. The Pope explained to us that he did not see his assignment in Córdoba as an "unjust" decision. A religious cannot think in this way, the Pope explained; on the contrary, he found in it a "way of God". For this reason it is even more remarkable that in the first lines of the book, Bergoglio wrote "the disturbing movements and the trials that once in a while threaten our fraternal communion, which can become moments of grace that strengthen our lives in Christ and make it believable". It was a remark and advice for religious in crisis, but could also be a picture of his own history. Fr. Jorge dedicated himself many times during his life and especially during his time in Córdoba, in room five, in the courtyard, while resting under the vine, in the historic chapel or in front of the statue of his beloved St. Joseph.

He prayed a lot and perhaps was able to transform a "chastisement" into a time of God's "gifts". The human virtues that are acquired after much effort make people more coherent, and the theological virtues, received from the summit of the humble and generous presentation of Christ, transform the person into witnesses that are obviously more credible.

"When we find ourselves in some difficult situation, at times silence is not an act of virtue. It simply is imposed upon us without any choice" Bergoglio says in the first lines of the book. "In such situations, any rebellion or release that one may seek is stifled by an impotence that could be an unmerited grace: *the grace of silence*".

The future Pope explains that St. Ignatius of Loyola counselled that one should only speak of another's fault when it would avoid that fault infecting souls with a public error, so that it might help the person at fault to "lift himself up". But the saint does not explain when to speak. "When the moment arrives, if we are inspired by the Good Spirit, then we are 'moved' from within". That is why silence ends up being a gift of God. "The Gospels show Our Lady (the Virgin Mary) keeping silent, meditating everything in her heart", he points out, and then explains the deep meaning of that image of the Virgin Mary that stayed with him since his time in Germany, the Virgin Undoer of knots: "Her hands are untying what is 'disordered' (...) 'the knot of disobedience of Eve was untied by the obedience of Mary; what was tied by the virgin Eve through her incredulity, the Virgin Mary untied through her faith'. Disorder that is created in the string of life of men and entire peoples, by these two things: disobedience and incredulity. This is what Mary unties and she does it with the hands of obedience and faith". Fr. Jorge explains that he is not concerned so much with the knots, since "no one is a stranger to disorder", but rather that we try to untie them with our own strength. When this happens the knots become even more tangled and "confusion is born of our own self sufficiency (...) which is the moment where our own project is strengthened instead of God's work".

"When this happens in an institution (...) we can say that we are in an internal struggle", he says and places as an example Argentina, which is inclined to create internal struggles, particularly in politics, where "the greatness of service is lost in the stinginess of personal interests". But Bergoglio points out that this also happens in religious life.

"The mother of all evil in any community is ambition", reads another paragraph of Reflections of Hope. Citing St. Ignatius, Bergoglio describes ambition as "a desire to receive honors, to be considered important, to be esteemed and the guest of honor"; he also identifies it with "those who seek a socially accepted luxury" in order to compensate their low self-esteem and "prove to themselves that they can do great things". And, finally, the most subtle ambition is that which changes religious life into a "business"; which is the case of those who seek the promotion of the Church but "they do it choosing the way beforehand", "a redemption 'on my terms'".

In harmony with this reflection written in Córdoba, when elected Pope, in his first visit to the Basilica St. Paul Outside the Walls on April 15, 2013, Francis denounced the "idols" of the modern world, "ambition, 'careerism', desire for success, putting oneself at the center, the pretention of being the only masters of our lives".

A month later, before the General Assembly of the Italian Episcopal Conference, the Pope condemned arrogance and warned the bishops that "without vigilance", they could be seduced by "the ambition of a career, of money, and surrendering to the spirit of the world". In this way a pastor "becomes a functionary, a government employee, more worried about himself, or for the organization and the structures, than for the good of the people of God".

Twenty years earlier, Fr. Jorge wrote that "Jesus also had the temptation to 'do his own thing'". The temptation will say to him "if you are the Son of God", come down from the cross and break the seals of the tomb. He reveals the solution to the conflict: "the answer Jesus gives for this temptation is illuminating. He does not enter into a theological dialogue with the tempter …Only when the moment comes, when 'The hour' arrives, will he break the seals of all human control with his Resurrection. Jesus responds with faith and obedience".

For Bergoglio "there is another option that encourages division: the lack of poverty". Citing once again St. Ignatius, he understands poverty as a "support of religions, which conserves them in their being and discipline" a "wall of religion" before the temptations of the devil. For this reason he suggests, along with the saint, that if there are to be adjustments in this matter, it should only be to seek greater poverty. At this point he cites the holy founder of the Order: "…all those that make profession in this Society promise to not alter what the Constitutions say about poverty, unless it were deemed necessary by the Lord to make them more strict". Bergoglio explains that "the Ignatian expression is severe. A superficial reading of it could lead one to accuse St. Ignatius of being a fundamentalist. On this point St. Ignatius wants to tie the hands of future companions: if there is a change, it should be only to make the poverty stricter".

There are many examples of this counsel in his life. From the decision to only have two pairs of socks and the same pair of shoes that will be repaired over and over while he was a priest and provincial, to rejecting the use of luxury cars with a chauffeur while archbishop of Buenos Aires or changing the pontifical apartments with their ten rooms, grand halls and marble floors for a room much more austere (and more accessible) in the internal hotel of the Vatican, as Pope.

He is so convinced of his decision that for him "to let up in decisions of poverty" is one "of the most common signs of proselytism" a habit of the political parties "to bring in more people". "But always in these types of actions, something is surrendered, precisely because there is a kind of tradeoff that takes away interior freedom", the text points out. Another sign of proselytism is replacing "the Feast day of the Lord" for a "party, the looking for 'bread and circuses' that also takes place in religious life, to its detriment".

Ambition and the lack of poverty usually are accompanied by two temptations, Bergoglio will say, "suspicion and a type of attachment to the dark". He explains: "suspicion creates in my heart a kind of urge before anything in my brother that I do not understand (...) and everything that is not understood or controlled ends up being a menace". The difference with a person who lacks confidence is that the latter "seeks the light somewhat, he feels himself weak, broken, and tries to survive taking light from whomever at the moment offers it to him (...). On the other hand the suspicious person has fallen in love with this attitude of not wanting things to be clarified because his life consists in confusing the scheme with reality". For this reason Fr. Jorge counsels to not stay long in the company of the suspicious.

On March 9, 2014, Pope Francis surprised the world getting on a bus with another eighty-two religious, Cardinals, bishops and priests; and travelled twenty miles to the Italian town of Ariccia to do a week of prayer with the Roman Curia. For the first time, this typical preparation that the Pope and Curia make during Lent to prepare for Holy Week was done outside the Vatican. It was also unheard of that the Pope travel in a bus, that each of the participants pay the expenses of the retreat from their own pocket, and even less that the Holy Father decided to celebrate his first year as Pope making the Spiritual Exercises.

As has been said throughout this book, the Spiritual Exercises are, for many, the most powerful weapon that St. Ignatius of Loyola left to his Society. He wrote them after spending eleven months in deep prayer in the town of Manresa and they consist in a method of prayer that lasts a month, although today they are also given in less time. They are based fundamentally in a re-reading of the Word of God, essentially what its meditation provokes in the soul of each person (which words "touched" him, which have given him joy or what emotion was provoked by them). And beginning with this "emotion" to discover what God is saying to each person. The objective is to discover, with the help of a Spiritual Director, and through a personal relationship with God, what direction to take in the decisions of one's life.

St. Ignatius says that his Exercises are "a way of examining the conscious, of meditating, of reasoning, of contemplating; every way of preparing and disposing the soul, to take away all the disordered affections (attachments, egoisms, etc.) with the end of seeking and finding the divine will". And if anything distinguishes the Jesuits, it should be precisely their ability to "discern", their capacity to decipher "the plan of God".

In 1990, Bergoglio wrote about this and underlined the fact that one can accept this plan or not; and he says that one way of not accepting God's plan is to try to "negotiate". "One looks to where one wants to arrive and in that direction, negotiating, one seeks to get as far as possible. It is a human means", the text points out. "In a negotiation there is a 'give and take', that is not always possible when one is dealing with God. There are things that one cannot negotiate and there are things that one cannot give in on, at least at the time". For this, St. Ignatius "submits all human means to the rule of 'in as much as'", which supposes a "vocation", a calling, to choose. He will explain more clearly that "it is not in the end my decision, but the decision of what God wants for me now. It goes beyond human prudence and reaches wisdom".

Bergoglio says, almost on a personal note: "When one enters the Society he renounces personal interests (...). If one renounces, necessarily one passes through the crucible of the cross and of abandonment to Divine Will". When we asked the Holy Father if in those paragraphs he was speaking about his own experience in Córdoba, he responded no. Yet, his reflections could well explain the submission and the obedience with which he faced a situation that many considered "humanly unjust". The future Pope will write: the renouncement of personal interest "will be a sign that one is seeking the good of the whole over that of the part".

"St. Ignatius bequeathed us the wisdom of discernment so as to rescue the will of God from the middle of life's ambiguities", he will later say. And he adds: "to know how to read the history of the faith, and to live it coherently, wearies the heart" that advances in the pilgrimage of faith. For Bergoglio this fatigue is the "night of faith", which he relates to the "interior darkness" of which St. Teresa of the Child Jesus, another of his favorite saints, speaks of in the book *Story of a Soul*: "When I want to rest my heart, wearied by the darkness that surrounds it, through the strengthening remembrance of the future eternal life... (chapter IX). It is inevitable to think that this is the same experience Bergoglio lived through at the time.

When one wants to read and live history anticipating the triumph "through other quicker means, through the means of a negotiated shortcut", without passing through the cross, "then one falls into *triumphalism*", Bergoglio wrote. "The Pharisee, on his feet, before God, is the image of the triumphalist: 'I thank you Lord, because I am not like this other man'". Triumphalists "like progress (...) but in the end they are persons that flee from the cross". Opposite to them, the author puts as an example Mary at the foot of the cross: "How heroic at that moment the obedience of faith... Look how she 'abandons herself in God' without reserve, 'lending homage of understanding and of the will to Him Whose ways are inscrutable!... By means of her faith Mary is perfectly united to Christ in his stripping of himself".

"There is a subtle form of triumphalism which is spiritual worldliness." Bergoglio alerts us. He will say it again when he was elected Pope, when he warned that one must not fall into "worldliness". The explication of these words are found in the writings of 1990, in which he cites the French Cardinal Henri de Lubac: "It is nothing other than a radically anthropocentric attitude (...) If this spiritual worldliness were to invade the Church and work to corrupt her attacking her at her roots, it would be infinitely more disastrous than any other simply moral worldliness; even that infamous leprosy that in certain moment of history disfigures so cruelly the beloved spouse, when religion seemed to bring scandal into the sanctuary itself and, represented by a libertine Pope, buried the face of Jesus Christ beneath precious stones, falseness and spies".

"We mustn't admit of dialogues with the world as Eve did with the serpent. Only Jesus comes away victorious after speaking with the devil, the world of the flesh (...). We ought not to despise any brother, no matter how worldly. We must love him and pray for him in silence, inviting the angels to come to his company", counsels Antonio Orbe, citing the then Fr. Jorge. He explained that "one has to get the evil spirit to reveal himself", but this "can only be done through the power of Jesus". For that, he says, "one must make room so that Jesus can, in concrete situations, realize his judgments make room for the light of God... there is only one way... emptying oneself, the *kenosis*. Be silent, pray, humble oneself... here there is no room for 'negotiating'; one either embraces it or rejects it", the text says. Bergoglio, who passed his time of purification wrote that when one "allows himself to be put on the cross with Jesus, aside from the obvious 'thrashing about', it is possible to fall —going over the thoughts about how 'they are mistreating me'— into a sort of spiritual victimization, and so one feels as though they are imitating the Lord and begins to feel sorry for himself: in that case there is no love and of course it is a subtle step toward pride".

In each paragraph there can be found references relative to the

210

moment of trial Bergoglio was living during his second period in
Córdoba. His attitude of recollection, silence, study and continual
prayer feed the theory of a dark night, although he insists on calling it
"purification". The Virgin Undoer of Knots must have worked without
rest with the insistent prayer of one of his most devoted sons who six
months after arriving at his exile in Córdoba, wrote: "In moments of
darkness and great trial, when the confusion and the 'knots' are unable
to be untied and things do not become clear, then one has to be silent:
the meekness of silence will reveal us to be weaker, and then it will be
the devil who will be encouraged and show himself in the light,
revealing his true intentions, no longer as an angel of light but rather
completely revealed". That is when the true "dimensions of the war are
revealed and who are the true protagonists". "This war is not yours but
God's", Bergoglio will say. And he will explain later: "When one gets
involved in a war of God, you end up badly. In the silence of the cross
we are only asked to protect the wheat and not that we go around
pulling up the weeds".

In that meditation destined to "help in the discernment of a
religious community that is passing through difficult circumstances",
he counsels that "in the internal struggles one should not enter because
animosity reigns... it is not a question of posing the question as
between good and evil. One easily forgets that on the cross, together
with the Just one, there was also an unjust man who was saved at the
eleventh hour". One has to choose God, he says. And he adds "While
we wait for the Lord's coming to calm the storm, we should ask
ourselves and others questions that imply a 'sign of hope' more than of
'certainties'".

In Him alone we place our hope

"What impressed you most about the reading of the *History of
the Popes* of Von Pastor, that today seems prophetic?", we asked Pope
Francis, in a phone conversation. From the other end of the line, he
answered firmly: "Without a doubt the figure of Mother Church".

Undoubtedly, reading this work during those years in Córdoba, impressed Fr. Jorge so much that he cited it in the second text of the most important book compiled during his time of purification. There, in a profound analysis on hope, the future Pope wrote something that could shed light on the direction his pontificate is taking: "Thus one understands that all through history, the true reforms of the Church, that which brings life to where it is needed, come from within the Church and not from the outside. Reforms from God come from where one can only hope against all hope".

Bergoglio reached this conclusion analyzing "the biblical experience of human life in history". He mentioned it in a conversation regarding this biography: "I was always impressed and liked working with biblical theology, especially that which deals with the Promise to the Covenant, up until the final encounter". Bergoglio had written in *Reflections of hope* that "all through Salvation history there are two groups of people: those that hope and put their strength in the Lord of the Promise and those who do not and seek a solution 'this side of the Promise". These are the two types of people (...) the first, even in the midst of problems and contradictions, are capable of maintaining hope —and even happiness— and they are capable of greeting the promises from afar. The others are discouraged with God because things are not going well, and they blame God for it".

"There is a tight relationship between hope, trials and the promise. It is precisely in the trials where hope emerges, for this reason we are encouraged to be, with the joy of hope, constant in tribulations, perseverant in prayer", the text states. "And this is the case because hope is in the play between the promise, failure, tribulation, temptation and retreat". Fr. Jorge explains that just like other virtues, hope is tempted in three ways: "According to Theophany the Recluse, the Devil tempts us with three horses. First, it begins with our passions. Second, it takes the form of an angel of light. Third, openly and revealed". He assures us that "the clearest and easiest to discover is the despair because of failure", where what is valid is "reality", "but understood as the result of the free play of the material world". More subtlety "and as an angel of light" is the temptation to pessimism. "Another bad way of handling failure is —in the midst of pain— to alienate oneself in any way that drugs the soul". The text continues: "one is able to breathe any air at all if it allows me to forget the failure".

"Hope is a theological virtue, and thus, it is given to us. We are incapable of obtaining it by ourselves. One has to ask for it", Bergoglio explains in his book published in 1991. "For this reason only by contemplating the Mystery of Christ do we get an idea of what theological hope means, which is revealed particularly when the circumstances remove all human hope, and one can only make room for the Lord to break forth 'against all hope'". In this way "the phenomenon of a 'descent' comes about, a descent of potentialities of achieving what is hoped for. The Precursor felt in his flesh this 'diminishing', his disciples were witnesses to this waning of human hope... 'the greatest man born of woman' ended by giving up his head", writes Bergoglio.

"From the moment of the Incarnation the Son of God did nothing other than 'descend', until he was the dead body of Jesus in the arms of Mary. "He is the 'Pietà' of God, that first was promise and now is consolidated in reality... She receives her Son, dead in the flesh...but, just as in the day of the Annunciation, she is receiving God, because the dead body of Jesus is not only a cadaver: therein lies the *suppositum divinum*' (the divine substratum)".

For the author, who today is Pope, the challenge is "to contemplate this 'degradation' and try to discover something there that does not appear" since the "the divine is hidden". "One must believe in the mystery of the strength of God in the *summum* of weakness, keeping silent before the greatest descent of all defeat: death".

In this way, Bergoglio points out that Holy Saturday is a day of silence for the Church, "and yet —he adds—, even here we are asked to have hope... hope in the victory. This unheard of victory, unimaginable, when the hearts of the disciples have already accepted the failure; when the defeat itself was guarded by soldiers and sealed" in the Holy Sepulcher. Faced with this, the Pope raises an alert: "Our heart, before the dead body of Jesus, can be tempted". The first way is "accepting as definitive the "sealing of the tomb": it is civil death... another temptation is to demand right away a resurrection ... another more subtle temptation would consist in accepting death with a certain condescension but not assuming it entirely". For this reason, ending his book, he invites us to look upon "the image of Mary with the dead body of her Son in her arms", And he exhorts us: "There we can say 'I know that my redeemer lives'... it is there we learn 'to keep firm in the confession of hope, because the author of the Promise is faithful', and there too, learn to proclaim, even if it be mumbling it and contrary to all human sentiment, that 'hope does not fail us'".

The Salesian roots and the catholic school

Many of the Cordobeses who participated in the Mass Bergoglio presided, in the Church of Society of Jesus, during those years might have asked themselves who was this Fr. Enrique Pozzoli that the Jesuit always named in the intercessions, after the consecration, together with the other faithful departed. "He was a worker in the Reign of God", Fr. Bergoglio would have responded if he were asked.

In the end, this name incarnated the profound influence of the Salesian charism in the family and in the formation of the future Pope. The key to understanding it is found in another of the texts Bergoglio wrote during his time in Córdoba.

On October 20, 1990, Fr. Jorge sat down, one more time, before his desk in room 5 of the Mayor Residence of the Society. He arranged his typewriter and typed: "Without writing an outline, I am writing what comes into my head".

It was the first of two letters that he sent to Fr. Cayetano Bruno, famous Salesian priest and a prizewinning historian[53] who had asked the ex-provincial to explain what his relationship with the Salesians was. The texts recounts the intimate relationship the whole Bergoglio family had with the Salesians, already seen in the first chapter. Their closeness to his grandparents and his father in Turin, Italy (city where the work of Don Bosco was born); the visits his father made to the Salesian house on Solís street, every time he travelled to Buenos Aires as an accountant of the family business in Paraná; the almost familiar relationship with the Salesian Enrique Pozzoli, who was his father's spiritual director, married his parents, baptized Jorge Bergoglio and three of his siblings. In the letter he also details how Fr. Pozzoli helped him discern his priestly vocation and how he was a frequent guest to dinner (of ravioli) in this family that had adopted him as a spiritual father. Pope Francis wrote in that letter in 1990, when he was a Jesuit priest who could never have imagined where God was leading him, "If my family today lives seriously their Christian life, it is because of him (Fr. Enrique Pozzoli). He was able to plant and strengthen the foundations of Catholic life", Bergoglio wrote. Bergoglio also attributes the religious vocations of his cousin Julio Picchi, his Jesuit nephew José Luis and his niece Maria Inés, Slave of the Sacred Heart to the influence of Pozzoli. For this reason he is thankful for this priest who "left a spiritual inheritance". "Every day —wrote the future Pope— I name him (Pozzoli) in the Divine Office when I pray for the dead... and believe me I enjoy the feeling of gratitude that the Lord grants me".

The second letter that Bergoglio sent to Cayetano Bruno puts an emphasis on his time as a Salesian student. Bergoglio spent the last portion of high school in the Wilfred Barón of the Holy Angels School, in Ramos Mejía. This text reveals, aside from his experiences, the characteristics that in his mind every catholic school should have. It may be because of this influence that when he began a profound

---

[53]Fr. Cayetano Bruno was born in Córdoba on July 23, 1912 and died in Buenos Aires on July 13, 2003. He was a Salesian priest, university professor in Argentina, Spain and Italy; prolific writer and investigator. For three decades he was member to the National Academy of History and wrote a brilliant and exhaustive History of the Church in Argentina, in 12 volumes. He met Bergoglio when he took office as provincial of the Society of Jesus and maintained with him an interesting exchange of letters.

reformation of the Formation House during his time as provincial, Fr. Jorge was sure that they accused him of "being a pro-Salesian Jesuit".

In 1949 Bergoglio was in sixth grade as a boarding student, under the direction of Fr. Emilio Cantarutti. For him, life in the school "was everything". He describes it: "By awakening consciousness of the truth of things, the school created a catholic culture that was not at all sanctimonious or in the clouds. The studies, the social values of living in community, the social references of the most needy (I remember having to deprive myself of things in order to give to others more in need than myself), the sports, the competition, the piety....everything was real, and everything formed habits that, together, formed a cultural form of life. We lived in the world but opened to the transcendence of another world". As part of this "catholic culture", Bergoglio explains that in this Salesian school he learned to study, to compete well, to "feel well", to have "a manly piety", "love for purity", creativity, to manage diverse crisis as well as the "sense of sin".

According to his description, the school routine included Mass early in the morning, later breakfast, study, classes, recreation and a simple but "key" moment for Pope Francis: the 'Good Night' of the school director. "Everything was done with a reason", the letter explains. "I learned there, almost unconsciously, to seek the meaning of things. One of the key moments (...) was the 'Good Night'. It was an activity that only the director did, although sometimes the inspector (Fr. Miguel Raspanti) did it, and one of them, at the beginning of October of 1949, particularly marked the young Bergoglio: "He had travelled to Córdoba because his mother had died... When he returned he spoke to us about death. Now, after almost fifty four years, I realize that this little night time talk is the reference point for all my life after that with regards to death. That night, without being afraid, I felt the fact that someday I would die, and that seemed entirely normal to me". Another talk that he remembered in great detail was that in which Fr. Cantarutti spoke to him about the need to pray to Our Lady to confirm our vocation. I remember that that night I went back to the dormitory praying intensely (...) and from that night on I never went to sleep without praying. It was a moment that was psychologically good to give a meaning to the day and to life".

"In High School I learned how to study", the letter continues. They had "study hours" daily where silence was supposed to reign. These were vital for him to create a habit of concentration, to dominate dispersion, which at this age is very strong. Sports were included in this pedagogical play: "We played a lot and well (...) there was a certain importance given to competition whether in sports or academics: we were taught to compete well and in a Christian spirit".

Another key dimension was "educating the sentiments". Bergoglio wrote: "A dimension that grew a lot in the years after high school was my capability to feel well; and I realized that a foundation was set in the year of boarding school (...) I am not referring to being emotional, but rather sentiment as a value of the heart. To not be afraid to feel and to tell oneself what one is feeling".

The "education in piety" was also underscored by Pope Francis. "A special mention of the devotion to Our Lady" that reaches from the consciousness of having a Mother in Heaven who takes care of me, to the praying of the three Hail Marys or the Rosary (...) they also inspired in us a respect and love of the Holy Father, and it remained ingrained in us".

Very united to love and devotion of the Virgin Mary was the "love of purity". Bergoglio will say: "They taught me to love purity without any kind of obsessive teaching. There was no sexual obsession in the school. I found more sexual obsession later on in other educators or psychologists that made a big deal of a 'laissez-passer' attitude (but that in the end they interpreted conducts in a Freudian key which smelled sex everywhere)".

The students also had times for hobbies such as arts and crafts, choir, theater, taxidermy, and sports championships all of which for Bergoglio, helped "educate in creativity". Finally Pope Francis emphasized the way the educators faced the adolescent crisis of their students. "They made us feel that they could have confidence in us, that they loved us; they knew how to listen, they gave us good, appropriate advice and they defended us from both rebellion and melancholy".

All these things contributed, for Bergoglio, to a "catholic culture" that was formed and transmitted. In that letter to Fr. Bruno, he underscores that a key to this culture was that "truth was never negotiated". He wrote regarding this: "The most typical case was with sin. It is part of the catholic culture the sense of sin (...). One later can be rebellious or atheist but in the end there is a sense of sin etched in the soul: a truth that cannot be thrown away so as to make things easier". The final paragraph of this letter that enumerates keys to what Francis considers characteristics of a truly catholic school, criticizes the possible capitulations that one can choose in seeking a "pastoral option". Bergoglio was saddened by the news that he received at the time of a Salesian priest who had confirmed his intention "to leave some schools in the hands of laypeople". But it was not simply the fact of letting the schools go that saddened Bergoglio, who in fact made the same determination with the Del Salvador University years before as provincial. What really upset him was that the religious congregation made the decision because "the young Salesians do not want to work in schools, they are not drawn by this apostolate".

Fr. Jorge responds to this vehemently making reference to priest teachers he had in school. He points out with certain irony: "I don't know if they 'were making gestures of insertion' (his Salesian teachers), but I do know that they wore themselves out every day and they had no time for a siesta. If these men that I knew in High School were able to create a 'catholic culture' it was because they had faith. They believed in Jesus Christ, and —a little because of their faith and little because they were audacious— they were able to 'preach', with their words, with their lives, with their work. They were unafraid to slap us with the language of the cross of Jesus, which is shame and crazyness for others". His words are severe and they remind one of the words he will use much later as archbishop, as cardinal or as Pope. For Bergoglio this "pastoral option" hid a claudication or a reductionism in the basic principles of Christianity: "I wonder: when a work languishes and loses its taste and its capability to leaven the bread, might it not be that it is because Jesus Christ was replaced by other types of options:

psychologists, sociologists, pastoralists? (…) I am always worried by the fact that —in order to make radical social insertions— we abandon our connection to the living Christ and to the consequent insertion into other areas, including education, which creates a catholic culture":

The writings of Fr. Bergoglio in Córdoba are already twenty-two years old. And in a certain way one can say they grew with him. But they have become best sellers just in the last few months, since the papal election of their author. It is to be expected. That unknown "morning" author who was going through a process of interior purification in a cold room in Córdoba, has become the most listened to man in the world, whose words —at times— are taken almost as though they were "word of God".

CHAPTER 7

THE STONE THAT THE BUILDERS REJECTED

A stony destiny

It is Fall in Córdoba and the vine of the courtyard in the Jesuit residence begins to lose its leaves. The weak rays of the sun struggle to warm up the morning and Fr. Jorge Bergoglio, who looks out at the patio through the window of his humble room n. 5, feels the desire to pray. He takes from his well-ordered desk the Breviary, the book of prayer that always accompanies him, wherever he goes, to pray during the different hours of the day. He goes to the Domestic Chapel where he feels "protected" by the mantle of Our Lady. He looks up at the arched ceiling of the historical chapel and meditated, one more time the little but significant image painted there of the Mother of God who sheltered her Jesuits. He whispers the phrase written below the picture: "Monstra te esse matrem" ("Show yourself as mother").

Bergoglio opens the breviary that contains, ordered, the seven moments of prayer of each day: "Office of Readings" for the dawn; "Lauds" for the beginning of each day; "Terse", "Sext" and "None" for midmorning, midday and midafternoon respectively; and "Vespers" for the evening, and finally the one called "Compline" that is prayed before sleep.

He looks at his watch and decides to pray "Terse". He makes the sign of the cross and prays, mentally, the initial invocation:

220

—Oh God, come to my assistance. Lord, make haste to help me.

The "Glory be to the Father..." follows and then a religious hymn that the priest meditates in silence:

—Spirit of God, Who fills the earth/the minds of men bathed in your light/ You who are light of God, divine fire/ fill every man with the strength of your cross.

The Jesuit, fifty-one years old, who is passing a time of trial, of purification, asks for the strength of the cross. What is the strength of the cross?

The antiphon of psalm 117 that the prayer of the Terse hour proposes answers to the transcendental question: "Christ, once risen from the dead, no longer dies. Alleluia". The strength of the cross is the resurrection of Christ.

Bergoglio prays the psalm. Like many others, it is attributed to King David and is a beautiful praise of God. And the future Pope, just as every praying believer knows, he is not praying alone. He knows that all over the world, in communities and monasteries, the same prayer is being offered:

"Give thanks to the Lord for he is good, / for his love endures forever./(...) I called to the Lord in my distress; / he answered and freed me./(...) I will thank you for you have answered / and you are my savior. / The stone which the builders rejected / has become the corner stone. / This is the work of the Lord, / a marvel in our eyes."

He doesn't know or suspect it, but in these last verses of the psalm some will find, years later, an explanation of his history: the stone that the constructors have rejected has become the corner stone.

Even though Pope Francis cannot accept the parallelism because of his humility, it is not difficult to notice that in the life of Jorge Bergoglio there is a stony path, a continuity of episodes that in some way appeared as a rejection that later ended up being something like the corner stone.

He felt that way when after entering the Jesuit Novitiate in Pueyrredon, his first Novice Master, Fr. Gaviña, suggested to him that he leave, that he abandon the Society. After some years, without looking for it, that novice who was close to being "rejected" was elected provincial, superior, head, corner stone of the Order in Argentina.

Later, that priest who had exercised a complicated mission as provincial with fidelity to the Church, found himself years later, rejected by the superiors who sent him chastised to Córdoba without any important pastoral responsibilities. From there, without seeking it, he was chosen for a larger mission, that of being a bishop, apostle, head of a portion of the Church, again a corner stone.

Almost in silence, the auxiliary bishop became coadjutor bishop and finally archbishop of the most important diocese of Argentina. John Paul II made him a Cardinal and shortly thereafter, the prelates of Argentina elected him president of the Episcopal Conference, "political" authority of the Church in the country, again "corner stone".

Then the time came for him to be rejected by the political power. President Nestor Kirchner, the "builder" of the so-called "national and popular project", rejected him as a pastor and identified him as an enemy, opposition, and almost the entire triumphant group of kirchnerist militants, including his wife Maria Cristina Fernandez, who was later president, joined in the diatribe against him.

Jorge Bergoglio had begun to reject himself when, after presenting his resignation as archbishop of Buenos Aires (as all bishops do when they reach seventy-five years of age), planned his retirement as a "builder" or worker in the Kingdom, and chose for it the humble room n. 13 of the priest's residence in the neighborhood of Flores in Buenos Aires, where he was convinced he would spend the last years of his life.

But the stone that all these builders, including Bergoglio had rejected, became the corner stone, the one that supports the arch of history, the stone upon which God builds his Church.

Fr. Angel Rossi agrees with this vision: "If someone had to choose a motto for Pope Francis, aside from the fact that he chose in his freedom to maintain '*Miserando atque eligendo*', it would be difficult to find a more *a propos* text than the psalm that speaks of the 'stone that the builders rejected is now the corner stone'. This defines what Bergoglio lived through with surprising clarity".

The reference to the rock that has been rejected and later converted into the corner stone is not only in the Davidic psalms of the Old Testament. It is also mentioned in the New Testament, the "parable of the unfaithful vineyard workers" that the Gospel writers put in the mouth of Jesus himself[54]. This parable speaks about the chosen People, the promises of God, of the leaders that lead them and how they mistook the way; but over all, it speaks about how they rejected the gifts God Himself was giving them all through history, even the unthinkable: that God became man.

For the Catholic Church, the Bible, the Gospels are not simply historical stories, but "living word". The Catechism explains that "God is the author of the Holy Scriptures" since the truths that it contains "were given by inspiration of the Holy Spirit". "God has inspired the human authors the sacred books", explains the text that is a collection of Catholic doctrine and was promoted by John Paul II. But this "Word" of God is not a dead letter but, through faith, becomes a source of life, of truth and of discernment even for the Christians of the 20th century.

---

[54] This Gospel text says: "There was a landowner who planted a vineyard, put a hedge around it, dug a wine press in it, and built a tower. Then he leased it to tenants and went on a journey. When vintage time drew near, he sent his servants to the tenants to obtain his produce. But the tenants seized the servants and one they beat, another they killed, and a third they stoned. Again he sent other servants, more numerous than the first ones, but they treated them in the same way. Finally, he sent his son to them, thinking, 'They will respect my son.' But when the tenants saw the son, they said to one another, 'This is the heir. Come, let us kill him and acquire his inheritance.' They seized him, threw him out of the vineyard, and killed him. What will the owner of the vineyard do to those tenants when he comes?" They answered him, "He will put those wretched men to a wretched death and lease his vineyard to other tenants who will give him the produce at the proper times." Jesus said to them, "Did you never read in the scriptures: 'The stone that the builders rejected has become the cornerstone; by the Lord has this been done, and it is wonderful in our eyes'? Therefore, I say to you, the kingdom of God will be taken away from you and given to a people that will produce its fruit. (The one who falls on this stone will be dashed to pieces; and it will crush anyone on whom it falls.)" When the chief priests and the Pharisees heard his parables, they knew that he was speaking about them. And although they were attempting to arrest him, they feared the crowds, for they regarded him as a prophet." (Matthew 21:33-46).

From this font Pope Francis drinks, as he has done throughout his life, each time that, as a child, he knelt before the tabernacle with his *Nonna* Rosa, or later on as a teenager, novice and priest, with important responsibilities or not. Even in the times of shadows and trials that he suffered, in prayer, in the Domestic Chapel of the Society of Jesus in Córdoba.

For the Catholic faith, it is the Holy Spirit, the third person of the Holy Trinity, Father, Son and Holy Spirit, Who governs the Church. Most of all when there is "*sede vacante*", where no human exercises the power of the keys of Peter – the apostle whom Jesus called "rock" upon which He would build his Church – because the Pope has died or has resigned, as happened with Benedict XVI, Joseph Ratzinger.

It is this divine Spirit that moves in each of the Cardinals that participates in the Conclave, so that, in a deeply prayerful atmosphere, pour out all their experience, their knowledge and vision of the Church as well as of the world, in order to propose a man to assume the immense responsibility of being the pope.

This is what the Church teaches. According to this doctrine, then, it was the Holy Spirit, the One who lead the Cardinals to elect the one among them "who came from the end of the world" to guide the People of God, to be the St. Peter (*Petrus*, rock in Latin) of the beginning of the 21st century. In the same Catholic doctrine it is understood that a vocation is precisely that, a *vocatum*, a call, and that a good son of God follows the steps that, through discernment, God Himself is pointing out for his life.

From this logic and in the light of things that are already history, it is not crazy to think that the rock that God had in mind to build and guide his Church at this time, at one time was "rejected" in a kind of cordobese "exile" that many considered "humanly unjust", but that Bergoglio himself accepted as the "will of God" so that he would be interiorly purified.

The intervention of Quarracino

Why should we not think that this rejected stone, after spending two years in the shadows, was unexpectedly rescued by Cardinal Antonio Quarracino[55] to be his right hand man, and later archbishop of Buenos Aires, then Cardinal Primate of Argentina, and finally, Pontiff of the Roman Catholic Apostolic Church?

"I knew Quarracino when I was Provincial of the Jesuits and he was bishop of La Plata", Francis told us. "He called me to consult some things about the Society of Jesus because we were working on a project. I met him there. Later, when I was in the Del Salvador University, he asked me to preach the spiritual exercises to the seminarians of the diocese of La Plata. To the theologians. So he came to see me about this".

Years later, in 1985, when Bergoglio was the rector of the Maximo College, in San Miguel, Buenos Aires, an International Congress on the Evangelization of the Culture and the Inculturization of the Gospel was organized. Quarracino participated in the event invited by the Jesuit priest and the Cardinal returned the favor, a few years later, inviting Bergoglio to preach a retreat to priests and bishops in Buenos Aires. Quarracino participated in this retreat and left convinced that the preacher had all the qualities and virtues to be a bishop. He was proved right with time. The intervention of Quarracino in the life of Bergoglio, and effectively, in the life of the Church is a paradox. This is because the Cardinal passed away leaving a less than favorable impression on many; an image probably exaggerated by the extensive diffusion by the media of some of the more controversial statements of the Cardinal about homosexual persons, as well as because of his relationship with some dark figures of

---

[55] Antonio Quarracino was born in the city of Pollica, in Salerno, Italy in August 1923, but at four years old came to Buenos Aires with his parents, where he grew up. He was ordained a priest in 1945 and in 1963 was designated bishop of the city 9 de Julio, in the province of Buenos Aires, by Pope John XXIII. He participated in Vatican II. Later he became bishop of Avellaneda, of La Plata, and finally of Buenos Aires. He was created Cardinal in 1991 and presided the Argentine Episcopal Conference. He died in Buenos Aires on February 28 of 1998.

political and economic power of menemism.

At the same time, Quarracino had an important participation in the life of the Latin-American Church in the second half of the 20th century, especially in what had to do with the application of Vatican II, the constant concern for social justice and the dialogue with Judaism.

Few remember it, but Quarracino was placed in charge of the investigation (apostolic visit) that the Vatican had called for in 1979 in El Salvador that cleared up the correct —and in the end sacrificial— actions and words with which the then archbishop of San Salvador, Oscar Arnulfo Romero faced the human rights violations during the civil war in this country. A year after the Quarracino's visit, on March 24, 1980, bishop Romero was assassinated by a military hit man, in spite of the fact that Quarracino had stated that he had never known a bishop as "holy" as Romero. As a result of the investigation, released a year later, Quarracino had recommended naming an apostolic administrator with full authority to coordinate the political matters in the Archdiocese of San Salvador, that had many divisive elements, but with Romero as archbishop in spiritual matters.

Without a doubt those documents that Quarracino prepared are among those being analyzed in the cause for beatification of Bishop Romero, which those close to Bergoglio say Pope Francis wants to promote.

Quarracino was a friend of another man very respected and loved by Bergoglio: the deceased Cardinal Eduardo Francisco Pironio[56], whose cause for beatification is also being promoted. Various ecclesiastical sources do not doubt that Pironio may have been one of those in Rome who supported the petition made by his friend Quarracino before Pope John Paul II to name the Jesuit Bergoglio as auxiliary bishop of Buenos Aires.

On May 13, 1992, Bergoglio was in his room in the Major

---

[56] Eduardo Francisco Pironio was born in the city of Nueve de Julio in the province of Buenos Aires, on December 3, 1920, and died at the Vatican on February 5,1998. He was the sixth argentine made cardinal and the first to occupy an important office in the Roman Curia.

Residence of the Society of Jesus in Córdoba, when they told him, from the front desk that he had an important phone call. The then apostolic nuncio in Argentina, bishop Ubaldo Calabresi, who habitually consulted the Jesuit about priests who were being considered for episcopal consecration, told him that he wanted to meet with him in the Córdoba airport, where he was going to quickly pass through.

In the book *El Jesuita*, Bergoglio himself describes the meeting: "Calabresi used to call me to consult about a few priests that were candidates to be bishop. One day he called and told me the consultation this time should be personal. Since the airline company had a flight Buenos Aires – Córdoba – Mendoza and back again, he asked me if we could meet at the airport while the plane went from Córdoba to Mendoza. So we talked there; he asked me about some serious matters and when the plane, already back from Mendoza was close to taking off to return to Buenos Aires and they were calling the passengers to present themselves at the gate, he mentioned: 'Ah…one more thing… you have been named auxiliary bishop of Buenos Aires, and the designation will be made public on the 20th'. That's the way he told me".

He did not know, but Antonio Quarracino had asked insistently that the Vatican designate Bergoglio as auxiliary bishop of the most important archdiocese of Argentina. The Cardinal from Buenos Aires understood that Bergoglio had acted firmly as well as prudently during his term as provincial in the Society of Jesus. He recognized his intelligence, his capability to govern and his deep spiritual life.

According to a the testimony obtained from a reliable source, it was in late 1991 when Quarracino asked Pope John Paul II for the appointment of four auxiliary bishops, since after the promotion to different Argentine dioceses of the bishops who previously had that office, there were only two auxiliary bishops left for the huge jurisdiction of Buenos Aires: Monsignor Eduardo Mirás and Monsignor Mario Serra. As required by canonical norms, Quarracino presented to the Apostolic Nuncio, Ubaldo Calabresi, four short lists of three names, in other words, 12 names of priests who could be bishops. In one of those Father Bergoglio was included.

On February 26 in 1992 two new auxiliary bishops were designated for the Archdiocese of Buenos Aires: Rubén Frassia and Héctor Aguer.   The following 20th of May the other two were appointed: Raúl Rossi and Jorge Bergoglio.

How did Bergoglio react to the news? Did he call any of his siblings in Buenos Aires with the news? Did he mention it to any of his brother Jesuits who lived in the community in Córdoba?

"When I returned to the Residence —Pope Francis remembered recently— it was late, around 8 p.m. I remember that I had dinner, and Fr. Castellano was there with Fr. Boasso, who was the superior of the house. The two were chatting at the table. I ate a little and then went to my room. I did not say anything until the news was made public some days later. I said nothing. It is not difficult for me to keep quiet, but it is no merit of mine".

In fact, since the pontifical secret was well kept, the news was publically known a week later, on May 20, 1992. Pope John Paul II had named Jorge Mario Bergoglio titular bishop of Auca and auxiliary bishop of Buenos Aires. It was the end of his "exile" in Córdoba.

Those last days, before leaving the city where his ignatian vocation dawned and where it was put to the test, Bergoglio went to greet the local archbishop, Cardinal Primatesta.   Francis himself remembered that at the end of the meeting, when he was leaving the chancery, a young auxiliary bishop approached him and Primatesta introduced him. It was Carlos Ñáñez, the now archbishop of Córdoba, who in this way met and greeted for the first time the man who today is his friend, brother in the episcopacy and Holy Father in the faith.

A "man to man" bishop

On June 27, 1992, in the Metropolitan Cathedral of Buenos Aires in front of Plaza de Mayo, Bergoglio received episcopal ordination by the laying on of hands of Cardinal Quarracino and the co-consecrating, the Nuncio Calabresi and the Bishop of Mercedes-Luján, Emilio Ogñénovich.

Picture 27 — Cardinal Quarracino and Bishop
Bergoglio, the day of his episcopal ordination.

When we asked Pope Francis why he had chosen the Nuncio and Ogñénovich, he explained: "When I had to choose two co-consecrating bishops I chose those who symbolized the Virgin and the Pope. That is why I chose Ogñénovich, Bishop of Mercedes-Luján, where there is the Shrine of the Virgin Mary, and the nuncio Calabresi, who was the representative of the Pope."

Over time, Cardinal Bergoglio would have an important and courageous gesture towards Ogñénovich, one of the most criticized bishops because of his political connections with president Menem and his environment. Bergoglio had met Ogñénovich "in passing", years before, when he lived in the Maximo College of San Miguel, Buenos Aires, and Ogñénovich went there to make his confession, as some bishops used to do during meetings of the Argentinian Episcopal Conference gathered at Casa María Auxiliadora of San Miguel.

However, the Pope himself recalls that the first formal conversation with Ogñénovich was when he invited him to be his co-consecrator as the head of the diocese where the Patroness of Argentina is.

The brave and charitable gesture of Bergoglio would come years later, when Ogñénovich after resigning for having reached the age of 75 years, moved to a Buenos Aires hotel owned by a friend of the bishop. When Bergoglio learned that Ogñénovich was living in a hotel, he called him and invited him to come to live in the Curia of Buenos Aires.

The Pope recalled the moment: "After a while I learned that Bishop Ogñénovich had gone to live in a hotel and it I did not feel right; so I invited him to live in the Curia of Buenos Aires. Although I cannot remember dates very well —added the Holy Father—, he was there some years until he had a fractured femur and underwent an operation. He made his recovery and rehabilitation in the Home for Priests of Flores and also rehabilitation. He returned for a while, but did not feel safe because of the steps of the Curia and finally decided to move to the Home for Priests, where he died a year later."

As soon as he was consecrated bishop he was informed that his principal pastoral assignment as auxiliary bishop would be in the neighborhood of his childhood, adolescence and youth. Quarracino designated him episcopal vicar of Flores, the area where he had been born, grew up and discovered his priestly vocation. Once again he returned to his origins. After his "exile" in Córdoba he returned to the city where he began his Jesuit vocation; and he passed through a trial of purification that allowed him to "return" to the deep source of his faith. Now, at fifty-five years old, he returned to the same people who watched him grow and become a man of God.

The building of the Flores Vicariate was only seven blocks from the parish of San José, which was the place where he found his vocation on "student's day" in 1953.

Bergoglio was one of six auxiliary bishops. With him were Héctor Aguer, Raúl Rossi, Rubén Fassia, Mario José Serra and Eduardo Mirás. But Quarracino soon showed his predilection for his new collaborator. Only a year and a half later, Bergoglio was named Vicar General, which in practice means being the second in the government of the archdiocese. On the day of his ordination, the motto that now many know was heard: *Miserando atque eligendo* ("He saw him with mercy and chose him"). It is the same one that he will later use as Pope.

The day he was ordained bishop many humble people from San Miguel came to greet him. They were his former neighbors of the Colegio Mayor, those that he had integrated into the life of the seminary when he was provincial and later rector. The warmth of these former neighbors contrasted with the cool reception that some of the religious gave to the news of his designation as bishop. They were perhaps victims of the "bad press" Bergoglio received before and during his time in Córdoba.

Yet, Fr. Jorge, who already at that time rejected being called "Monsignor", which is a common way of referring to bishops in Argentina, would adopt the same personal relationship with each priest that consulted him, always ready to respond personally or with a telephone call to all of the messages recorded by the two secretaries. Imitating those priests that had marked him as a young man in his priestly formation, he too wanted to becme a "man to man" pastor.

Only a year and a half after his arrival in Buenos Aires, on December 21, 1993, he was named Vicar General of the archdiocese, and three and a half years later the apostolic nuncio, bishop Ubaldo Calabresi called him again. The meeting was described by Bergoglio himself to the journalists Sergio Rubín and Francesca Ambrogetti for the book *El Jesuita*. "On May 27, 1997, at midmorning, Calabrese called me and invited me to lunch. When we were having coffee, and I was about to thank him for the invitation and leave, I see that they are bringing over a cake and a bottle of champagne. I thought it was his birthday and almost wished him a happy birthday. But when I asked him I received a big surprise. 'No, it is not my birthday —he responded with a big smile—, it's that you are the new coadjutor bishop of Buenos Aires'".

Once again he was surprised with an unexpected and important announcement: from that moment on he was to be the successor of Quarracino. The Cardinal passed away eight months later and Bergoglio became head of the principal archdiocese in Argentina. Only five years had passed since his twenty two months of "exile" in Córdoba.

He rejected every sign of privilege and opted to "blend in" with the people. Marks of his time as bishop were his travelling by bus to the poorest neighborhoods where he would go periodically and, aside from praying and sharing *mates*, he promoted the manifestations of religious popularity. In this way, important moments of his pastoral work were the multitudes that celebrated St. Cajetan every 7th of August, the pilgrimages to the Marian sanctuary of Our Lady of Lujan, patroness of Argentina, the feast day of St. Raymond Nonato every 31st of August and the *Te Deum* that would become the moral compass for the political action of the nation.

He also strengthened his relationship with the so-called "slum" priests, faithful to his own missionary style that is proper to his Jesuit formation and the early Salesian influence. In 1994 he met Fr. "Pepe" Di Paola, an emblem of the priests that moved into the slums to spiritually and materially assist the poorest of Buenos Aires. Three years later, Quarracino named Di Paola pastor of Villa 21, and he decided to enthrone the image of Our Lady of Caacupé, patroness of the Paraguayans. The celebration included taking the image in procession from the Metropolitan Cathedral to the neighborhood of Barracas. Fr. Pepe headed the procession and no one noticed that bishop Bergoglio was in the crowd with a poncho and a rosary in his hands. From that time on he personally accompanied his work, convinced that in those little streets the true treasure of the Church could be found. The poor are an example of faith and perseverance for Bergoglio, and so he elevated their gestures of popular religiosity participating in person in many of them and joining them to the rest of the city by including them in the archdiocesan calendar. For example the washing of the feet on Holy Thursday of the most poor in the slums 1-11-14 or Villa 21 became a classic each year.

During his management as archbishop the number of priests assigned to this work doubled and the visits of the archbishop —with or without notice— became routine in order to celebrate Baptisms, Confirmations First Communions or to participate in the patronal feast days or processions. He went down all the aisles, he drank *mate*, he spoke with all of them and blessed all regardless of their condition.

One of the last (and rare) interviews he gave before becoming Pope, was on November 1, 2012 to the radio of the parish Our Lady of Caacupé in the slum 21-24. He confessed there that "the most beautiful moments" he had spent as a priest, he spent with "the people". And he added "What it gave my heart is this: having walked together with the people who are seeking Jesus and have listened to so many things and have learned so much fidelity from them".

Austerity, politics and commitment

Faithful to his style, Bergoglio never moved to the Archbishop's Residence located in the aristocratic neighborhood of Olivos. He chose to stay in a simple room of the Chancery, in front of the Plaza de Mayo. He rejected police protection, the official car and chauffer, and continued to travel by bus or subway. In his attempt not to change the simple austere style he adopted from the time he was a Jesuit in the cordobese novitiate in the Pueyrredon neighborhood, he also did not use the official office of the archbishop, large and elegant, but rather moved his office into a small simple room. The official residence he changed into a retreat house and the official office he used to store books and boxes with food and donations for the poor.

He already adopted the phrase that will distinguish him throughout the world: "Pray for me". But he also accompanied it with a constant invitation to prayer to everyone who came to him, especially his priests whom he encouraged to pray and to be open to their faithful. As was the case with other things in his life, before recommending something to others, he had already long before put it into practice. Each day he got up a little after four in the morning to pray and work, in an exhausting routine that Bergoglio as Pope still maintains today.

His days were (and still are) arduous, filled with meetings and audiences, and he never took vacations.

His low profile many times made him look like someone who is closed, but after speaking with him a while, many are sure to have met a bishop who is close to them, concerned about everyone and with a warm and cordial demeanor.

His style of government always provoked two parallel opinions. While some priests describe him as a "fatherly and loving" man, others categorize his public actions where he moves like a "political animal". Always with a low profile, archbishop Bergoglio never stopped speaking with politicians, union heads and businessmen, with whom he tried to extend bridges without abandoning his direct way of speaking, without hypocrisies. His sermons on the occasions of the *Te Deums* on the national holiday each May 25 always left people commenting on his words. Several presidents (Carlos Menem, Fernando De la Rúa, Eduardo Duhalde, Nestor Kirchner and Cristina Fernández de Kirchner) heard his ideas and arguments against corruption, and his accusations due to of the lack of commitment to the common good. The greatest tension came when Néstor Kirchner was in the central Government. Unhappy with Bergoglio's strong words during the first *Te Deum* in which he participated, Kirchner decided to break with tradition and not participate any more in the religious ceremony where the authorities and the Church give thanks to God for the country. As was said earlier, the deceased president (he died suddenly on October 27, 2010, in El Calefate in the Santa Cruz province) even identified the then Cardinal Bergoglio as the "leader of the opposition". The wife and successor of the man from Santa Cruz, only returned to the liturgical celebrations in the Metropolitan Cathedral when Bergoglio had been elected Pope.

One of the actions that cemented the then archbishop's image in social and political commitment came about during the deep crisis that exploded in Argentina in 2001. Bergoglio was one of the promotors in forming the Argentine Dialogue Table which became key in confronting the social disintegration that the country faced. Coordinated by the Church, the experience united different religious confessions, politicians, union heads, and other people who represented a wide variety of ideologies, and it became the source of consensus and political decisions in a state where violence and a dangerous loss of authority and legitimacy on the part of politicians and the institutions was making the country ungovernable.

On December 30, 2004 one of the worst tragedies in the history of Argentina took place. A roman candle ignited in the middle of a rock concert brought about a fire in the *Republic of Cromagnon* disco which left 194 dead and 1432 wounded, almost all young people. That same night, Bergoglio went to the morgue to pray with the victim's families and went to each of the hospitals to give spiritual assistance to the wounded and their families. His presence was constant during the following years, to support the demand for justice. Five months later, during the celebration of Corpus Christi, the Cardinal spoke strong words denouncing the authorities who were questioned because of the lack of control that permitted the tragedy. "Do not buy and sell our young people. Do not experiment with our young. If you want to experiment, put yourselves in the test tube", he told them at the time. On the first anniversary of the tragedy he presided a Mass where he asserted: "Buenos Aires needs to weep (...) Distracted city, divided city, egoistic city: weep, you need to be purified through tears". His presence also reached the members of the band *"Callajeros"* playing that night, accused as coauthors of the crime of "destruction and manslaughter".

The then archbishop took the same attitude more recently in the train accident at the Once station, when an eight wagon train slammed into the contention rail at rush hour in this Buenos Aires station. That Wednesday February 22, 2012, 51 people died and more than 700 were wounded. Once again Bergoglio came to console.

International pastoral work

Many feel that Bergoglio, with his profile as an austere, honest and committed pastor, began to be renowned internationally at the end of 2001 when he was called on to replace his colleague in New York, Cardinal Edward Michael Egan as the general rapporteur in the Bishop's Synod that was celebrated in the Vatican in October of that year. The reason for the substitution is famous and dramatic: the terrorist attack on the Twin Towers of New York, on September 11, 2001.

With the approval of John Paul II, Cardinal Egan decided to remain in his country to assist the victims of the attack and from the Vatican the Argentine bishop was asked to take the key position of general Moderator of the Synod. Bergoglio's performance in the Synod left a very good impression on the bishops and cardinals from all over the world that participated in the meeting. After that experience, he was designated in various commissions of the Vatican curia.

On April 2, 2005, after a long illness, Karol Wojtyla, Pope John Paul II, passed away, and gave way to a popular and heartfelt farewell to the pontiff who had won the hearts and respect of everyone, as well as to the preparations to elect his successor. Bergoglio assisted at the funeral of the Polish Pope who had designated him bishop and created him cardinal, and then participated as an elector in the Conclave that began on April 18. In the meetings prior to the Conclave he had to defend himself from accusations that arrived in a dossier from Argentina that stated he was an "accomplice" to the last military dictatorship. The same "document" resurfaced eight years later in the last Conclave and is founded on the texts of the journalist Horacio Verbitsky.

In spite of the lobby against him, already in 2005 Bergoglio was voted by many of the Cardinals and became the surprise of the Conclave, the principal alternative to the German Joseph Ratzinger, one of the principal collaborators in the pontificate of John Paul II in the Pontifical Congregation for the Doctrine of the Faith.

Because of the silence imposed upon the electors, the journalistic accounts were never confirmed, but it was reported that in the second to the last vote, Bergoglio had stepped aside and asked that they not vote for him. He feared, according to some observers, that his surprise candidacy would slow down the Conclave and give an image of a divided Church after the death of the man who had governed the Church for twenty-six years. Immediately after this decision, Ratzinger became Benedict XVI, the 265th pontiff in history.

Returning home, the Cardinal was named President of the Argentine Episcopal Conference, a responsibility that he exercised for two terms of three years until 2011. The consolidation of his silent international leadership began with his hard work in the Fifth General Conference of the Episcopal Counsel of Latin-American and the Caribbean (CELAM), celebrated in 2007 in the Sanctuary of Our Lady of Aparecida, in Brazil. This meeting in which hundreds of bishops from all over the continent participated, was inaugurated by Pope Benedict XVI himself, and had Bergoglio as the president of the committee for the writing of the final document. For such an intense job, the cardinal relied upon the key collaboration of a cordobese priest (born in Alcira Gigena) Victor Manuel Fernández, today archbishop and rector of the Argentine Catholic University. Bergoglio worked with Cardinals Claudio Hummes (from Brazil) and Oscar Andrés Rodríguez Maradiaga (from Honduras), who became friends with the Argentine. In eighteen days they produced a document of 550 points that sought "to promote a new Pentecost (...) a renewal of action in the Church". At the time no one imagined that the text would become the plan of action for a future pope. And even less could they have imagined that Bergoglio would do it as the successor of Peter.

The document defines the concept of "Disciples and Missionaries", and states that "the most valuable patrimony of the cultures of our countries is the faith in God Who is Love". It proposes "to renew the Church" by means of "the joy of being called to announce the Gospel", "the call to holiness", "the communion of the whole People of God", and it offers an "itinerary" that considers, among other things, the richness of "popular piety". In the third part it confirms the preferential option for the poor and excluded and it recalls the Second General Conference of CELAM celebrated in Medellin in 1968; "new faces of the poor" are recognized in the unemployed, the immigrants, the abandoned, the sick, and it promotes "international justice and solidarity". It also speaks of "the culture of love in married couples and the family, and a culture of respect for life" as well as encourages the "political commitment of laypeople", solidarity with the indigenous peoples and afro-descendants. It also exhorts to "an evangelical action that shows the way to reconciliation, fraternity and integration " to form "a regional community of nations". Here also, for the first time appears the phrase: "The sweet and comforting joy of evangelizing". A concept that arose to encourage all to "communicate the love of the Father (...) and the joy of being Christians" in Latin-America, but that after being repeated in Rome in 2013, it will become the new mission of the Church.

That document, as is the case with each of those written in Latin America, was not ignored in the rest of the world. It consolidated the prestige of Cardinal Bergoglio and it became a true plan for the pastoral governing for Francis. In fact, Cardinal Humme had an important role in the Conclave of 2013; Maradiaga was chosen by Pope Francis to coordinate a group of eight Cardinals from all the continents to help him reform the Curia and to make decisions for the Church; and, as has been said, Fernández was the first bishop designated by the new Pope, on May 13, 2013.

Between retirement and Rome

"His plans for the future were, once his resignation was accepted and his successor named, to go and live in the home we have in Buenos Aires for elderly and sick priests", pointed out Bishop Eduardo García, auxiliary of Buenos Aires, speaking of Cardinal Bergoglio's plans. In fact, the man who today guides the Church in the whole world had already chosen room 13 of the Home for Priests in the neighborhood of Flores, where he hoped to retire once Benedict XVI accepted his resignation that he submitted when he turned 75 years of age. It was a question of waiting.

The room that no longer is waiting to house the Cardinal is located on the ground floor, it is simple and has a bed, a night stand, a closet, bathroom and a small room next door with a desk and book shelves that was destined to be a place of study and to receive guests. In the end, very much like his residence now, only a lot more peaceful and a lot less worldwide exposure.

His plan was to lead a life of prayer, giving spiritual direction and to continue visiting parishes but without the responsibility of governing. But something unexpected happened that shook up the world as well as the structures of the Church and "threw out" —once again— the plans of Bergoglio himself.

"Being very conscious of the seriousness of this act, with full freedom, I resign from the ministry of the Bishop of Rome, Successor of St. Peter, that was confided to me by the Cardinals on April 19, 2005", Benedict XVI said in perfect Latin, on February 11 of 2013. His words and action created a stir that went across the globe.

Everyone spoke of an historic crisis in the Church. A pope resigned for the first time in 598 years and did it after living with and fighting incessantly with scandals during a large part of his pontificate. The world received, through the media, an image of a pope who was seen as involved in the accusations of corruption in the Vatican bank, for cases of pedophile priests and for the betrayal of his own private secretary who had revealed secret letters and a world of intrigues and shameful lobbies.

"Starting February 28, 2013, at 8 p.m., the see of Rome, the see of Peter will be vacant and there must be a conclave, convened by the competent authority, for the election of a new Supreme Pontiff", the German pontiff said in his most valiant and revolutionary decision.

With that, all eyes were upon the Vatican. A historical event had occurred and another about to begin. Only a week after the decree of the vacant chair of Peter, the 116 electing Cardinals and a few who did not have the right to vote for the new pope, had already come to Rome to participate in the General Congregations, meetings in which the prelates exchange opinions and their ideas about the situation of the

Church that constitutes the threshold of a Conclave.

Bergoglio arrived from Buenos Aires and he went to the International House of the Clergy, a simple hostel where priests stay who are passing through Rome. He was a frequent guest and they always reserved the same room, n. 203. During those cold and rainy days of March, each morning he left the building located on *Via della Scofra* 70 and walked the tiny cobbled streets, crossing the Tiber river on the *Victor Emanuelle II* bridge and, avoiding the gazes of the journalists and onlookers, avoiding the *Via della Conciliazione,* he arrived directly at the gate located on the left of St. Peter's Square. It was about eighteen irregular blocks that the cardinal walked, praying with his black overcoat covering his red cassock. Few noticed his passing and those that did knew of his reluctance to speak with reporters. On one occasion, a journalist form Buenos Aires that he trusted asked him to give him some idea of what was going on inside the Vatican and who were the candidates in the extraordinary election. The cardinal responded: "Pray for me". It was an expression that those who know him would have expected, but for the vast majority it was an inappropriate response since it put a finger on what was, for many, the least noticeable dimension of the story, the faith. "Pray for me".

The conclave according to a Cordobese journalist

Together with the prelates, a multitude of journalists, technicians, cameramen and women, photographers and producers of mass media from all over the world arrived in Rome. For the beginning of the Conclave there were already 5,085 men and women of the press, from sixty five nations; among them, Sebastián Pfaffen, one of the authors of this book who was the special envoy from Channel 12 of Córdoba. What follows is the account of the most transcendental event he lived during that unforgettable experience where an Argentine, who had been, for four years, a neighbor in Córdoba, was transformed into a the first Latin-American –and Jesuit— Pope in history.

In a Rome in upheaval, with the *Città del Vaticano* filled with people, the most powerful media in the world were occupying different corners of the impressive *Via della Conciliazione* as well as the terraces and balconies of hotels and buildings that have a privileged view of St. Peter's square. The accredited journalists doubled the stable population of the Vatican, this walled territory of a little more than 100 acres, which is a great complex of buildings, plazas and parks of incalculable cultural and historic value. And, at the same time, this city state is inside the capital of Italy.

The first impression is striking. The majesty of its architecture, the wide avenue "of the Conciliation" that guides the visitor towards the enormous Plaza of St. Peter; the Bernini columns that "envelop" the visitors with a welcoming embrace, guarded by the one hundred and forty statues of saints of all the ages that crown the galleries. Behind rises the imposing basilica where, among others, the remains of the fisherman who followed Jesus and was called "Peter", the "rock" upon which Christ built and still builds his Church. Everyone was there, two thousand years after that personal encounter, to know who would be the successor of the fisherman.

So much history in one glance makes one tremble.

Fifteen miles away, in Castel Gandolfo, the summer pontifical residence, the now Pope *emeritus* Benedict XVI began what he described as a "life dedicated to prayer". And his decision, which at first was interpreted as a capitulation to pressures from the scandals, began to take on its true dimension as a gesture of humility and greatness. "After having examined my conscience many times before God —Benedict himself expressed announcing his resignation—, I have come to the certainty that my strength, given my advanced age, no longer correspond with the adequate exercise of the petrine ministry".

The general congregations began on March 7, at 9:30 a.m., in the enormous Paul VI Hall. In the first press conference, the spokesman for the Vatican, Fr. Federico Lombardi, a Jesuit like Bergoglio, assured us that all the Cardinals wanted to speak, although he did not reveal the contents of the deliberations. The speculations grew with the anxiety.

The "vaticanists" (secular journalists of mass media that habitually give information and analysis on what goes on in the Vatican) spoke of "Vatileaks" and of the three hundred page report that Cardinals Julian Herrans, Josez Tomko and Salvatore De Giorgi had written at the request of Pope Benedict. In this report, all the witnesses and writings connected to the leak of the reserved documents of the Vatican were gathered. Benedict wanted the dossier to be private and only available for the next pope to read. But the three Cardinals who were in charge were also present in the Conclave and they were questioned by the other prelates.   This was acknowledged by Fr. Lombardi, who explained: "In the time prior to the Conclave the cardinals meet, they counsel one another and can analyze elements they deem relevant to the evaluation in choosing the successor of the Pope, without showing any specific document that remains reserved as such to the successor. Everything that makes up the reality of the Church is part of the deliberations".

The strict silence that is imposed on the prelates heightened the mystery as well as the mystique that surrounds every Conclave. The press exacerbated the imagination and while inside the silence was respected, outside there was a lottery of "*papabiles*". Among the "front runners" the Italian Cardinal Angelo Scola, archbishop of Milan was considered, along with the archbishop of San Paolo, Odilio Pedro Scherer; and the Canadian Marc Ouellet.

The meetings ran on one after the other during days that were as tense as they were cold and rainy. The cardinals came to and from the Vatican and always passed a dozen or more workers who with their hard hats and white aprons, worked on the scaffolding that covered a large part of the columns of Bernini. Almost no one noticed them, even though their work served as an apt metaphor for what was happening in the Church, inside.   The workers were cleaning with incredible delicacy every inch of those historic columns. They sprayed a little water and dried them with sponges, which they avoided rubbing on the marble so as not to wear them down any more than the passing of time had. It was a slow, meticulous work that seemed unending. The smog had damaged the work of Bernini but it never passed through the mind of anyone the thought of tearing those columns down. Because of its beauty, its value, its artist, the columns deserved to be restored to its original splendor. The same was going on in the Church at the time.

Four days after the beginning, nine general congregations had passed with 161 interventions of Cardinals from all over the world. That morning, the College of Cardinals accepted the justifications of two absent Cardinals. That day there were tens of interventions, among them one from the Argentine Cardinal Bergoglio. Immediately it transcended that it was a brief and simple intervention that had caused a deep impact among those that were there who applauded it with surprising enthusiasm. "The sweet and comforting joy of evangelizing" was the title of Bergoglio's intervention, which made reference to a renowned phrase of Paul VI. In his speech, which lasted only three minutes, he made reference to concepts that later became famous: "The Church is called to go out of herself and reach the peripheries, not only the geographic ones, but also the existential peripheries". He warned that "when the Church does not go out of itself to evangelize, it becomes auto referential and becomes sick...it considers Jesus Christ only in herself and does not let Him out". In the third and fourth brief points he stated: "The Church, when it is auto referential, without knowing it, believes it has its own light... and it gives way to the very great evil of spiritual worldliness" that would be "a Church that lives in itself, of itself and for itself" and uses this deformation as the basis of possible changes and reforms that it should make "for the salvation of souls". Bergoglio closed his brief intervention speaking of the profile that for him the next pope should have: "A man that, from the contemplation of Jesus Christ and from the adoration of Jesus Christ helps the Church go out of herself and toward the existential peripheries, that helps her be a fertile mother that lives in the sweet and comforting joy of evangelizing".

The speech caused an ovation and remained for the time in secret. Today we can read it entirely since Bergoglio gave a copy of it to the archbishop of Havana, Cardinal Jaime Ortega who released it to the public several months later, with the authorization of Pope Francis.

After this the Cardinals decided it was time to close the deliberations and to begin the election on Tuesday, March 12. They also reserved Sunday March 10 to rest and pray, and celebrate Mass in different parishes and basilicas in Rome. The church of St. Andrew *del Quirinal*, in the center of Rome, was one of the churches that drew the most faithful and journalists that Sunday. A multitude received the Brazilian Cardinal Odilio Pedro Scherer, considered one of the Latin American *"papabili"*. The same occurred in Our Lady of Victory church, where the charismatic archbishop of Boston, Cardinal Sean O'Malley celebrated Mass. There, the capuchin who enchanted many with his brown habit and his leather sandals, asked: "Let us pray that the Holy Spirit illuminate the Church in the election of a pope that will confirm us in our faith and make visible the love of the Good Shepherd". Another of the churches with a lot of people was that of the Twelve Holy Apostles. There the cardinal Angelo Scola presided, the archbishop of Milan and protagonist of a formidable media campaign that made him appear as though he were already elected pope. The three Argentine cardinals drew much smaller crowds: the cordobese Stanislaus Karlic, who celebrated in the Argentine church; Leonardo Sandri who was then prefect of the Congregation for the oriental Churches and substitute Secretary of State during John Paul II's pontificate; and Jorge Bergoglio who, faithful to his low profile, did everything possible so that the church assigned to him to celebrate the last Mass prior to the election would not be known.

Between prophesies and prayers

On Monday, March 11, the cardinals came together one last time to prepare the Conclave. It was the tenth meeting in the New Hall of the Synod where the electors debated the reform of the roman Curia, the financial situation of the Holy See, the crisis of the Catholic Church in the world and the scandal of the Vatileaks.

This time, the prelates had more difficulty going through the journalists, photographers and onlookers who registered their every move. In the crowd there was a homeless man who was noticed when he waved a sign in front of the television cameras. The sign had a message that turned out being an incredible prophesy: "Francis I, pope". There was no Cardinal with this name; the homeless man seemed to be the only fan of a team that did not exist, but many interviewed him and he became a "colorful moment" for much of the world's media. In his statements, the poor man insisted that the Church needed a new St. Francis, not from Assisi, but from Rome. The solitary "protestor" turned out to be a man who struggled to make a living collecting cardboard and paper from the streets of Rome and the Vatican, just as some friends of Bergoglio did in Buenos Aires.

The next day, Rome dawned with even more cold and rain. 12 days had passed since the beginning of the "*sede vacante*". The Cardinals arrived at the Vatican with umbrellas in their hands and with a small bag. This time only the "electors" participated, the cardinals that had not reached eighty years of age and they brought a bag because they did not know when they were going to leave the Vatican. The rules of the process they were about to begin were even more strict, so much so that this part of the election is referred to as a "conclave", from the Latin "*cum-clave*" that translates into English as "with or under key". The cardinals remained enclosed, virtually isolated from the world, without telecommunication, without newspapers, or internet, in an atmosphere of prayer and silence, with the sole objective of voting twice in the morning and twice in the evening until someone was voted the new pope with at least two thirds of the vote. This time there were 115 "present and electors" so 77 votes were necessary to elect the successor of Peter. Before being "enclosed", the 115 cardinals concelebrated the Mass *Pro eligendo Pontifice*. In St. Peter's Basilica, filled with faithful, Cardinal Angelo Sodano, the dean of the College of Cardinals, presided the ceremony and gave the homily. Sodano, who was eighty five and did not participate in the election, said: "We want to beg Our Lord that through the pastoral request of the cardinal fathers, He might soon give us another Good Shepherd". Then he made reference to the mission that the successor of Peter has and cited the prophet Isaiah: "I have been sent to bring good news to the poor, to heal hearts that are broken, to proclaim freedom to the slaves, freedom for the imprisoned". The cardinal explained that this prophesy was fully realized in Jesus, but "the mission of mercy is a commitment for every priest and bishop, but especially for the Bishop of Rome, Shepherd of the universal Church". He also mentioned the duty to keep safe the unity of the Church that is reflected in the letter to the Ephesians written by the apostle Paul from imprisonment in Rome, in the year 62 A.D. This text exhorts us "to behave with humility and gentleness, with patience, bearing with one another through love, striving to preserve the unity of the spirit through the bond of peace". Finally, Sodano pointed out that "the fundamental attitude of the shepherds of the Church is love". He continued: "that love that moves us to offer our life for our brothers". This is true "especially for the Successor of St. Peter (…) because the higher and more universal the pastoral office gets, the greater must be the charity of the Shepherd". Each word was followed carefully by the electors and by millions of viewers around the world who began to follow the historic process on television, as well as by the faithful who, quietly, began to congregate in St. Peter's plaza.

While the mass media spoke about the restlessness prior to the voting, few noticed that thousands of faithful were sitting silently on the steps and around St. Peter's square. There were men and women of different nationalities as well as religious men and women with strange vestments. They could be confused with tired tourists who were spending some time to rest from walking the obscure streets of Rome; but in reality, they were faithful who arrived there to pray. They formed small groups; some had signs, others, lighted candles; many prayed the rosary in silence. Although none of it was commented on in the newspapers, millions of Catholics all over the world were praying while the cardinals were coming and going to the Vatican. Thousands of Masses were celebrated simultaneously and even virtual campaigns sprung up where faithful could "adopt" a cardinal and pray especially for him during the election of the new pope.

Among the pilgrims were a group of Franciscans that looked like they were taken out of a history book. Their habits were brown, but of a rustic, coarse material. They had a rope around their waist from which large wooden rosaries hung. In spite of the cold and persistent rain, the friars wore sandals and their heads were crowned by the typical haircut that one sees on the "poor man of Assisi": the tonsure. One of them was different from the others. He had a habit made of jute, he carried a walking stick, a bag on his shoulder and no shoes. He had walked from Assisi, that is, over a hundred and ten miles, on days that the temperatures were below freezing at night. His feet were swollen. Humble and patient, he knelt in the middle of St. Peter's square, on a drain, under the constant rain, sleet and cold, and prayed for hours. It looked as though St. Francis himself were there praying, awaiting the new pope. His image was identical to the *poverello*, the patron saint of Italy, but his name is different: Massimo Coppo, an Italian of seventy-four years, member of a Franciscan community since he was thirty-two, when he converted to Catholicism and left everything, including his chair as a university professor.

A man who arrived trying to find his relatives decided to accompany him in prayer and knelt beside him. A woman, moved at the sight, also came closer to offer them a little shelter with her umbrella. There the three of them stayed another long hour and a half.

On March 12th, just hours before electing the new pope, the praying friar explained to some journalists why he was praying: "If we kneel in prayer before God, He provides for us, He gives us everything. It is most of all important to be united in prayer to seek the mercy of Jesus. These times many people suffer, many people really are living in difficulties and they do not know how to get out of it.... The Church has so much to offer, it is more than a human institution, although the people sometimes get confused. This is not an election for a Head of State, it is not a political thing, it is spiritual, it is to the Holy Spirit that one has to pray so that he give us a pope for the poor and that he be close to them, that he speak to us of eternity, of Hell and of the return of Christ."

The conclave

At 4:30 p.m., Rome time, the 115 cardinals from fifty-one countries entered the Sistine Chapel. The world followed, live, the captivating images that the Vatican Television Center transmitted. The prelates took their positions in the long lines of desks located along the sides of the impressive church that the Church and the universal culture owe to pope Sixtus IV, who ordered its definitive construction between 1473 and 1481.

Then, with a hand on the Bible and repeating a formula in Latin, each one of the electors swore to maintain secret everything that would happen in the Conclave and fervently defend the rights of the Church if elected. Then those present that were not electors and the cameramen moved back to the door while the Master of Ceremonies walked toward them proclaiming in Latin *"extra omnes"* ("everyone out"), and the front doors were solemnly shut. It was 5:30 in the afternoon in Rome. From that moment on the secret voting began and the only means of communication between the cardinals and the rest of the world, in this 21st century, was a simple chimney.

The eyes of the world were fixed on the tile roof of the Sistine Chapel. The chimney was a lot smaller than many imagined and stood at some 200 yards distance. It had been placed there a week earlier and seemed too simple for the important role it played: to inform the world that a pope had been elected or not. If it spewed black smoke, then it meant that no one had received two thirds of the vote; if the smoke was white then everyone would let up a cheer because there was a new pontiff.

The news reporters reminded everyone that the smoke comes from burning the papers which the cardinals used to write their votes; little white cards where each prelate writes the last name of his candidate and then places it ceremoniously in a golden urn placed on a table which has as a backdrop Michelangelo's imposing fresco of the *Last Judgment.*

After counting the votes, a secretary who is elected among the cardinals pierces them with a needle and thread to avoid confusions and after finalizing the count, whatever the outcome was, it is burned in a stove installed for this purpose in a room next to the chapel. If there is no pope elected the smoke comes out black because together with the ballots are burned little pellets of rubber. If it is white, another chemical is added to avoid confusion.

That Tuesday the Vatican norms required having two votes and at the end the first "*fumata*". In the square there were thousands of people that had to take shelter under the gallery of Bernini's columns because, at times, the rain was a down-pour, with lightning and even hail. The temperature dropped considerably. At 7:41 p.m. the chimney let out the first puffs of smoke. Many were in doubt at first because the smoke at the beginning came out grey and then turned to deep black. The crowd understood the signal and expressed its disappointment. There was still no pope. It would have been a miracle that 77 of the 115 cardinal electors agreed in the first ballot.

On Wednesday the ritual repeated itself starting in the early morning. The cardinals began the day with a private Mass inside the Vatican. For the liturgical calendar it was Wednesday of the Fourth Week of Lent, a time when the Church remembers the forty days of Jesus in the desert fasting, praying and overcoming the temptations of the devil.

That day the cardinals, as well as the priests and faithful all over the world read the biblical text of Isaiah 49, 8-15 in which the prophet repeats the words he has heard from God: "In a time of favor I answer you, on the day of salvation I help you, To restore the land and allot the desolate heritages, Saying to the prisoners: Come out! To those in darkness: Show yourselves!"

It was impossible not to think again about the scaffolding that covered sections of the columns of travertine marble, this ridged stone full of pores where the humidity and dust accumulate and corrode its shape and beauty. How could one avoid the evident parallelism between what was happening in the façade of the monument and that which was going on in the heart of the Church? In a kind of solemn ritual, the restorers of the travertine marble took away with infinite patience and a small brush the remains of dirt, they filled the deeper wounds of the rock with a new material so as to recover its strength and finally they protected it against the imperceptible but merciless action of water and other temporal agents. In the heart of this city there is also a State, the cardinals returned to concentrate on the interior restauration, as well as in seeking one who will motivate her according to the designs of the Great Restorer of Whom Isaiah spoke.

Beginning this day four votes were to take place, two in the morning and another two in the afternoon. Outside the people began to enter the square early on and by midday they numbered tens of thousands. The expectation was growing in this never before seen history in the making, the election of the 266th pope while a pope *emeritus* was alive and watching the proceedings on television and praying.

At 11:39 a.m., roman time, the chimney "spoke" again. It communicated the results of the morning's voting and once more, consensus had not been reached. The huge screens installed in different points of the square reproduced the news that was already going around the world, which showed the faithful, having seen the black smoke, begin to withdraw slowly from the plaza under a persistent drizzle, to return later that afternoon.

The most important news report of my life

Something tells me that the end of the historic Conclave is getting closer even though the *fumata* of the morning was dark. I literally run to send the news, in order to warm up and prepare myself for what is coming. A technical problem worries me and my cameraman: due to security measures all cell phone signal is blocked in the area around the Vatican. It is impossible to receive key information and we have to be there, with papers that are becoming useless because of the rain, trying to guess the most important news of our lives. I go over the biographies of the cardinals mentioned as *"papables"*, although everyone knows there may be surprises. There were too many signals and well based opinions that warn of a possible change, of a non-European pope, perhaps Latin American. My nerves do not permit me to memorize much more and as a last resort, I pray. Minutes before leaving and walking the 20 blocks that separate us from St. Peter's square, I go over carefully the personal history and the most important work in the life of Cardinal Jorge Mario Bergoglio. Just in case. Why not?

After the midday rest, the expectation has multiplied as much as the people have who at 5:00 p.m. already fill the square and part of the *Via della Conciliazione*. It is difficult to reach the plaza. The locals calculate that there are a hundred thousand people. Under a cover of umbrellas, all are staring at the chimney. Three ballots had passed and eight years earlier, Benedict XVI was voted on the fourth.

While it was getting dark, everyone calculated that thirty-six hours had passed since the beginning of the conclave. Nervously we repeat over and over the phrases we had memorized so as to avoid confusion at the moment we had to announce the story. No one wants to make a mistake with such an important story. Suddenly the whole plaza erupts with applause and cheers. We get goose bumps as we see the smoke begin to come out of the small chimney. It's white smoke! Expressions of joy explode in all sorts of strange languages, and the applause grows as the bells of the Basilica of St. Peter's confirm the news: a new pope has been elected. At 7:06 p.m. on March 13, 2013 the 266th pope in history has been elected. I am thankful to be present to tell the story.

Among the yelling and hugs, those of us who had been outside the plaza run forward to find a place closer to the central balcony where the traditional announcement of *habemus Papam* will be made. Only then will we know the name of the new pontiff.

Seventy-five unending minutes passed before the proto-deacon cardinal, the Frenchman Jean Louis Tauran, came out on the balcony to read, in Latin, the phrase that is already part of history: "*Annuntio vobis gaudium magnum: habemus Papam*".

The crowd erupts in applause that raises the tension and the anxiety. And the announcement that moved the world, but especially, the Argentines: "*Eminentissimum ac Reverendissimum Dominum, Dominum Georgium Marium Sanctae Romanae Ecclesiae Cardinalem Bergoglio qui sibi nomen imposuit Franciscum*".

My emotion chokes me at the most inopportune moment. There are several of us that are paralyzed and slow to react. We had come to Rome to relate an important news story but we were not prepared to report this unique and unrepeatable news. We yelled out the news: "Cardinal Bergoglio, a Jesuit, is the new pope of the Catholic Church!"

A small group of Argentines wave hysterically their flag. The rest of the people in the plaza are silent and ask themselves who is this Bergoglio. It is obvious that they do not know him and they are curious about the name he has chosen: Francis or Francis I since until now no pope has used that name.

Without entirely getting over our initial surprise we begin to spill out in front of the cameras the information we went over before leaving the hotel, and we report that "the cardinals have just elected for the first time a Latin American pope. What many thought might happen did, it is not a European pope. But the surprise is bigger since it is a pope from our country, cardinal Bergoglio is now pope, the leader of the Catholic Church".

❦

The few details that came out over the next few days allow one to reconstruct what the argentine cardinal might have lived inside. Four ballots had passed, when the cardinals shared a frugal lunch in the *Domus* Santa Marta. They say that Bergoglio had lost his appetite because, although no one reached 77 votes, he had been the most voted that morning. The great favorite, Angelo Scola, remained "stuck" at 50 votes, and according to the Italian newspapers, Scola himself asked that they not vote for him in order to facilitate the designation of the one who had most support: Bergoglio. It was the same thing the Argentine cardinal had done in the Conclave of 2005, when his name appeared among the most voted but was an obstacle in defining the election of Ratzinger. Now he was the one elected.

Without a doubt, Bergoglio put himself once more under the protection of St. Joseph and the Virgin Mary, and in spite of considering himself "a poor guy", as he would tell us in a conversation some months later, he accepted the mission that, for many, is the most important in the world.

The pope himself spoke about those moments prior to and after his election. He remembered for example that when the cardinals returned to the Sistine Chapel for the first ballot of the afternoon, he sat down beside his friend, the Brazilian cardinal Claudio Hummes, archbishop *emeritus* of San Paolo. While this was happening inside the Conclave, outside the rain continued as well as "signs". To calm the anxiety of the waiting, the pilgrims and journalists enjoyed watching a sea gull that sat insistently on the chimney of the Sistine Chapel. All sorts of speculation and jokes ensued. The bird is called a spy, as well as an emissary sent from God Himself announcing that the result of the Conclave is imminent. But the sea gull hides another sign: he belongs to a species whose scientific name is *Larus Argentinus*. *Larus* for the generic name given to sea gulls and *argentinus* for its silver color, the same origin of the name of the country from where the new pope comes: *Argentum*.

The sixth ballot went on without difficulty and the principal protagonist recreated the scene three days later, before a multitude of journalists in the Paul VI hall: "In the election —the Pontiff recalled— at my side was the archbishop *emeritus* of Sao Paolo, who is also the Prefect *emeritus* of the Congregation for the Clergy, Cardinal Caludio Hummes, a great friend. When it began to become 'dangerous', he consoled me. And when the votes reached two thirds, there was the normal applause because a pope had been elected. He hugged me, gave me a kiss and told me: 'do not forget the poor'. And those words entered here —the pope said signaling his heart—. The poor, the poor. Then, right away, I thought in relation with the poor I thought of St. Francis of Assisi. Then I thought of the wars, while the counting continued, until it finished. And Francis is a man of peace. The man who loved and took care of creation, at this time when the relationship we have with creation is not a good one. He is the man who gives us this spirit of peace, the poor man. Oh, how I would love a poor Church and a Church for the poor!"

The counting ended and, according to the news leaks, Bergoglio had well more than 80 votes. The Cardinals approach him to embrace him and joke a little: "You should call yourself Adrian, because Adrian VI was a reformer, and there is need to reform" another prelate said according to Francis. "Another told me 'no, no, your name should be Clement... Clement XV, that way you can avenge Clement XIV who suppressed the Jesuits!'"

Cardinal Giovanni Batista Re was in charge of completing the ritual by asking Bergoglio if he accepts the canonical election as Supreme Pontiff. To this question Bergoglio responded: "I am a great sinner, but confiding in the mercy and patience of God, suffering, I accept it". Immediately he is asked by what name he wants to be called and Bergoglio answers: "Francis".

The cardinals understand that this name is special, but they do not know the reasons for it. Some think he may be honoring the great disciple of St, Ignatius of Loyola, St. Francis Xavier, the Jesuit who was sent to the orient as the young Bergoglio dreamed of doing. But no. It was the other Francis. The same one whose name was on the cardboard sign of the beggar on the *Via della Conciliazione*, the same who inspired the very humble pilgrim from Assisi who prayed kneeling on the gutter of St. Peter's Square. It was the name of the *poverello*, the holy patron of Italy, and it embodied a clear message and contained a real governing program.

This message will be even clearer with the decisions that the new pontiff will make seconds after the election. In the so-called "crying room", which is really the sacristy of the Sistine Chapel, the small room that every church has to keep the liturgical vestments, Bergoglio did not weep. He had accepted, serenely, once again the will of God. He chose the traditional white cassock among the three sizes that were offered, but rejected the red *mozzetta*, a kind of short cape that his predecessors used. He also did not accept the red shoes but remained with his now famous and worn black orthopedic shoes. He rejected the golden pectoral cross that historically characterized the pontiffs and kept his own, of cheap silver, as well as his ring as archbishop of Buenos Aires. These decisions could have passed unnoticed by the majority of the faithful and onlookers that awaited him in St. Peter's square, but they had an enormous meaning for those who had just elected him.

Still, the signs were just beginning. Starting then, a revolution of small gestures began. The Rite indicates that the new Pontiff receive the greeting and embrace of each of the Cardinals but Bergoglio went over to embrace the archbishop *emeritus* of Bombay, Ivan Dias, who was very ill and in a wheel chair. Then he stopped other cardinals several times from kneeling before him to acknowledge his authority and promise him fidelity and obedience. It was he himself who knelt in a gesture of reverence and kissed the rings of the cardinals of Vietnam and China, in a moving gesture that was also an act of justice. While the Church moved for years among the scandalous lobbies, accusations of wasting millions of dollars and the whitewashing of capital of mafia mobsters who had managed to infiltrate the Vatican bank, the Church that they represented suffered persecution, arbitrary detentions and even martyrdom in areas that were hostile to the faith.

Love at first sight

It was after all of this that Cardinal Tauran announced the election and Bergoglio arrived at the principal balcony of St. Peter's to present himself to the multitude that applauded him. From up there, the view is impressive; from below, pressed in on all sides by the people, the experience is imposing. Even more so when the compatriot who is now nothing less than the pope decides to inaugurate his pontificate with a simple and unforgettable greeting: "*Fratelli e sorelle, buonasera*" ("Brothers and sisters, good evening"). The answer was an ovation. We never imagined that such simple words could mean so much and provoke such a reaction in tens of thousands of people. It was love at first sight.

"You know that the duty of a Conclave is to give you a bishop of Rome. It appears that my brother cardinals went to look for him to the end of the world", he said in Italian, taking away some of the solemnity of the occasion and deliberately avoiding speaking of himself as the "Supreme Pontiff". Then he continued: "Here we are. Thank you for the warm welcome. The diocesan community of Rome has a bishop: thank you!"

From now on the pope would be a "bishop". It was another great definition. He did not come to govern a kingdom, but rather came to coordinate the government of the universal Church but in a certain way, being another bishop. For those who understood, it was a sign of respect for the collegiality in the government of the Church and a calling out to his brother bishops to collaborate in this responsibility, as they had asked in the meetings prior to the Conclave.

Then he asked everyone to pray for Benedict XVI, who he called "bishop *emeritus*": "Let us all pray together for him, that the Lord bless him and the Virgin Mary protect him"; and he invited all to pray, just like a father would to his children putting them to bed, an Our Father, Hail Mary and a Glory be. When the ovation once again died down he continued, speaking like a teacher and in a fatherly way: "And now, we begin this walk: bishop and people. This walk of the Church of Rome which is that which presides all the churches in charity. It is a way of fraternity, of love, of confidence between us". His words created an atmosphere of intimacy, of closeness. "Let us pray for one another. Let us pray for the whole world, that there might be a great fraternity. I wish that this walk of the Church that we begin today and in which my vicar who is here with me will help, may be fruitful for the evangelization of this beautiful city".

At this point the connection between the people and their new shepherd was evident but the best was yet to come. Francis prepared to give the first blessing, the one known by its Latin words *urbi et orbi* ("to the city and to the world"); a blessing that is given once in a while from the chair of Peter and that carries with it a plenary indulgence.

Before giving this blessing which was highly expected by the majority of those present, Bergoglio again made a gesture that surprised even the atheists watching. "Now I would like to give the blessing, but before I do I ask a favor of you: before the bishop of Rome blesses the people, I ask that you pray to the Lord to bless me; the prayer of the people, asking the blessing of their bishop. Let us make this your prayer for me in silence". The response was a tremendous silence and to the surprise of those around him on the balcony, the pope bowed deeply toward the people to receive with a greater gesture of solemnity the sought after prayer from the multitude that looked on perplexed.

Finally, he lifted his right hand, and prayed reading from an enormous book the rite of the solemn blessing and there was a great applause. "Brothers and sisters, I am leaving. Thank you very much for your welcome, pray for me and I will see you soon. We will see you soon. Tomorrow I would like to go pray to Our Lady, that she may protect all of Rome. Good night and sleep well".

The stone that the builders rejected became the corner stone. Bergoglio was Pope Francis, the new *Petrus* of the 21st century. On him, Christ was building his Church.

The first day of his pontificate, Francis began to show his *"Bergoglian* style" in the city of Rome. Wearing the simplest cassock he could find, he got in a car considered "undignified" for a Roman Pontiff and left quickly for the center of the eternal city to look for his suitcase, pay his bill at the hotel, offer a floral offering to the image of Our Lady in the basilica of St. Mary Major and on his way back, say hello to some children going into school. In only twelve hours, the Argentine pope had upset all the pomp and ostentation of the Vatican protocol, to the despair of the guards and the delight of everyone else: romans, foreigners, faithful, atheists and journalists.

The gestures followed one after another and the communicators spoke of a pope who is humble, simple, close to the people. They looked into his life and found again that they were mistaken. The first steps of Francis were not made as part of a "publicity campaign" or a strategy for the purposes of proselytism, but rather that this man, while he was still called Bergoglio, acted in the same way.

Soon to the gestures were added words. Francis began to give clues as to the direction he wanted to take his pontificate. He spoke to the cardinal electors of a Church that has to walk, go out, build and confess its faith in Jesus Christ, because otherwise it would spread the worldliness of the devil. He asked the elder cardinals to renew their hope and to the faithful he gave the best face of God: His Mercy. Once again, with simplicity, without undecipherable quotes, appealing to stories from daily life, and even humor, he explained that God loves us always, that he never tires of forgiving. The problem is that we get tired of asking forgiveness.

Before all this, the pope decided to receive all of us journalist that covered the Conclave. He offered us the first general audience of his pontificate. There with a clear dominion of his audience, he revealed the origin of his name. It was impossible not to recall the poor man and the monk in the square, and ask ourselves who sent them. Francis is named thus for the saint of Assisi, the one who stripped himself of all that he had to be shamelessly Christian and scandalously coherent with the message of Jesus.

There is a story told that the first Francis had gone out to meditate in the fields and passed close by the chapel of St. Damian, that was destroyed. He felt the need to enter and kneel before the crucifix that was still fixed to one of the ruined walls. It was there that St. Bonaventure, who wrote what is considered the "definitive" biography of St. Francis, known as the *Major Legend*, described what happened: "With his eyes full of tears, he looked at the cross of the Lord, and he heard with his corporeal ears a voice from the cross that said to him three times 'Francis, go and repair my house, which as you can see, is almost entirely in ruins!'" Francis took the words literally and began to restore, first the chapel of St. Damian, then another dedicated to St. Peter and finally one of Our Lady of the *Porciuncula*. But a little time later he understood that the true meaning of the words which St. Bonaventure describes thus: "the divine voice was referring principally to the reparation of the Church that Christ acquired with His blood".

Perhaps this new Francis has inherited something from his grandparents, aunts and uncles who came from Italy to Argentina and founded their construction company. Perhaps our Francis, the one who lived in Córdoba, who walked our streets, who prayed in our churches, who heard our sins and with the grace of God forgave them; perhaps this new Francis is also a constructor and restorer. He too was reconstructed and restored with patience; at times with pain, with lights and shadows such as what happened in his two times in Córdoba. After all we all are. Even the Church that Bergoglio serves as "servant of the servants of God" from a call that is also an exhortation: the one that over twenty centuries ago the Galilean repeated three times to the fisherman:

—"Do you love me more than these?"

— "Yes Lord. You know that I love you."

EPILOGUE

"None of us lives for oneself, and no one dies for oneself"
(Romans 14,7)

Francis and Brochero

Romano Guardini, the theologian preferred by Pope Francis, on whose work he wrote his never finished doctoral thesis, taught that for people of faith there is no such experience of "fate", that is, unlucky or lucky circumstances. For those who believe in this personal God who loves each person as a "generous dad", Guardini said, all that happens in our pilgrimage "is providence"; a loving design that absolutely respects the freedom of the beloved.

After having examined the life in Córdoba of Jorge Bergoglio, after having accompanied him in experiences that molded his heart as a pastor, there is no other option than to surrender to the evidence of the guardinian perspective: everything in the life of the now Pope Francis has had a deep meaning, a pro-vidence; and nothing that happened has been without meaning, neither pure coincidence nor pure chance. Who could have anticipated that that boy, almost an adolescent, with political concerns, standing on a Buenos Aires street corner waiting for the arrival of someone to sell him a socialist newspaper *La Vanguardia*, that only four years later he would be on the edge of a hospital bed in Córdoba, dressed in a black cassock, accompanying an old Jesuit who spoke to him of an active mountain priest who was an authentic priestly model?

Who could have known, that this young man listening carefully to an older Jesuit who spoke to him, that fifty years later one of them will be Pope who will authorize the beatification of the country priest of whom they were speaking?

There is a providential link between Pope Francis and blessed Cura José Gabriel del Rosario Brochero; a link that goes beyond the "smell of the sheep" pastoral style that both men have, as we have seen in these pages, and it is a good example of what the Church refers to as the "communion of saints".

Jorge Bergoglio did not get on the band wagon of Brochero's cause at the last minute as some suspect. Nor did he simply do his duty that he would have had to do in any case, for example as President of the Argentine Episcopal Conference. Providentially, the Argentine who is today the "rock" upon which the Catholic Church sits, knew Brochero's work and the heroism of his apostolic adventures, form the mouth of one who was almost a direct witness, at a time when the now famous cordobese blessed was practically unknown in the majority of the Argentine provinces. Fr. Antonio Aznar had already published the first of his books on the eminent cordobese priest, around the year 1958, when the 21 year old novice arrived at the Jesuit residence in the Pueyrredon neighborhood who listened to him carefully every time he spoke of the adventures of Brochero. Not only that, but the year that the novice and the elderly Jesuit met, Aznar was working on an article that would be very important in the cause of Brochero entitled "Brochero's bad words" which was published in the Argentine Academy of the Arts in 1958. In this article, Fr. Aznar put to rest the objection some theologians had that his language was vulgar, but in truth, it was simply the language the mountain folks used who Brochero evangelized.

Since Pope Francis knows that more people are reached when he uses language the young missionaries will understand such as the famous "*hagan lío*"[57] or "*callajeros de la fe*"[58], Brochero also knew in

---

[57] Literally: "make a mess"; it is used in Argentina similar to the way the stadiums in the United States, before an important play, will invite the crowd to "make noise".
[58] Literally: "street riots of the faith", used in Argentina to mean being on the streets, close to the people, not shut in.

his time, that his faithful would understand better when he used their way of speaking. For example, when he spoke of the gratuitousness of divine grace he used the normal country image of the goats that climb on the round earthen bread ovens to relieve themselves, and from there the manure spreads all over.

The well known bergoglian pontifical exhortation to *"no chusmear"*[59] or *"no sacar cuero a nadie"*[60] that few imagined in the mouth of a Pope, has the same theological and human sense and foundation as did that pronounced by Brochero in a Mass in 1892, in the church of Our Lady of Ransom in the center of Córdoba. Surprising many who listened to him that day, among them the then governor Manuel Pizzaro, Brochero said that "those women of a long tongue with which they stab their neighbor who, even if they pray will go to hell with petticoats and all…"

Another strong link between Brochero and Bergoglio is through the ignatian spirituality. The humility and self-knowledge that the practice of the Spiritual exercises of St. Ignatius imparts, gave both these pastors a "smell of the sheep" and worn-out shoes.

When Brochero found out through a friend's letter that may have been included in a shortlist of candidates for the future bishop of Córdoba, he did not hesitate to respond: "I am a halfwit, without capacities nor virtues". When we asked Pope Francis if in Córdoba he had passed through a kind of "dark night of the soul" such as St. John of the Cross and St. Teresa of Avila experienced, the Holy Father responded: "I would not say that. Those things are for saints. I am just a poor guy".

There are many, many sayings and gestures that support the idea of a close "communion" between the co-protagonists of this epilogue. It is no coincidence that Bergoglio went in 2008 to the land evangelized by Brochero until he dropped and gave his life for them. Nor is it a coincidence that five years later, Brochero ended up being

---

[59] Very informal way of saying not to gossip.
[60] Literally: "Do not take leather off anyone", an even more informal way of saying "do not gossip".

the first blessed in the pontificate of Francis.

The then cardinal Bergoglio visited Villa Cura Brochero, in the west of the province of Córdoba, from September 9 – 11, 2008, on the occasion of the National Meeting of Priests taking place there. He arrived in Córdoba on a commercial bus. Fr. Gustavo Zanchetta, a close collaborator with Bergoglio in Buenos Aires, had arrived the day before to the small town in the mountains of the province and asked to borrow a car to look for him at the humble bus terminal in Villa Cura Brochero. Black bag in hand, the Cardinal, at the time President of the Argentine Episcopal Conference, got in the car gratefully, and was taken to *La Palmita* hostel, where other bishops were also lodging, among them, the archbishop of Córdoba, Carlos Ñañez.

Marcelo Nesteruc, son of the owners of the tourist complex, Hugo and Julia, remembers the details of that "low profile" visit that wound up being so special. The picture that his parents took with Bergoglio and Ñañez (see picture n. 28) today holds a prominent place in the hostel. Not only because it is a picture with the pope, but also because it was taken by the bishop of Cruz del Eje, Santiago Olivera, who is devoted to and promotes the cause for the canonization of the Cura Gaucho. "It is really very special to know that here, in our hostel, the man who today is pope lodged", Marcelo commented, and he pointed out the humility of that visitor who spent most of his time there receiving visitors who wanted to greet him.

Picture 28 — Cardinal Bergoglio and the Archbishop of Córdoba, Carlos Ñáñez, with the owners of the *Hostería La Palmita* in Villa Cura Brochero. *Picture by kind permission of the Nesteruk family.*

At that encounter, Bergoglio gave a talk on "The idea of the presbyter in Aparecida", a reflection on the priesthood in the light of the final document of the Fifth Conference of the Episcopal Conference of Latin America and the Caribbean (CELAM) that took place in the city of Aparecida, Brazil. The basis of the talk given by the then Cardinal Bergoglio is the priestly model of Brochero who always knew and lived evangelical poverty together with a commitment that moved him to go out in search of those in need.

Brochero was generous in his virtues and gives the key to what Bergoglio described then as vital to the life of a good priest. "That the option for the poor is 'preferential' means that it must be a part of all our pastoral structures and priorities", he said. Then he added: "The Church must be companion to all our most needy brethren, even to martyrdom. It invites us to be friends with the poor, with a closeness that makes us friends, since today we defend too much our spaces for privacy and enjoyment, and we let ourselves be infected easily by individualistic consumerism. For this reason, our option for the poor runs the risk of remaining on a theoretical or purely emotional level, without true incidence in our lives or our decisions. With sound realism, Aparecida asks us to dedicate time to the poor. Thus one can draw a profile of a priest who 'goes out' to the abandoned peripheries, recognizing in each person an infinite dignity. This option to become close to the poor does not mean pastoral successes, but rather fidelity to the Teacher, who is always close, always available for everyone, wanting to fill all the corners of the earth with life."

Five years after that talk, Bergoglio had to again speak of Brochero. The memories of Fr. Aznar, of Fr. Bustos Zambrano, of his life in Córdoba, of the many poor that he always visited where ever God took him, all came to his mind and heart. On this occasion his words were not only heard by a hundred or so priests as was the case in 2008. His writing, dated in the Vatican on September 14, 2013, spread through the world like "the manure of the goat off the round bread oven." Of course, it was the voice of the Pope. It was the voice of the pope, speaking precisely of the humblest —and for this reason the greatest— cordobese priest.

A deep silence took over the valley on the other side of the mountains of Córdoba, invaded for the occasion by pilgrims from all over the country united by the grace of Brochero. Pope Francis, the argentine Pope, the same who incarnated the virtues of this mountain priest, had sent a message for the beatification. With these words that the Holy Father sent to the now president of the Argentine Episcopal Conference, José María Arancedo, for all the friends of Brochero, we will end this book. It is like a message from the Pope to every reader:

"Dear brother:

That Brochero finally is among the blessed is a great joy and blessing for Argentines and devotees of their pastor with the smell of the sheep, who made himself poor among the poor, who fought continually to be very close to God and to the people, that did and continues to do so much good which is like a caress of God to our suffering people.

It does me good to imagine today Brochero as pastor on his mule "*malacara*", travelling through the long arid and desolate paths of the hundred and twenty-five square miles of his parish, looking house to house for the grandparents and great grandparents of all of you, to ask them if they needed anything and to invite them to make the Spiritual Exercises of St. Ignatius of Loyola. He knew every inch of his parish. He did not remain in his sacristy to comb the sheep.

Fr. Brochero was a visit from Jesus himself to each family. He brought with him the image of Our Lady, the book of prayers with the Word of God, things to celebrate daily Mass. They invited him in to have *mate*, they talked and Brochero spoke to them in a way they all understood because he spoke from the heart, from his faith and the love he had of Jesus.

José Gabriel Brochero centered his pastoral action in prayer. As soon as he arrived at his parish, he began to take men and women to the city of Córdoba to make the spiritual exercises with the Jesuit fathers. How much sacrifice was involved in order to cross the high sierras, snow covered in the winter, to pray in the capital of Córdoba. How much work it took them to build the Holy House of the Exercises in the parish! There, they prayed a long time in front of the crucifix to know, feel and taste the love so great of the heart of Jesus, and it all ended in the forgiveness of God in confession, with a priest full of charity and mercy. A lot of mercy!

This apostolic courage of Brochero, so full of missionary zeal, this bravery in his compassionate heart just like Jesus' that allowed him to say: "Woe is me if a devil ever robs a soul!", moved him to win over for God even people of bad lives and difficult country folk. Thousands of men and women abandoned fighting and vices, thanks to the priestly work of Brochero. All received the sacraments during the spiritual exercises and, with them, the strength and the light of the faith to be good sons of God, good brothers and sisters, good fathers and mothers of families, in a large community of friends committed to the common good of all, who respected and helped one another.

In a beatification the pastoral relevance of the person is very important. Cura Brochero has the relevance of the Gospel; he is a pioneer in moving out to the geographic and existential peripheries to take love, the mercy of God, to everyone. He did not remain in the parish office, he spent himself on his mule and wound up with leprosy, because of seeking the people, like a street priest of the faith. This is what Jesus wants today, missionary disciples, street rioters of the faith!

Brochero was a normal man, fragile, just like all of us, but he knew the love of Jesus, he allowed his heart to be worked over by the mercy of God. He was able to leave the cave of "I-me-mine-with me-for me" little egoisms that we all have, conquering himself, overcoming with the help of God those interior forces that the devil used to chain us to comforts, to seek to live the moment well, to take work out of life. Brochero listened to the call of God and chose the sacrifice of working for his kingdom, for the common good that the enormous dignity of each person is worthy of as a child of God and he was faithful to the end: he continued to pray and celebrate Mass even while blind and a leper.

Let us allow Brochero to enter, mule and all, into the home of our hearts and invite us to prayer, to the encounter with Jesus, that he might free us from what binds us so as to go out to the streets and seek our brother, to touch the flesh of Christ in those that suffer and need God's love. Only in this way will we taste the joy that Cura Brochero had, which is anticipation of the happiness that he now enjoys as a blessed in heaven. I ask the Lord that He might give you this grace, that He bless you and I pray that the Holy Virgin take care of you.

With affection,

Francis

Vatican, September 14, 2013".

Picture 29 — Blessed José Gabriel del Rosario Brochero.

SPECIAL   THANKS

To the Holy Father,
for supporting and helping us to tell his fascinating story.
To our Father and Bishop, Carlos Ñáñez,
and to Father and friend Ángel Rossi SJ. Without them, without their
confidence and generosity, this book would have a heart but little soul.

Picture 30 – Pope Francis with the original Spanish edition in his hands

From Javier Cámara:

To my wife and our daughters, Juli, Agus e Miqui
sweet and kind supporters of this book.
To Sebastián Pfaffen and his beautiful family,
for helping me in becoming the other author of this book.
To everybody that, in different ways, has collaborated with this work:
to my parents-in-law, always taking care of our needs. To my brothers
and my sisters, in particular to Jorge Cámara, first reader and reviewer.
To my sisters-in-law, my brothers-in-law,
nephews and godchildren, for their love.
To my friends and their families;
they know to whom I am talking about.
To my co-workers of mission from *Periódico Encuentro*,
with and special mention for Gustavo Loza and Leonardo Altamirano:

268

without their generosity, this work would have be finished twice in time.
To Father Carlos Cravenna SJ: witht his memories and patience "he has open the door" of the disapear Novitiate of Pueyrredón Quarters where Pope Francis and him began to be Jesuits.

Picture 231 - Pope Francis with Javier Cámara, Sebastián Pfaffen and their wifes

For their support and prayers, to the priests: Munir Bracco, friend and advisor of *Periódico Encuentro*;
Alfonso Gómez SJ, rector of the Catholic University of Córdoba;
Dante Simón, judicial vicar of the Archdiocesis of Córdoba;
to the Sisters of the Sacred Family of Urgel, always close in affection to me and my family.
To my my *little patron*s and companions of *Casa de la Bondad*, for having teached me to live.
To my companions of *La Voz del Interior*, for their support.
To those who have given their essential testimonies collected for this book, but also for life itself:
Dr. Margarita Schweizer, Father Juan Etulain, Father Andrés Swinnen, Horacio Lescano, Engineer Diamanti and wife, Néstor Giraudo.
To Ricardo Spinassi, Irma Peralta and Lucila Tejeda, witnesses that Jesus works in the world through other people.
To Lita, for her contagious enthusiasm and for her prayers.
To Jorge Cuadrado, for consenting me to show the faces of a Chruch and a Faith unknown for him.
To Sergio Chius, my first teacher of Philosophy and Theology, whom

even not seeing him for 20 years, is the cause of my intellectual passion for the work of Leopoldo Marechal and Romano Guardini, authors that, by Providence, have contributed to the building of the enormous intellect and immeasurable faith of Jorge Bergoglio, today Pope Francis.

To Miguel Pérez Gaudio, for having taught me, over 20 years ago, how to become a journalist with faith.

Picture 32 - Pope Francis and Sebastián Pfaffen in St. Martha's House in The Vatican

From Sebastián Pfaffen:

To each and every one of those mentioned by Javier Cámara, whom I thank for his generous invitation to participate in this incredible project.

My wife Elizabeth Aeschlimann, for being my support in faith, my life partner, column of the family and for the tremendous efforts to make this book a reality.

To my parents, Orlando Pfaffen and Ana María Vetti for their example, their love and constant support and encouragement.

My brothers: Francisco, María Julia, Agustín, María Clara and my uncles, cousins, friends and co-workers for rejoice in my joy.

To Daniel Carlos Lasa, for letting me find out the reasons of faith and mark forever my life "in the shared commitment to seek the truth".

ABOUT THE AUTHORS

Javier Cámara is a journalist since 1993 and writes on the newspaper *La Voz del Interior* of the city of Córdoba, Argentina. In 1996 he founded the Catholic journal *Encuentro*. He is the President of the "Asociación Civil Encuentro". In 2000 he coordinated the press room of the National Eucharistic Congress with which the Church in Argentina celebrated the Great Jubilee. He later was sent to international events such as the Jubilee of 2000 in Rome, presided over by John Paul II and the Fifth Conference of CELAM in Aparecida, Brazil (2007), presided over by Benedict XVI, whose final document was drawn up under the supervision of the then Cardinal Jorge Bergoglio, now Pope Francis.

Twitter: @camarajavier

Sebastián Pfaffen is is a journalist. From 1995 to 2000 he was coordinator and speaker of Canal 2 of Villa María, Córdoba. Since 2000, he has been working as a news reporter for Canal 12 of Córdoba. He collaborates with the journal *Encuentro*. He was sent to cover press information for the Conclave of 2013 in which was elected Pope Francis, as well as the first apostolic visit of the Pope for the World Youth Day in Rio de Janeiro, Brazil.

Twitter: @SPfaffen